D1478041

What Your Colleagues Are Saying . . .

"At last, the Common Core Mathematics Companion is available for Grades 6–8! Having used the Common Core Mathematics Companions for Grades K–2 and 3–5, our math partners were awaiting the guide for Grades 6–8. The guidance as to what the teacher does and what the students do will support our teachers in using instructional strategies that support the deep understanding called for in the Common Core State Standards and instructional practices reflected in our teaching framework. Since a cornerstone of our lesson planning is identifying and planning how to address student misconceptions and common errors, the section on student misconceptions and common errors will be invaluable to teachers, especially our new teachers who don't have any of this background knowledge. Thanks to Ruth Harbin Miles and Lois Williams for providing the field with such a valuable resource."

—Cathy Martin, **Director of PreK–12 Mathematics**
Denver Public Schools, Denver, CO

"The book breaks down the CCSS in mathematics by using practical, accessible language and offers concrete mathematical examples to assist educators in gaining a deep understanding of the discrete components of each standard. By presenting clear language to describe 'what the teacher does' and 'what the students do,' the authors offer a helpful tool that clearly outlines for teachers the recommended instructional actions in concrete and measurable terms. In each chapter of the book, the authors identify key instructional activities to differentiate instruction and target learning for both students who are struggling and those who are more advanced in their understandings of the content at hand. Having specific adaptations for students who may not perform a given activity on grade-level offers teachers multiple methods and opportunities to reach ALL learners in their classrooms."

—Elizabeth Greninger, **PhD**
Managing Associate, edCount, LLC

"This book offers accommodations for struggling students and suggestions for how to deal with common student misconceptions and errors. These are critical when working with special needs populations. It is a special education teacher's dream for mathematics."

—Diane Stave Civerchia
Special Education Teacher, KY

The Common Core Companion
at a Glance

Suggested Materials for This Domain: Provides teachers with a list of materials that will be helpful in introducing the concepts in this domain.

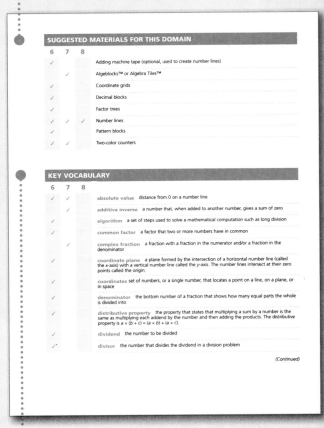

Domain Overview: Gives a brief description of the big ideas, allowing you to see how the mathematical ideas develop across grade levels.

Key Vocabulary: Vocabulary included in the domain with grade levels indicated. This terminology can be used for building a word wall in the classroom. Students should be able to use these terms in talking about mathematics. Standard for Mathematical Practice 6: Attend to Precision calls for students to use mathematical terminology appropriately.

Domain: General mathematical topic for this group of standards.

Identifying number for this cluster: Grade, domain, cluster

Cluster: Statements that summarize groups of related standards. Note that standards from different clusters may sometimes be closely related, because mathematics is a connected subject.

6 = Grade
NS = Domain
B = Cluster

Standards: Mathematical statements that define what students should understand and be able to do.

Domain

The Number System
6.NS.B

Cluster B

Compute fluently with multi-digit numbers and find common factors and multiples.

STANDARD 2   **6.NS.B.2:** Fluently divide multi-digit numbers using the standard algorithm.

STANDARD 3   **6.NS.B.3:** Fluently add, subtract, multiply, and divide multi-digit decimals using the standard algorithm for each operation.

STANDARD 4   **6NS.B.4:** Find the greatest common factor of two whole numbers less than or equal to 100 and the least common multiple of two whole numbers less than or equal to 12. Use the distributive property to express a sum of two whole numbers 1–100 with a common factor as a multiple of a sum of two whole numbers with no common factor. *For example, express 36 + 8 as 4(9 + 2).*

The Number System   6.NS.B

Cluster B: Compute fluently with multi-digit numbers and find common factors and multiples.
Grade 6 Overview

Fluency and accuracy with multi-digit addition, subtraction, and division is the focus for this cluster along with a spotlight on greatest common factors and least common multiples. The cluster also builds on previous learning of the multiplicative structure as well as prime and composite numbers.

Standards for Mathematical Practice
SFMP 2. Reason abstractly and quantitatively.

Students are able to understand the meaning of a division problem.

SFMP 7. Look for and make use of structure.

Sixth graders apply division algorithms to divide multi-digit numbers.

SFMP 8. Look for and express regularity in repeated reasoning.

Students consider the reasonableness of an estimated quotient.

Related Content Standards

5.NBT.B.6   5.NBT.B.7   7.NS.A.2.b   7.NS.A.2.c   7.NS.A.2.d   7.NS.A.3

Notes

Each cluster begins with a brief description of the mathematics in that cluster.

Related Content Standards: Provides a list of standards connected to this topic in other grade levels as well as standards in this grade level related to this topic that are in other domains. Consider the related standards as you plan instruction for each cluster.

Standards for Mathematical Practice: Although it is likely you will use a variety of Standards for Mathematical Practice in teaching each cluster, this section gives examples of how you might incorporate some of the practices into your instruction on this topic.

You will find the following components for each standard in the cluster:

Standard: The standard as written in the Common Core, followed by an explanation of the meaning of the mathematics in that standard, including examples.

What the TEACHER does: An overview of actions the teacher might take in introducing and teaching the standard. This is not meant to be all-inclusive, but rather to give you an idea of what classroom instruction might look like. Illustrations may be included, detailing how to use materials to teach a concept when using models and representations called for in the standard.

Addressing Student Misconceptions and Common Errors: Each standard concludes with a misconception or common student error around the standard and suggested actions to address those misconceptions or errors.

STANDARD 5 (6.NS.C.5)

Understand that positive and negative numbers are used together to describe quantities having opposite directions or values (e.g., temperature above/below zero, elevation above/below sea level, credits/debits, positive/negative electric charge); use positive and negative numbers to represent quantities in real-world contexts, explaining the meaning of 0 in each situation.

In this standard, students investigate positive and negative numbers (integers) in real-world scenarios as being opposite values or opposite directions such as 10° below zero (−10) and 10° above zero (+10). They use vertical and horizontal number lines to show all rational numbers and must explain that the meaning of zero is determined by the real-world context.

What the TEACHER does:

- Explore with multiple examples and experiences using positive and negative integers to represent real-world situations such as a bank account with credits and debits, temperature, and above and below sea level.

- Investigate the use of both vertical and horizontal number lines to illustrate examples such as, "*Our football team lost 7 yards on the first down.*" Or, "*It is freezing outside today and is 10 degrees below zero.*" Or, "*The bank statement for the middle school football team has a balance of $4,026. The coach bought new equipment for the team for a total of $4,400. How much money should the coach deposit into the football account in order to stop the account from being overdrawn?*"

- Have students create their own examples to show on their number lines and explain the meaning of 0 in each situation.

- Pose questions such as, "*When you look at the number line, what do you notice about the location of the negative numbers?*" which will lead students to discover that all negative numbers are less than zero.

What the STUDENTS do:

- Understand that zero represents a position on the number line.

- Discover that every negative integer is less than zero.

- Understand that the meaning of zero is determined by the real-world context. For example, on a Celsius thermometer, everything below zero is negative, and everything above zero is positive.

- Represent real-world scenarios such as bank account balances, temperature, and sea level with integers.

- Use precise mathematical vocabulary to discuss positive and negative numbers.

Addressing Student Misconceptions and Common Errors

Some sixth graders may believe the greater the magnitude of a negative number, the greater the number. To help with this misconception, continue to use the number line. Have the students trace a horizontal number line with a finger starting at a positive number such as 10 and moving left one number at a time. Ask the student each time the finger moves one number left if the number is getting larger or smaller. Continue across 0. By then, a pattern of numbers getting smaller as you move left on the number line should be established.

Notes

Notes: Included is blank space beneath each standard for taking notes while studying the mathematical content. This might include vocabulary, materials, resources you want to use, or an explanation of the standard in your own words.

What the STUDENTS do: Some examples of what students may do as they explore and begin to understand the standard. This is not intended to be directive, but rather to frame what student actions may look like.

Sample Planning Page: Provided is a complete sample planning page for one standard at the end of each grade level. While these are not complete lesson plans, they provide ideas, activities, and a structure for planning.

Goal: The purpose of this activity and how it connects to previous and future ideas is stated.

Standards for Mathematical Practice: The Mathematical Practices emphasized in this sample plan are included.

Planning Page: A planning template is provided at the end of each grade level.

Sample PLANNING PAGE   6.G.A

Geometry
Cluster A: Solve real-world and mathematical problems involving area, surface area, and volume.

Standard: 6.G.A.4. *Represent three-dimensional figures using nets made up of rectangles and triangles, and use the nets to find the surface area of these figures. Apply these techniques in the context of solving real-world and mathematical problems.*

Standards for Mathematical Practice:

SFMP 4. Model with mathematics.
Students use real-world three-dimensional objects to create nets and find surface area.

SFMP 6. Attend to precision.
Students use correct vocabulary to talk about the parts of the nets and describe how to find surface area. Correct units should also be used.

SFMP 8. Look for and express regularity in repeated reasoning.
Students find repetition in the dimensions of the individual rectangles that make up the three-dimensional box.

Goal:
Students find surface area by using what they already know about area and composite figures using nets.

Planning:

Materials: 1 cardboard box per pair of students (cereal box, USPS mailing box, etc.), rulers, scissors

Sample Activity:

• Model cutting apart a box to find its net. Then, allow students to cut apart their own boxes to find the nets.
• Review the concept of area. As students measure and find the areas of the individual rectangles on their nets, direct them to write the areas on the respective faces on both sides of the net.
• Fold the nets back into the three-dimensional boxes and ask students to find the total outside area of their boxes. Then, introduce the term *surface area.*
• Discuss anything students noticed that helped them calculate the surface area. Some students may notice shapes that were repeated as well as the location of those repeated shapes.

Questions/Prompts:

• Are students able to see the composite shapes that make up the net? Ask, *"What shapes make up your net?"*
• Are students using the correct units? Ask, *"Which units represent area?"*
• Are students noticing that their nets have pairs of congruent rectangles? Ask, *"How do the areas of the rectangles compare? Where are the congruent shapes located? Why do you think that is so?"*

Differentiating Instruction:

Struggling Students: Some students may have difficulty physically cutting a box. In this case, the teacher may need to assist them. Other students may have weaknesses in measuring and may need to be shown how to round their measures. The many steps involved in calculating surface area may overwhelm some learners. Creating a list for the areas of the faces of the box will help.

Extension: Challenge students to formalize how they calculated the surface area of their boxes into a formula that will work for all rectangular prisms.

PLANNING PAGE   6.G.A

Geometry
Cluster A: Solve real-world and mathematical problems involving area, surface area, and volume.

Standard:

Standards for Mathematical Practice:

Goal:

Planning:
Materials:

Sample Activity:

Questions/Prompts:

Differentiating Instruction:
Struggling Students:

Extension:

Materials: The materials used in the Sample Activity are listed.

Questions/Prompts: This section provides questions or prompts you may use to help build student understanding and encourage student thinking.

Differentiating Instruction: Suggestions to address the need of struggling learners along with extension ideas to challenge other students are included here.

Sample Activity: An example of an activity that addresses this standard is provided.

Resources: In the Resources section at the end of the book you will find tables outlining the Standards for Mathematical Practice and Effective Teaching Practices from NCTM's *Principles to Actions*, the CCSS Where to Focus Mathematics, and reproducibles.

Table 1　Standards for Mathematical Practice

Standard for Mathematical Practice	What the Teacher Does	What the Students Do
1. Make sense of problems and persevere in solving them.	• Provide students with rich tasks and real-world problems that focus on and promote student understanding of an important mathematical concept. • Provide time for and facilitate the discussion of problem solutions. 　o What are you asked to find? 　o Have you solved a similar problem before? 　o What is your plan for solving the problem? 　o Can you explain how you solved the problem? 　o Does your answer make sense? 　o Did you use a different method to check your answer?	• Actively engage in solving problems by working to understand the information that is in the problem and the question that is asked. • Use a variety of strategies that make sense to solve the problem. • Try a different strategy if the first strategy does not work. • Ask themselves if they used the most efficient way to solve the problem. • Ask themselves if their solution makes sense. • Solve real-world problems through the application of algebraic and geometric concepts.
2. Reason abstractly and quantitatively.	• Provide real-world scenarios to use real numbers and variables in mathematical expressions, equations, and inequalities. • Help students decontextualize to manipulate symbolic representations by applying properties of operations. • Help students understand the meaning of the number or variable as related to a problem.	• Use varied strategies, models, and drawings to think about the mathematics of a task and example. • Represent a wide variety of real-world situations through the use of real numbers and variables in mathematical expressions, equations, and inequalities. • Contextualize to understand the meaning of the number or variable as related to the problem and decontextualize to manipulate symbolic representations by applying properties. • Examine patterns in data and assess the degree of linearity of functions.
3. Construct viable arguments and critique the reasoning of others.	• Provide tasks that encourage students to construct mathematical arguments. • Expect students to explain their strategies and mathematical thinking to others. • Expect students to listen to the reasoning of others and respond to their thinking. • Help students to compare strategies and methods by asking questions such as: 　o How can you prove that your answer is correct? 　o What do you think about _____'s strategy? 　o How is your method different from _____'s? How is it similar? 　o Why is this true? Does it always work?	• Explain orally or in writing their strategies and thinking using models, drawings, or symbolic representations. • Critique and evaluate their own thinking and the thinking of other students. • Ask questions to one another and to the teacher to clarify their understanding. • Look for similarities among different ways to solve problems. • Construct arguments using verbal or written explanations for expressions, equations, inequalities, models, and graphs, tables, and other data displays.

Table 2　Effective Teaching Practices

Teaching Practice	Purpose	What the Teacher Does	What the Students Do
1. Establish mathematics goals to focus learning.	• Set the stage to guide instructional decisions. • Expect students to understand the purpose of a lesson beyond simply repeating the words in the Standard.	• Consider broad goals as well as the goals of the unit and the lesson, including: 　o What is to be learned? 　o Why is the goal important? 　o Where do students need to go? 　o How can learning be extended?	• Make sense of the new concepts and skills, making connections to previously learned Grades 6–8 concepts. • Experience connections among the Standards and across domains. • Deepen their understanding and expect what they are learning makes sense.
2. Implement tasks that promote reasoning and problem solving.	• Provide opportunities for students to engage in exploration and make sense of important mathematics. • Encourage students to use procedures in ways that are connected to understanding.	• Choose tasks that: 　o are built on current student understandings, 　o have various entry points with multiple ways for the problems to be solved, 　o are interesting to students.	• Work to make sense of the task and persevere in solving problems. • Use a variety of models and materials to make sense of the mathematics in the task. • Convince themselves and others the answer is reasonable.
3. Use and connect mathematical representations.	• Lead students to connect conceptual understanding of procedural skills using models and representations.	• Use tasks that allow students to use a variety of representations. • Encourage the use of different representations, including concrete manipulatives, models, and symbolic representations that support students in explaining their thinking and reasoning.	• Use materials to make sense of problem situations. • Connect representations to mathematical concepts and the structure of big ideas for ratios and proportional relationships, expressions, and equations, the number system, statistics, and probability, geometry, and functions.
4. Facilitate meaningful mathematical discourse.	• Provide students with opportunities to share ideas, clarify their understanding, and develop convincing arguments. • Allow discussion to advance mathematical thinking for the whole class.	• Engage students in explaining their mathematical reasoning in small group and classroom discussions. • Facilitate dialog among students that supports sense making of a variety of strategies and approaches. • Scaffold classroom discussions so that connections between representations and mathematical ideas occurs.	• Explain their ideas and reasoning in small groups and with the entire class. • Listen to the reasoning of others. • Ask questions of others to make sense of their ideas.

CCSS Where to Focus Grade 6 Mathematics

CCSS WHERE TO FOCUS GRADE 6 MATHEMATICS

MATH · 6 · F

This document shows where students and teachers should spend the large majority of their time in order to meet the expectations of the Standards.

Not all content in a given grade is emphasized equally in the Standards. Some clusters require greater emphasis than others based on the depth of the ideas, the time that they take to master, and/or their importance to future mathematics or the demands of college and career readiness. More time in these areas is also necessary for students to meet the Standards for Mathematical Practice.

To say that some things have greater emphasis is not to say that anything in the Standards can safely be neglected in instruction. Neglecting material will leave gaps in student skill and understanding and may leave students unprepared for the challenges of a later grade.

Students should spend the large majority[1] of their time on the major work of the grade (■). Supporting work (□) and, where appropriate, additional work (◉) can engage students in the major work of the grade.[2,3]

MAJOR, SUPPORTING, AND ADDITIONAL CLUSTERS FOR GRADE 6

Emphases are given at the cluster level. Refer to the Common Core State Standards for Mathematics for the specific standards that fall within each cluster.

Key: ■ Major Clusters □ Supporting Clusters ◉ Additional Clusters

6.RP.A	■	Understand ratio concepts and use ratio reasoning to solve problems.
6.NS.A	■	Apply and extend previous understandings of multiplication and division to divide fractions by fraction.
6.NS.B	◉	Compute fluently with multi-digit numbers and find common factors and multiples.
6.NS.C	■	Apply and extend previous understandings of numbers to the systems of rational numbers.
6.EE.A	■	Apply and extend previous understandings of arithmetic to algebraic expressions.
6.EE.B	■	Reason about and solve one-variable equations and inequalities.
6.EE.C	■	Represent and analyze quantitative relationships between dependent and independent variables.
6.G.A	□	Solve real-world and mathematical problems involving area, surface area, and volume.
6.SP.A	◉	Develop understanding of statistical variability.
6.SP.B	◉	Summarize and describe distributions.

HIGHLIGHTS OF MAJOR WORK IN GRADES K–8

K–2	Addition and subtraction – concepts, skills, and problem solving; place value
3–5	Multiplication and division of whole numbers and fractions – concepts, skills, and problem solving
6	Ratios and proportional relationships; early expressions and equations
7	Ratios and proportional relationships; arithmetic of rational numbers
8	Linear algebra and linear functions

REQUIRED FLUENCIES FOR GRADE 6

6.NS.B.2	Multi-digit division
6.NS.B.3	Multi-digit decimal operations

1 At least 65% and up to approximately 85% of class time, with Grades K–2 nearer the upper end of that range, should be devoted to the major work of the grade. For more information, see Criterion #1 of the K–8 Publishers' Criteria for the Common Core State Standards for Mathematics www.achievethecore.org/publisherscriteria.

2 Refer also to criterion #3 in the K–8 Publishers' Criteria for the Common Core State Standards for Mathematics www.achievethecore.org/publisherscriteria.

3 Note, the critical areas are a survey of what will be taught at each grade level; the major work is the subset of topics that deserve the large majority of instructional time during a given year to best prepare students for college and careers.

STUDENT ACHIEVEMENT PARTNERS
Find additional resources at achievethecore.org

Source: Created by Student Achievement Partners (SAP). http://achievethecore.org/content/upload/SAP_Focus_Math_6.pdf

---

CCSS Where to Focus Mathematics: The major content focus for each grade level is identified on the grade-level focus charts included in the Resources.

Reproducibles: A variety of reproducibles can be downloaded from the companion website at **resources.corwin.com/mathematicscompanion6-8** and used by students in the classroom when working with concrete materials.

Reproducible 1. Percent Wheel

Directions: Cut out two wheels on cardstock. Cut along the dotted line to the center of each wheel. Insert the wheels into each other through the cuts. Position the wheels so the lines face out. You should be able to see the lines on each side when the wheels are together.

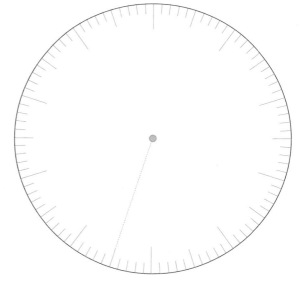

Copyright © 2016 by Corwin. All rights reserved. Reprinted from *The Common Core Mathematics Companion: The Standards Decoded, Grades 6–8: What They Say, What They Mean, How to Teach Them* by Ruth Harbin Miles and Lois A. Williams. Thousand Oaks, CA: Corwin, www.corwin.com. Reproduction authorized only for the local school site or nonprofit organization that has purchased this book.

Quick Reference Guide

GRADE 6

A. Understand ratio concepts and use ratio reasoning to solve problems.

1. Understand the concept of a ratio and use ratio language to describe a ratio relationship between two quantities. *For example, "The ratio of wings to beaks in the bird house at the zoo was 2:1, because for every 2 wings there was 1 beak." "For every vote candidate A received, candidate C received nearly three votes."*

2. Understand the concept of a unit rate $\frac{a}{b}$ associated with a ratio $a{:}b$ with $b \neq 0$, and use rate language in the context of a ratio relationship. *For example, "This recipe has a ratio of 3 cups of flour to 4 cups of sugar, so there is $\frac{3}{4}$ cup of flour for each cup of sugar." "We paid $75 for 15 hamburgers, which is a rate of $5 per hamburger."*[1]

   1. Expectations for unit rates in this grade are limited to non-complex fractions.

3. Use ratio and rate reasoning to solve real-world and mathematical problems, e.g., by reasoning about tables of equivalent ratios, tape diagrams, double number line diagrams, or equations.

   a. Make tables of equivalent ratios relating quantities with whole-number measurements, find missing values in the tables, and plot the pairs of values on the coordinate plane. Use tables to compare ratios.

   b. Solve unit rate problems including those involving unit pricing and constant speed. *For example, if it took 7 hours to mow 4 lawns, then at that rate, how many lawns could be mowed in 35 hours? At what rate were lawns being mowed?*

   c. Find a percent of a quantity as a rate per 100 (e.g., 30% of a quantity means $\frac{30}{100}$ times the quantity); solve problems involving finding the whole, given a part and the percent.

   d. Use ratio reasoning to convert measurement units; manipulate and transform units appropriately when multiplying or dividing quantities.

A. Apply and extend previous understandings of multiplication and division to divide fractions by fractions.

1. Interpret and compute quotients of fractions, and solve word problems involving division of fractions by fractions, e.g., by using visual fraction models and equations to represent the problem. *For example, create a story context for $\frac{2}{3} \div \frac{3}{4}$ and use a visual fraction model to show the quotient; use the relationship between multiplication and division to explain that $\frac{2}{3} \div \frac{3}{4} = \frac{8}{9}$ because $\frac{3}{4}$ of $\frac{8}{9}$ is $\frac{2}{3}$. (In general, $\frac{a}{b} \div \frac{c}{d} = \frac{ad}{bc}$.) How much chocolate will each person get if 3 people share $\frac{1}{2}$ lb of chocolate equally? How many $\frac{3}{4}$-cup servings are in $\frac{2}{3}$ of a cup of yogurt? How wide is a rectangular strip of land with length $\frac{3}{4}$ mi and area $\frac{1}{2}$ square mi?*

B. Compute fluently with multi-digit numbers and find common factors and multiples.

2. Fluently divide multi-digit numbers using the standard algorithm.

3. Fluently add, subtract, multiply, and divide multi-digit decimals using the standard algorithm for each operation.

4. Find the greatest common factor of two whole numbers less than or equal to 100 and the least common multiple of two whole numbers less than or equal to 12. Use the distributive property to express a sum of two whole numbers 1–100 with a common factor as a multiple of a sum of two whole numbers with no common factor. *For example, express 36 + 8 as 4(9 + 2).*

C. Apply and extend previous understandings of numbers to the system of rational numbers.

5. Understand that positive and negative numbers are used together to describe quantities having opposite directions or values (e.g., temperature above/below zero, elevation above/below sea level, credits/debits, positive/negative electric charge); use positive and negative numbers to represent quantities in real-world contexts, explaining the meaning of 0 in each situation.

6. Understand a rational number as a point on the number line. Extend number line diagrams and coordinate axes familiar from previous grades to represent points on the line and in the plane with negative number coordinates.

   a. Recognize opposite signs of numbers as indicating locations on opposite sides of 0 on the number line;

recognize that the opposite of the opposite of a number is the number itself, e.g., $-(-3) = 3$, and that 0 is its own opposite.

b. Understand signs of numbers in ordered pairs as indicating locations in quadrants of the coordinate plane; recognize that when two ordered pairs differ only by signs, the locations of the points are related by reflections across one or both axes.

c. Find and position integers and other rational numbers on a horizontal or vertical number line diagram; find and position pairs of integers and other rational numbers on a coordinate plane.

7. Understand ordering and absolute value of rational numbers.

a. Interpret statements of inequality as statements about the relative position of two numbers on a number line diagram. *For example, interpret $-3 > -7$ as a statement that is located to the right of -7 on a number line oriented from left to right.*

b. Write, interpret, and explain statements of order for rational numbers in real-world contexts. *For example, write $-3\ °C > -7\ °C$ to express the fact that $-3\ °C$ is warmer than $-7\ °C$.*

c. Understand the absolute value of a rational number as its distance from 0 on the number line; interpret absolute value as magnitude for a positive or negative quantity in a real-world situation. *For example, for an account balance of -30 dollars, write $|-30| = 30$ to describe the size of the debt in dollars.*

d. Distinguish comparisons of absolute value from statements about order. *For example, recognize that an account balance less than -30 dollars represents a debt greater than 30 dollars.*

8. Solve real-world and mathematical problems by graphing points in all four quadrants of the coordinate plane. Include use of coordinates and absolute value to find distances between points with the same first coordinate or the same second coordinate.

Expressions and Equations　　　　　　6.EE

A. Apply and extend previous understandings of arithmetic to algebraic expressions.

1. Write and evaluate numerical expressions involving whole-number exponents.

2. Write, read, and evaluate expressions in which letters stand for numbers.

a. Write expressions that record operations with numbers and with letters standing for numbers. *For example, express the calculation "Subtract y from 5" as $5 - y$.*

b. Identify parts of an expression using mathematical terms (sum, term, product, factor, quotient, coefficient); view one or more parts of an expression as a single entity. *For example, describe the expression $2(8 + 7)$ as a product of two factors; view $(8 + 7)$ as both a single entity and a sum of two terms.*

c. Evaluate expressions at specific values of their variables. Include expressions that arise from formulas used in real-world problems. Perform arithmetic operations, including those involving whole-number exponents, in the conventional order when there are no parentheses to specify a particular order (Order of Operations). *For example, use the formulas $V = s^3$ and $A = 6s^2$ to find the volume and surface area of a cube with sides of length $s = \frac{1}{2}$.*

3. Apply the properties of operations to generate equivalent expressions. *For example, apply the distributive property to the expression $3(2 + x)$ to produce the equivalent expression $6 + 3x$; apply the distributive property to the expression $24x + 18y$ to produce the equivalent expression $6(4x + 3y)$; apply properties of operations to $y + y + y$ to produce the equivalent expression $3y$.*

4. Identify when two expressions are equivalent (i.e., when the two expressions name the same number regardless of which value is substituted into them). *For example, the expressions $y + y + y$ and $3y$ are equivalent because they name the same number regardless of which number y stands for.*

B. Reason about and solve one-variable equations and inequalities.

5. Understand solving an equation or inequality as a process of answering a question: which values from a specified set, if any, make the equation or inequality true? Use substitution to determine whether a given number in a specified set makes an equation or inequality true.

6. Use variables to represent numbers and write expressions when solving a real-world or mathematical problem; understand that a variable can represent an unknown number, or, depending on the purpose at hand, any number in a specified set.

7. Solve real-world and mathematical problems by writing and solving equations of the form $x + p = q$ and $px = q$ for cases in which p, q and x are all nonnegative rational numbers.

8. Write an inequality of the form $x > c$ or $x < c$ to represent a constraint or condition in a real-world or mathematical problem. Recognize that inequalities of the form $x > c$ or $x < c$ have infinitely many solutions; represent solutions of such inequalities on number line diagrams.

C. Represent and analyze quantitative relationships between dependent and independent variables.

9. Use variables to represent two quantities in a real-world problem that change in relationship to one another; write an equation to express one quantity, thought of as the dependent variable, in terms of the other quantity, thought of as the independent variable. Analyze the relationship between the dependent and independent variables using graphs and tables, and relate these to the equation. *For example, in a problem involving motion at*

constant speed, list and graph ordered pairs of distances and times, and write the equation $d = 65t$ *to represent the relationship between distance and time.*

Geometry   6.G

A. Solve real-world and mathematical problems involving area, surface area, and volume.

  1. Find the area of right triangles, other triangles, special quadrilaterals, and polygons by composing into rectangles or decomposing into triangles and other shapes; apply these techniques in the context of solving real-world and mathematical problems.

  2. Find the volume of a right rectangular prism with fractional edge lengths by packing it with unit cubes of the appropriate unit fraction edge lengths, and show that the volume is the same as would be found by multiplying the edge lengths of the prism. Apply the formulas $V = lwh$ and $V = bh$ to find volumes of right rectangular prisms with fractional edge lengths in the context of solving real-world and mathematical problems.

  3. Draw polygons in the coordinate plane given coordinates for the vertices; use coordinates to find the length of a side joining points with the same first coordinate or the same second coordinate. Apply these techniques in the context of solving real-world and mathematical problems.

  4. Represent three-dimensional figures using nets made up of rectangles and triangles, and use the nets to find the surface area of these figures. Apply these techniques in the context of solving real-world and mathematical problems.

Statistics and Probability   6.SP

A. Develop understanding of statistical variability.

  1. Recognize a statistical question as one that anticipates variability in the data related to the question and accounts for it in the answers. *For example, "How old am I?" is not a statistical question, but "How old are the students in my school?" is a statistical question because one anticipates variability in students' ages.*

  2. Understand that a set of data collected to answer a statistical question has a distribution which can be described by its center, spread, and overall shape.

  3. Recognize that a measure of center for a numerical data set summarizes all of its values with a single number, while a measure of variation describes how its values vary with a single number.

B. Summarize and describe distributions.

  4. Display numerical data in plots on a number line, including dot plots, histograms, and box plots.

  5. Summarize numerical data sets in relation to their context, such as by:

    a. Reporting the number of observations.

    b. Describing the nature of the attribute under investigation, including how it was measured and its units of measurement.

    c. Giving quantitative measures of center (median and/or mean) and variability (interquartile range and/or mean absolute deviation), as well as describing any overall pattern and any striking deviations from the overall pattern with reference to the context in which the data were gathered.

    d. Relating the choice of measures of center and variability to the shape of the data distribution and the context in which the data were gathered.

GRADE 7

Ratios and Proportional Relationships   7.RP

A. Analyze proportional relationships and use them to solve real-world and mathematical problems.

  1. Compute unit rates associated with ratios of fractions, including ratios of lengths, areas and other quantities measured in like or different units. *For example, if a person walks $\frac{1}{2}$ mile in each $\frac{1}{4}$ hour, compute the unit rate as the complex fraction $\frac{\frac{1}{2}}{\frac{1}{4}}$ miles per hour, equivalently 2 miles per hour.*

  2. Recognize and represent proportional relationships between quantities.

    a. Decide whether two quantities are in a proportional relationship, e.g., by testing for equivalent ratios in a table or graphing on a coordinate plane and observing whether the graph is a straight line through the origin.

    b. Identify the constant of proportionality (unit rate) in tables, graphs, equations, diagrams, and verbal descriptions of proportional relationships.

    c. Represent proportional relationships by equations. *For example, if total cost* t *is proportional to the number* n *of items purchased at a constant price* p, *the relationship between the total cost and the number of items can be expressed as* $t = pn$.

    d. Explain what a point (x, y) on the graph of a proportional relationship means in terms of the situation, with special attention to the points $(0, 0)$ and $(1, r)$ where r is the unit rate.

  3. Use proportional relationships to solve multistep ratio and percent problems. *Examples: simple interest, tax, markups and markdowns, gratuities and commissions, fees, percent increase and decrease, percent error.*

The Number System   7.NS

A. Apply and extend previous understandings of operations with fractions to add, subtract, multiply, and divide rational numbers.

1. Apply and extend previous understandings of addition and subtraction to add and subtract rational numbers; represent addition and subtraction on a horizontal or vertical number line diagram.

   a. Describe situations in which opposite quantities combine to make 0. *For example, a hydrogen atom has 0 charge because its two constituents are oppositely charged.*

   b. Understand $p + q$ as the number located a distance $|q|$ from p, in the positive or negative direction depending on whether q is positive or negative. Show that a number and its opposite have a sum of 0 (are additive inverses). Interpret sums of rational numbers by describing real-world contexts.

   c. Understand subtraction of rational numbers as adding the additive inverse, $p - q = p + (-q)$. Show that the distance between two rational numbers on the number line is the absolute value of their difference, and apply this principle in real-world contexts.

   d. Apply properties of operations as strategies to add and subtract rational numbers.

2. Apply and extend previous understandings of multiplication and division and of fractions to multiply and divide rational numbers.

   a. Understand that multiplication is extended from fractions to rational numbers by requiring that operations continue to satisfy the properties of operations, particularly the distributive property, leading to products such as $(-1)(-1) = 1$ and the rules for multiplying signed numbers. Interpret products of rational numbers by describing real-world contexts.

   b. Understand that integers can be divided, provided that the divisor is not zero, and every quotient of integers (with non-zero divisor) is a rational number. If p and q are integers, then $-\frac{p}{q} = \frac{p}{-q} = \frac{-p}{q}$. Interpret quotients of rational numbers by describing real-world contexts.

   c. Apply properties of operations as strategies to multiply and divide rational numbers.

   d. Convert a rational number to a decimal using long division; know that the decimal form of a rational number terminates in 0s or eventually repeats.

3. Solve real-world and mathematical problems involving the four operations with rational numbers.[1]

---

1. Computations with rational numbers extend the rules for manipulating fractions to complex fractions.

Expressions and Equations   7.EE

A. Use properties of operations to generate equivalent expressions.

1. Apply properties of operations as strategies to add, subtract, factor, and expand linear expressions with rational coefficients.

2. Understand that rewriting an expression in different forms in a problem context can shed light on the problem and how the quantities in it are related. *For example,* $a + 0.05a = 1.05a$ *means that "increase by 5%" is the same as "multiply by 1.05."*

B. Solve real-life and mathematical problems using numerical and algebraic expressions and equations.

3. Solve multi-step real-life and mathematical problems posed with positive and negative rational numbers in any form (whole numbers, fractions, and decimals), using tools strategically. Apply properties of operations to calculate with numbers in any form; convert between forms as appropriate; and assess the reasonableness of answers using mental computation and estimation strategies. *For example: If a woman making $25 an hour gets a 10% raise, she will make an additional $\frac{1}{10}$ of her salary an hour, or $2.50, for a new salary of $27.50. If you want to place a towel bar $9\frac{3}{4}$ inches long in the center of a door that is $27\frac{1}{2}$ inches wide, you will need to place the bar about 9 inches from each edge; this estimate can be used as a check on the exact computation.*

4. Use variables to represent quantities in a real-world or mathematical problem, and construct simple equations and inequalities to solve problems by reasoning about the quantities.

   a. Solve word problems leading to equations of the form $px + q = r$ and $p(x + q) = r$, where $p, q,$ and r are specific rational numbers. Solve equations of these forms fluently. Compare an algebraic solution to an arithmetic solution, identifying the sequence of operations used in each approach. *For example, the perimeter of a rectangle is 54 cm. Its length is 6 cm. What is its width?*

   b. Solve word problems leading to inequalities of the form $px + q > r$ or $px + q < r$, where $p, q,$ and r are specific rational numbers. Graph the solution set of the inequality and interpret it in the context of the problem. *For example: As a salesperson, you are paid $50 per week plus $3 per sale. This week you want your pay to be at least $100. Write an inequality for the number of sales you need to make, and describe the solutions.*

Geometry   7.G

A. Draw, construct, and describe geometrical figures and describe the relationships between them.

1. Solve problems involving scale drawings of geometric figures, including computing actual lengths and areas from a scale drawing and reproducing a scale drawing at a different scale.

2. Draw (freehand, with ruler and protractor, and with technology) geometric shapes with given conditions.

Focus on constructing triangles from three measures of angles or sides, noticing when the conditions determine a unique triangle, more than one triangle, or no triangle.

3. Describe the two-dimensional figures that result from slicing three-dimensional figures, as in plane sections of right rectangular prisms and right rectangular pyramids.

B. Solve real-life and mathematical problems involving angle measure, area, surface area, and volume.

4. Know the formulas for the area and circumference of a circle and use them to solve problems; give an informal derivation of the relationship between the circumference and area of a circle.

5. Use facts about supplementary, complementary, vertical, and adjacent angles in a multi-step problem to write and solve simple equations for an unknown angle in a figure.

6. Solve real-world and mathematical problems involving area, volume and surface area of two- and three-dimensional objects composed of triangles, quadrilaterals, polygons, cubes, and right prisms.

Statistics and Probability   7.SP

A. Use random sampling to draw inferences about a population.

1. Understand that statistics can be used to gain information about a population by examining a sample of the population; generalizations about a population from a sample are valid only if the sample is representative of that population. Understand that random sampling tends to produce representative samples and support valid inferences.

2. Use data from a random sample to draw inferences about a population with an unknown characteristic of interest. Generate multiple samples (or simulated samples) of the same size to gauge the variation in estimates or predictions. *For example, estimate the mean word length in a book by randomly sampling words from the book; predict the winner of a school election based on randomly sampled survey data. Gauge how far off the estimate or prediction might be.*

B. Draw informal comparative inferences about two populations.

3. Informally assess the degree of visual overlap of two numerical data distributions with similar variabilities, measuring the difference between the centers by expressing it as a multiple of a measure of variability. *For example, the mean height of players on the basketball team is 10 cm greater than the mean height of players on the soccer team, about twice the variability (mean absolute deviation) on either team; on a dot plot, the separation between the two distributions of heights is noticeable.*

4. Use measures of center and measures of variability for numerical data from random samples to draw informal comparative inferences about two populations. *For example, decide whether the words in a chapter of a seventh-grade science book are generally longer than the words in a chapter of a fourth-grade science book.*

C. Investigate chance processes and develop, use, and evaluate probability models.

5. Understand that the probability of a chance event is a number between 0 and 1 that expresses the likelihood of the event occurring. Larger numbers indicate greater likelihood. A probability near 0 indicates an unlikely event, a probability around $\frac{1}{2}$ indicates an event that is neither unlikely nor likely, and a probability near 1 indicates a likely event.

6. Approximate the probability of a chance event by collecting data on the chance process that produces it and observing its long-run relative frequency, and predict the approximate relative frequency given the probability. *For example, when rolling a number cube 600 times, predict that a 3 or 6 would be rolled roughly 200 times, but probably not exactly 200 times.*

7. Develop a probability model and use it to find probabilities of events. Compare probabilities from a model to observed frequencies; if the agreement is not good, explain possible sources of the discrepancy.

a. Develop a uniform probability model by assigning equal probability to all outcomes, and use the model to determine probabilities of events. *For example, if a student is selected at random from a class, find the probability that Jane will be selected and the probability that a girl will be selected.*

b. Develop a probability model (which may not be uniform) by observing frequencies in data generated from a chance process. *For example, find the approximate probability that a spinning penny will land heads up or that a tossed paper cup will land open-end down. Do the outcomes for the spinning penny appear to be equally likely based on the observed frequencies?*

8. Find probabilities of compound events using organized lists, tables, tree diagrams, and simulation.

a. Understand that, just as with simple events, the probability of a compound event is the fraction of outcomes in the sample space for which the compound event occurs.

b. Represent sample spaces for compound events using methods such as organized lists, tables and tree diagrams. For an event described in everyday language (e.g., "rolling double sixes"), identify the outcomes in the sample space which compose the event.

c. Design and use a simulation to generate frequencies for compound events. *For example, use random digits as a simulation tool to approximate the answer to the question: If 40% of donors have type A blood, what is the probability that it will take at least 4 donors to find one with type A blood?*

GRADE 8

The Number System   8.NS

A. Know that there are numbers that are not rational, and approximate them by rational numbers.

1. Know that numbers that are not rational are called irrational. Understand informally that every number has a decimal expansion; for rational numbers show that the decimal expansion repeats eventually, and convert a decimal expansion which repeats eventually into a rational number.

2. Use rational approximations of irrational numbers to compare the size of irrational numbers, locate them approximately on a number line diagram, and estimate the value of expressions (e.g., π^2). *For example, by truncating the decimal expansion of $\sqrt{2}$, show that $\sqrt{2}$ is between 1 and 2, then between 1.4 and 1.5, and explain how to continue on to get better approximations.*

Expressions and Equations   8.EE

A. Work with radicals and integer exponents.

1. Know and apply the properties of integer exponents to generate equivalent numerical expressions. *For example,*
$$3^2 \times 3^{-5} = 3^{-3} = \frac{1}{3^3} = \frac{1}{27}.$$

2. Use square root and cube root symbols to represent solutions to equations of the form $x^2 = p$ and $x^3 = p$, where p is a positive rational number. Evaluate square roots of small perfect squares and cube roots of small perfect cubes. Know that $\sqrt{2}$ is irrational.

3. Use numbers expressed in the form of a single digit times an integer power of 10 to estimate very large or very small quantities, and to express how many times as much one is than the other. *For example, estimate the population of the United States as 3 times 10^8 and the population of the world as 7 times 10^9, and determine that the world population is more than 20 times larger.*

4. Perform operations with numbers expressed in scientific notation, including problems where both decimal and scientific notation are used. Use scientific notation and choose units of appropriate size for measurements of very large or very small quantities (e.g., use millimeters per year for seafloor spreading). Interpret scientific notation that has been generated by technology.

B. Understand the connections between proportional relationships, lines, and linear equations.

5. Graph proportional relationships, interpreting the unit rate as the slope of the graph. Compare two different proportional relationships represented in different ways. *For example, compare a distance-time graph to a distance-time equation to determine which of two moving objects has greater speed.*

6. Use similar triangles to explain why the slope m is the same between any two distinct points on a non-vertical line in the coordinate plane; derive the equation $y = mx$ for a line through the origin and the equation $y = mx + b$ for a line intercepting the vertical axis at b.

C. Analyze and solve linear equations and pairs of simultaneous linear equations.

7. Solve linear equations in one variable.

   a. Give examples of linear equations in one variable with one solution, infinitely many solutions, or no solutions. Show which of these possibilities is the case by successively transforming the given equation into simpler forms, until an equivalent equation of the form $x = a$, $a = a$, or $a = b$ results (where a and b are different numbers).

   b. Solve linear equations with rational number coefficients, including equations whose solutions require expanding expressions using the distributive property and collecting like terms.

8. Analyze and solve pairs of simultaneous linear equations.

   a. Understand that solutions to a system of two linear equations in two variables correspond to points of intersection of their graphs, because points of intersection satisfy both equations simultaneously.

   b. Solve systems of two linear equations in two variables algebraically, and estimate solutions by graphing the equations. Solve simple cases by inspection. *For example, 3x + 2y = 5 and 3x + 2y = 6 have no solution because 3x + 2y cannot simultaneously be 5 and 6.*

   c. Solve real-world and mathematical problems leading to two linear equations in two variables. *For example, given coordinates for two pairs of points, determine whether the line through the first pair of points intersects the line through the second pair.*

Functions   8.F

A. Define, evaluate, and compare functions.

1. Understand that a function is a rule that assigns to each input exactly one output. The graph of a function is the set of ordered pairs consisting of an input and the corresponding output.[1]

   1. Function notation is not required for Grade 8.

2. Compare properties of two functions each represented in a different way (algebraically, graphically, numerically in tables, or by verbal descriptions). *For example, given a linear function represented by a table of values and a linear function represented by an algebraic expression, determine which function has the greater rate of change.*

3. Interpret the equation $y = mx + b$ as defining a linear function, whose graph is a straight line; give examples of functions that are not linear. *For example, the function $A = s^2$ giving the area of a square as a function of its side length is not linear because its graph contains the points $(1,1)$, $(2,4)$ and $(3,9)$, which are not on a straight line.*

B. Use functions to model relationships between quantities.

4. Construct a function to model a linear relationship between two quantities. Determine the rate of change and initial value of the function from a description of a relationship or from two (x, y) values, including reading these from a table or from a graph. Interpret the

rate of change and initial value of a linear function in terms of the situation it models, and in terms of its graph or a table of values.

5. Describe qualitatively the functional relationship between two quantities by analyzing a graph (e.g., where the function is increasing or decreasing, linear or nonlinear). Sketch a graph that exhibits the qualitative features of a function that has been described verbally.

Geometry   8.G

A. **Understand congruence and similarity using physical models, transparencies, or geometry software.**

1. Verify experimentally the properties of rotations, reflections, and translations:

   a. Lines are taken to lines, and line segments to line segments of the same length.

   b. Angles are taken to angles of the same measure.

   c. Parallel lines are taken to parallel lines.

2. Understand that a two-dimensional figure is congruent to another if the second can be obtained from the first by a sequence of rotations, reflections, and translations; given two congruent figures, describe a sequence that exhibits the congruence between them.

3. Describe the effect of dilations, translations, rotations, and reflections on two-dimensional figures using coordinates.

4. Understand that a two-dimensional figure is similar to another if the second can be obtained from the first by a sequence of rotations, reflections, translations, and dilations; given two similar two-dimensional figures, describe a sequence that exhibits the similarity between them.

5. Use informal arguments to establish facts about the angle sum and exterior angle of triangles, about the angles created when parallel lines are cut by a transversal, and the angle-angle criterion for similarity of triangles. *For example, arrange three copies of the same triangle so that the sum of the three angles appears to form a line, and give an argument in terms of transversals why this is so.*

B. **Understand and apply the Pythagorean Theorem.**

6. Explain a proof of the Pythagorean Theorem and its converse.

7. Apply the Pythagorean Theorem to determine unknown side lengths in right triangles in real-world and mathematical problems in two and three dimensions.

8. Apply the Pythagorean Theorem to find the distance between two points in a coordinate system.

C. **Solve real-world and mathematical problems involving volume of cylinders, cones, and spheres.**

9. Know the formulas for the volumes of cones, cylinders, and spheres and use them to solve real-world and mathematical problems.

Statistics and Probability   8.SP

A. **Investigate patterns of association in bivariate data.**

1. Construct and interpret scatter plots for bivariate measurement data to investigate patterns of association between two quantities. Describe patterns such as clustering, outliers, positive or negative association, linear association, and nonlinear association.

2. Know that straight lines are widely used to model relationships between two quantitative variables. For scatter plots that suggest a linear association, informally fit a straight line, and informally assess the model fit by judging the closeness of the data points to the line.

3. Use the equation of a linear model to solve problems in the context of bivariate measurement data, interpreting the slope and intercept. *For example, in a linear model for a biology experiment, interpret a slope of 1.5 cm/hr as meaning that an additional hour of sunlight each day is associated with an additional 1.5 cm in mature plant height.*

4. Understand that patterns of association can also be seen in bivariate categorical data by displaying frequencies and relative frequencies in a two-way table. Construct and interpret a two-way table summarizing data on two categorical variables collected from the same subjects. Use relative frequencies calculated for rows or columns to describe possible association between the two variables. *For example, collect data from students in your class on whether or not they have a curfew on school nights and whether or not they have assigned chores at home. Is there evidence that those who have a curfew also tend to have chores?*

Standards for Mathematical Practice (6–8)

1. Make sense of problems and persevere in solving them.

2. Reason abstractly and quantitatively.

3. Construct viable arguments and critique the reasoning of others.

4. Model with mathematics.

5. Use appropriate tools strategically.

6. Attend to precision.

7. Look for and make use of structure.

8. Look for and express regularity in repeated reasoning.

The Common Core Mathematics Companion: The Standards Decoded, Grades 6–8

The Common Core Mathematics Companion: The Standards Decoded, Grades 6–8

What They Say, What They Mean, How to Teach Them

Ruth Harbin Miles

Lois A. Williams

Series Creator: Jim Burke

Mathematics Series Creator: Linda M. Gojak

Name: _____

Department: _____

Learning Team: _____

A JOINT PUBLICATION

FOR INFORMATION:

Corwin

A SAGE Company

2455 Teller Road

Thousand Oaks, California 91320

(800) 233-9936

www.corwin.com

SAGE Publications Ltd.

1 Oliver's Yard

55 City Road

London EC1Y 1SP

United Kingdom

SAGE Publications India Pvt. Ltd.

B 1/I 1 Mohan Cooperative Industrial Area

Mathura Road, New Delhi 110 044

India

SAGE Publications Asia-Pacific Pte. Ltd.

3 Church Street

#10-04 Samsung Hub

Singapore 049483

Series Creator: Jim Burke

Mathematics Series Creator: Linda M. Gojak

Acquisitions Editor: Erin Null

Editorial Development Manager: Julie Nemer

Senior Associate Editor: Desirée A. Bartlett

Editorial Assistants: Andrew Olson and Nicole Shade

Production Editor: Melanie Birdsall

Copy Editor: Gillian Dickens

Typesetter: C&M Digitals (P) Ltd.

Proofreader: Jennifer Grubba

Cover Designer: Scott Van Atta

Marketing Manager: Rebecca Eaton

Copyright © 2016 by Corwin

All rights reserved. When forms and sample documents are included, their use is authorized only by educators, local school sites, and/or noncommercial or nonprofit entities that have purchased the book. Except for that usage, no part of this book may be reproduced or utilized in any form or by any means, electronic or mechanical, including photocopying, recording, or by any information storage and retrieval system, without permission in writing from the publisher.

All trademarks depicted within this book, including trademarks appearing as part of a screenshot, figure, or other image, are included solely for the purpose of illustration and are the property of their respective holders. The use of the trademarks in no way indicates any relationship with, or endorsement by, the holders of said trademarks.

Common Core State Standards cited throughout © copyright 2010 National Governors Association Center for Best Practices and Council of Chief State School Officers. All rights reserved.

Printed in the United States of America

Library of Congress Cataloging-in-Publication Data

Names: Miles, Ruth Harbin. | Williams, Lois A. | National Council of Teachers of Mathematics.

Title: The common core mathematics companion : the standards decoded, grades 6–8 : what they say, what they mean, how to teach them / Ruth Harbin Miles, Lois A. Williams.

Description: Thousand Oaks, California : Corwin, [2016] | "A joint publication with National Council of Teachers of Mathematics." | Includes bibliographical references.

Identifiers: LCCN 2015045169 | ISBN 9781506332192 (spiral : alk. paper)

Subjects: LCSH: Mathematics—Study and teaching (Middle school)—Standards—United States. | Language arts (Middle school)—Standards—United States.

Classification: LCC QA135.6 .M546 2016 | DDC 510.71/273—dc23 LC record available at http://lccn.loc.gov/2015045169

This book is printed on acid-free paper.

Certified Chain of Custody
Promoting Sustainable Forestry
www.sfiprogram.org
SFI-01268

SFI label applies to text stock

19 20 10 9 8 7

DISCLAIMER: This book may direct you to access third-party content via Web links, QR codes, or other scannable technologies, which are provided for your reference by the author(s). Corwin makes no guarantee that such third-party content will be available for your use and encourages you to review the terms and conditions of such third-party content. Corwin takes no responsibility and assumes no liability for your use of any third-party content, nor does Corwin approve, sponsor, endorse, verify, or certify such third-party content.

Contents

Part 3. Expressions and Equations

Part 4. Functions

Resources

Reproducibles

Additional Resources   263

About the Authors   265

For downloadable versions of the Quick
Reference Guide, Reproducibles, and a Planning Page Template,
visit the companion website at
resources.corwin.com/mathematicscompanion6-8.

Acknowledgments

A very special thank you is due to the very best teacher I have ever known, my incredible father, Dr. Calvin E. Harbin, who taught me to value my education and at the age of 99 is still modeling lifelong learning. Acknowledgment and thanks must also be given to my extraordinary mentors, Dr. Ramona Anshutz and Dr. Shirley A. Hill, who both inspired me to become a mathematics educational leader. Their influence and guidance changed my life's work. Words could never express the thanks and credit I owe my dear colleagues and writing partners, Linda Gojak, Dr. Ted H. Hull, and Dr. Don S. Balka, who are simply the best! Most important, I thank my incredible husband, Sam Miles, for *always* being there for me.

—Ruth Harbin Miles

Special thanks to all of my mentors who have guided me to this point in my career: Joe Garofalo, John Van De Walle, Ann Stafford, and Maria Timmerman. A piece of what each of you has taught me is in this publication. I also thank my husband, Mike, for always standing by me.

—Lois A. Williams

Publisher's Acknowledgments

Corwin gratefully acknowledges the contributions of the following reviewers:

Betty Brandenburg
Retired Educator and Consultant
Department of Defense Schools
Guston, KY

Amanda McKee
Mathematics Instructor
Florence County School District 5
Johnsonville, SC

Letter to Grades 6–8 Teachers

Dear Teachers of Grades 6–8,

The Common Core Mathematics Companion: The Standards Decoded, Grades 6–8: What They Say, What They Mean, How to Teach Them is designed to provide support as you help your students learn what they need to know and be able to do. This book includes critical mathematical ideas for each grade and is intended to be your guide to both the Content Standards and the Mathematical Practices. A brief overview for each standard, along with effective teaching practices, mathematics vocabulary, suggested models, manipulatives, representations, and ideas for each standard, is included. This book is intended to help you make sense of the Content Standards and Mathematical Practices.

The Common Core Mathematics Content Standards and the Standards for Mathematical Practice were developed to promote student achievement and have the potential for changing traditional classroom instruction across the United States. This is significant as the Content Standards will help ensure students deeply understand the mathematics they are expected to learn. The Content Standards are a foundation for the development of a rigorous, relevant, and coherent mathematics curriculum for every student and will help ensure all students are ready for their futures, including college and the workforce.

The Common Core State Standards for Mathematics (CCSSM) promote conceptual understanding and reasoning as well as skill proficiency. It is organized around domains, clusters, and standards. The domains for Grades 6–8 mathematics include: The Number System, Expressions and Equations, Geometry, and Statistics and Probability. Ratios and Proportional Relationships is a domain in Grades 6 and 7. Functions is an additional domain in Grade 8. The standards under each domain include developing conceptual understanding, skills based on that understanding, and application of key ideas. Clusters are groups of related standards for each domain. Also included in the CCSSM document are eight Standards for Mathematical Practice. These standards describe the mathematical habits of mind that proficient students demonstrate in doing mathematics with understanding. The Standards for Mathematical Practice are as follows:

1. Make sense of problems and persevere in solving them.
2. Reason abstractly and quantitatively.
3. Construct viable arguments and critique the reasoning of others.
4. Model with mathematics.
5. Use appropriate tools strategically.
6. Attend to precision.
7. Look for and make use of structure.
8. Look for and express regularity in repeated reasoning.

When students are engaged in the Standards for Mathematical Practice, they are learning meaningful, high-quality mathematics.

It is suggested that you work with your grade-level colleagues and use this book when you are studying the standards to decide upon the sequencing and clustering of the standards as well as the selection of appropriate instructional resources. Be sure to study the content for the grade before and after the one you teach so you will understand what students should have learned and what they will be learning the next year. Keep in mind that implementation of the standards and practices is a process and may take time to do well. Your devotion to teaching the standards will make a difference for students who will be learning to reason and apply the mathematics you have taught them.

We hope you will find this book a helpful resource and a valuable companion as you work to help your students become successful mathematics learners.

Sincerely,

Ruth Harbin Miles

Lois A. Williams

Letter to Middle School Principals

Dear Middle School Principal,

The Common Core Mathematics Companion: The Standards Decoded, Grades 6–8: What They Say, What They Mean, How to Teach Them is designed to support teachers in their learning and implementation of the Common Core Mathematics Standards. The book focuses on the critical ideas of Grades 6–8 mathematics, including a meaningful explanation of each standard along with effective teaching practices and learning activities. Mathematics vocabulary and suggested teaching materials are highlighted for each standard. The book is not only a reference but also a guide to help teachers more deeply understand all aspects of the standards.

As a principal, you can clearly explain and help teachers understand that student success and achievement are the goals for implementing the Common Core Mathematics Standards and the Standards for Mathematical Practice. You can also support teachers as they engage in professional learning to study both the Content and the Practice Standards they will be teaching. Teachers will need guidance to understand the depth and the sequencing of each standard as well as the content before and after their levels. You can help teachers recognize that the Common Core Mathematics Standards have the prospect of ensuring equity and access to high-quality mathematics for every student.

The CCSSM define what students should understand and be able to do in Grades 6–8. Implemented properly, these standards are the foundation for the concepts and skills students will be expected to know in Grades 9–12. The standards are organized around domains, clusters, and standards. The domains for Grades 6–8 mathematics include: The Number System, Expressions and Equations, Geometry, and Statistics and Probability. Ratios and Proportional Relationships is a domain in Grades 6 and 7. Functions is a domain in Grade 8. The standards under each domain include developing conceptual understanding, skills based on that understanding, and application of key ideas. Clusters are groups of related standards for each domain. Also included in the CCSSM document are eight Standards for Mathematical Practice. These standards describe the mathematical habits of mind that proficient students demonstrate in doing mathematics with understanding. The Standards for Mathematical Practice are as follows:

1. Make sense of problems and persevere in solving them.
2. Reason abstractly and quantitatively.
3. Construct viable arguments and critique the reasoning of others.
4. Model with mathematics.
5. Use appropriate tools strategically.
6. Attend to precision.
7. Look for and make use of structure.
8. Look for and express regularity in repeated reasoning.

When students are actively engaged in using the Practice Standards, they are learning meaningful, high-quality mathematics.

Middle schools, professional learning communities, individual classrooms, and special education teachers will all have different knowledge, various skills, and distinct ideas about using *The Common Core Mathematics Companion: The Standards Decoded, Grades 6–8: What They Say, What They Mean, How to Teach Them.* You may wish to supply every teacher with a personal copy of the book for use as a schoolwide initiative or book study. Such a study will help improve both content knowledge and understanding of the mathematics teachers are expected to teach. Providing the opportunity for teachers to engage and use the book in grade-level planning with colleagues will allow teachers to dig deeply into the standards. Use of this resource will add cohesiveness and consistency, ensuring all Grades 6–8 students will benefit from similar instruction. Be sure to invite teachers to bring this resource to all planning and professional development work. You may even want teachers to start or end a meeting with a lesson they have planned based on the suggestions and strategies in this reference guide. As a result of the book study, *The Common Core Mathematics Companion: The Standards Decoded, Grades 6–8: What They Say, What They Mean, How to Teach Them* will influence professional practice at both the classroom and school levels and will help teachers transform instruction.

Sincerely,

Ruth Harbin Miles

Lois A. Williams

Introduction

A Brief History of the Common Core

Mathematics standards are not new. In fact, they have been around for more than 25 years. In 1989, the National Council of Teachers of Mathematics introduced *The Curriculum and Evaluation Standards for School Mathematics*, followed by the updated set of standards, *Principles and Standards for School Mathematics*, in 2000. Both of these documents provided a vision for K–12 mathematics and were the foundation for most of the states' grade-level standards.

In 2008, the National Governors Association and the Council of Chief State Schools Officers met to discuss the Common Core State Standards Initiative with the purpose of developing a set of common standards across states with the focus of balancing the quality of mathematics instruction and learning. Following that meeting, the process of writing the Common Core Standards began, led by William McCallum, Phil Daro, and Jason Zimba with a writing team including mathematicians, mathematics educators, mathematics education researchers, and classroom teachers. The process provided an open invitation for feedback from the National Council of Teachers of Mathematics, state mathematics associations, mathematics educators, and the general public. This feedback was considered and much of it was incorporated into the final document released in June 2010. Following the release of the standards, individual states reviewed and adopted the Common Core State Standards for Mathematics.

The Common Core State Standards for Mathematics

"The Common Core State Standards are a clear set of shared goals and expectations for the knowledge and skills students need in English language and mathematics at each grade level so they can be prepared to succeed in college, career, and life" (www.corestandards.org/about-the-standards/frequently-asked questions/#faq-2303).

The Common Core State Standards for Mathematics (CCSSM) include two critical components for learning mathematics: (1) the Content Standards and (2) the Standards for Mathematical Practice. The first component, the Content Standards, explicitly outlines the mathematics students should know and be able to do at each grade level. The Content Standards of the Common Core are fewer in number than most previous state standards. At the same time, the expectation is that students will develop *deeper* understanding of the content, so less time is spent on reteaching from year to year. Additionally, the standards were carefully constructed to show connections among ideas at a grade level as well as vertical progressions across grades. For example, the standards in Grade 6 develop from the mathematical work students completed in previous grades. It is important for teachers to be knowledgeable of the standards not only at the level they are teaching but also at the preceding and following grade levels.

The second component of the CCSSM are the Standards for Mathematical Practice. These standards describe the habits of mind that students should develop as they do mathematics. These eight standards are the same across all grades levels, K–12. When planning lessons, teachers should consider how students will use the practices in learning and doing mathematics.

The Common Core Standards are *not* a curriculum. Decisions about mathematics programs, textbooks, materials, sequencing topics and units, and instructional frameworks are decisions to be made by local school districts. The standards *do not* tell teachers how to teach but rather describe what students need to know and be able to do. Schools and teachers know best how to help students reach both the Content and the Practice Standards.

The Common Core Standards *do not* dictate specific assessments. Many states will be using assessments developed by the PARCC (Partnership for Assessment of Readiness for College and Careers) or SBAC (Smarter Balanced Assessment Consortium). Some states will develop and use their own assessments. For additional information, check out http://www.corestandards.org.

Instructional Shifts

The standards do not call for a particular model or philosophy. They are based on the best of existing standards. What makes them different is the call for specific instructional shifts: *focus, coherence, and rigor.*

Focus: The Content Standards call for greater focus on fewer topics. An examination of the mathematics standards of high-performing countries indicate that fewer, more focused topics are taught at a grade level to allow students to deepen understanding of the mathematics and gain a stronger foundation for ongoing study of mathematics. Within the standards, the major mathematical work of each grade level has been identified (www.corestandards.org). That means that not all of the content within a grade is emphasized equally among the Content Standards. The list of Content Standards for a grade is not linear or a checklist. Some clusters require greater emphasis than others. Some clusters may need more time for students to master with depth of understanding. The major work of Grades 6–8 includes ratios and proportional relationships, expressions and equations, arithmetic of rational numbers, and linear algebra and linear functions. This means that the majority of instructional time in Grades 6–8 (65%–85%) must be spent on these mathematical topics. This does not mean that other standards should be skipped. Rather, the supporting standards should be taught to connect mathematical ideas among the essential standards. The additional standards provide students with experiences that will be foundational to work in future grades. Neglecting material will leave gaps in student skill and understanding.

Coherence: Mathematics must be thought of as a coherent body of knowledge made up of topics that are all connected and build on each other. The call for coherence in the Content Standards ensures that there are carefully constructed progressions from grade to grade so students build new understanding on the foundations built in previous years. Each standard is not a new topic but an extension of previous learning. In addition to the progressions across grade levels, the standards incorporate specific connections within a grade level.

Rigor: The third instructional shift, *rigor*, refers to how we support students in developing deep understanding of each standard. Understanding does not develop by assigning more worksheets or with more difficult examples and problems. Rather, it calls for instructional practices that balance conceptual understanding, procedural skills, and applying mathematical ideas to a variety of contexts.

The following descriptions of each component of rigor are from www.corestandards.org.

Conceptual understanding: The standards call for conceptual understanding of key Grade 6 concepts such as ratios and proportional relationships and early expressions and equations. In Grade 7, the major concepts are ratios and proportional relationships and arithmetic of rational numbers. Grade 8 calls for linear algebra and linear functions. Students must be able to access concepts from a number of perspectives in order to see mathematics as more than a set of rules or procedures.

Procedural skills and fluency: The standards call for speed and accuracy in calculation. Students must practice core skills such as basic multidigit division and multidigit decimal operations in order to have access to more complex concepts and procedures. Fluency is built upon conceptual understanding, and with students, through the development of ideas using representations, models, and symbols.

Applications: The standards call for students to use mathematics in situations that require mathematical knowledge. Correctly applying mathematical knowledge depends on students having a solid conceptual understanding and procedural fluency.

Major Work of Grades 6–8

At least 65% to 85% of instructional time should focus on the major work for each grade level. Areas of major work include the following:

Grade 6: Understand ratio concepts and use ratio reasoning to solve problems. Apply and extend previous understandings of multiplication and division to divide fractions by fractions. Apply and extend previous understandings of numbers to the system of rational numbers. Apply and extend previous understandings of arithmetic to algebraic expressions. Reason about and solve one-variable equations and inequalities. Represent and analyze quantitative relationships between dependent and independent variables.

Grade 7: Analyze proportional relationships and use them to solve real-world and mathematical problems. Apply and extend previous understandings of operations with fractions to add, subtract, multiply, and divide rational numbers. Use properties of operations to generate equivalent expressions. Solve real-life and mathematical problems using numerical and algebraic expressions.

Grade 8: Work with radicals and integer exponents. Understand the connections between proportional relationships, lines, and linear equations. Analyze and solve linear equations and pairs of simultaneous linear equations. Define, evaluate, and compare functions. Use functions to model relationships between quantities. Understand congruence and similarity using physical models, transparencies, or geometric software.

Common Core Word Wall

The language of the Common Core differs from traditional standards. Familiarity with the terms *standards*, *clusters*, and *domains* is critical.

Standards define what students should understand and be able to do.

Clusters summarize groups of related standards. Be aware that standards from different clusters may sometimes be closely related as mathematics is a connected subject.

Domains are larger groups of related standards. Be aware that standards from different domains may sometimes be closely related.

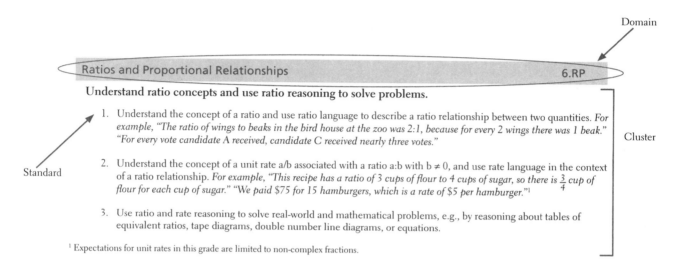

Source: Common Core State Standards for Mathematics (www.corestandards.org).

The Common Core Standards for Mathematical Practice

The Common Core Standards for Mathematical Practice describe eight ideas teachers must incorporate in classroom instruction to develop a depth of understanding of critical mathematical concepts in their students. The Mathematical Practices are not intended to be taught in isolation but should be integrated into daily lessons. Some of the lessons may focus on developing one or two of these Standards, and others may incorporate all eight Standards. The eight Standards are not explicitly taught but exemplify the type of mathematical thinking and doing students should practice as they develop mathematical understanding.

Throughout the following chapters, examples of the Mathematical Practices intended to be used are included in each cluster. The listed Practices are not meant to limit lessons by using only those Practices but are examples of key practices that can be included in lessons around that particular cluster. It is likely that teachers will use all of the Practices throughout the cluster and domain.

The eight Standards for Mathematical Practice (SFMP), briefly explained below, are essential for student success. If students are actively engaged in using these eight Practices, they are learning rigorous, meaningful mathematics.

SFMP 1. Make sense of problems and persevere in solving them.

Grades 6–8 students should work to understand what a problem is asking, choose a strategy to find a solution, and check the answer to make sure it makes sense.

SFMP 2. Reason abstractly and quantitatively.

Grades 6–8 students must make sense of quantities and their relationships in problem situations. At this level, students can model problem solutions.

SFMP 3. Construct viable arguments and critique the reasoning of others.

Grades 6–8 students often use stated assumptions, definitions, and established results in constructing arguments. At this level, students must justify and communicate their conclusions as well as listen to other students' explanations.

SFMP 4. Model with mathematics.

Grades 6–8 students should use various representations, models, and symbols to connect conceptual understanding to skills and application. Students should use the mathematics they know to solve problems in everyday life, society, and the workplace. At this level, students may write an equation or may connect representations and explain the connections.

SFMP 5. Use appropriate tools strategically.

Grades 6–8 students consider the available tools when solving a mathematics problem. At times, students may choose to solve problems with mental calculations, with paper and pencil, or with other technology.

SFMP 6. Attend to precision.

Grades 6–8 students communicate precisely with others. At this level, students explain their knowledge of mathematical symbols that explicitly connect to using the correct mathematical vocabulary.

SFMP 7. Look for and make use of structure.

Grades 6–8 students look closely to discern patterns and structure.

SFMP 8. Look for and express regularity in repeated reasoning.

Grades 6–8 students notice if calculations are repeated and make generalizations. At this level, students discover shortcuts through making the generalizations and understanding why they work.

Effective Teaching Practices

Quality mathematics teaching is a critical key for student success. In *Principles to Actions* (2014), the National Council of Teachers of Mathematics outline eight valuable practices every teacher *must* incorporate to guarantee student achievement. These eight research-informed practices, briefly explained below, provide a foundation for effective common core mathematics teaching and learning.

1. Establish mathematics goals to focus learning.

Establishing learning goals sets the stage and helps guide instructional decisions. Teachers must keep in mind what is to be learned, why the goal is important, where students need to go (the trajectory), and how learning can be extended. Students must clearly understand the purpose of the lesson.

2. Implement tasks that promote reasoning and problem solving.

Implementing tasks that promote reasoning and problem solving provides opportunities for students to engage in exploration and encourages students to use procedures in ways that are connected to concepts and understanding. The tasks teachers choose should be built on current student understandings and have various entry points with multiple ways for the problems to be solved.

3. Use and connect mathematical representations.

Using and connecting representations leads students to deeper understanding. Different representations should be introduced, discussed, and connected to support students' abilities to justify and explain their thinking and reasoning.

4. Facilitate meaningful mathematical discourse.

Facilitating meaningful discourse provides students with opportunities to share ideas, clarify understandings, and develop convincing arguments. Talking and sharing aloud can advance the mathematical thinking of the whole class.

5. Pose purposeful questions.

Posing purposeful questions reveals students' current understanding of a concept and encourages students to explain, elaborate, and clarify thinking. Asking good questions makes the learning of mathematics more visible and accessible for student examination.

6. Build procedural fluency from conceptual understanding.

Building procedural fluency from conceptual understanding allows students to flexibly choose from a variety of methods to solve contextual and mathematical problems.

7. Support productive struggle in learning mathematics.

Supporting productive struggle in learning mathematics is significant and essential to learning mathematics with understanding. Productive struggle allows students to grapple with ideas and relationships.

8. Elicit and use evidence of student thinking.

Eliciting and using evidence of student thinking helps teachers access learning progress and can be used to make instructional decisions during the lessons as well as help to prepare what will occur in the next lesson.

The overall goal of this book is to help teachers more deeply understand the mathematical meaning of clusters and standards within the domains of Grades 6–8. The intent of the resource is to use it as your personal toolkit for teaching the mathematics standards. Blank space on numerous pages has been left for you to take notes, add ideas, and reference other resources that may be helpful.

Each part of the book explains one domain and begins with an overview of how the domain progresses across Grades 6 through 8. A list of helpful materials, reproducibles, and key vocabulary from the domain is included in the overview as well.

Every domain is tracked across sixth, seventh, and eighth grades with a page for each cluster and the standards within the cluster. A description of the cluster and how the Standards for Mathematical Practice can be incorporated into your teaching of the cluster follows. Because the standards are intentionally designed to connect within and across domains and grade levels, a list of related standards is included in the cluster overview. As you prepare work on a cluster, we suggest you look at these standards to have a better idea of the mathematics students learned in previous grades and where they are going in the future. A list of all of the Standards is found in the Quick Reference Guide at the beginning of the book.

Each standard within a cluster is explained with a section called *What the TEACHER does* followed by a description of *What the STUDENTS do*. It is important to note that most standards will take several days, and you should be connecting conceptual understandings across standards and domains as you teach for understanding.

Addressing student misconceptions and common errors in developing student understanding of a concept concludes the contents for each standard.

At the end of each grade-level domain, you will find a sample planning page based on one standard for that domain. Also included are planning page templates for each cluster within the domain for you to duplicate and use for planning.

In the resource section, you will find reproducible key materials. These are designed to be samples, and we encourage you to use them or redesign them to best meet the needs of your students. A list of our favorite resource books and high-quality online resources that are particularly useful to developing mathematical ideas in Grades 6–8 is also included.

We believe that this can become your common core bible. Read it and mark it with questions, comments, and ideas. We hope that this resource will help you use these standards and good teaching practices to lay the essential foundation that will ensure your students success not only in your grade but in all of their future study of mathematics.

Reflection Questions

1. How are the three instructional shifts called for by the Common Core similar to your current instructional practice?

   - What is conceptual understanding?
   - How is it different from procedural skills?
   - What do you need to consider to teach for conceptual understanding?
   - How can you connect conceptual understanding to help students develop procedural skills?

2. The Standards for Mathematical Practice describe the habits of mind that students need for thinking about and doing mathematics. While not every practice will be in every lesson, select one standard at your grade level and consider some ways you can incorporate these practices in a lesson for that standard.

   - How will these practices provide you with information about student understanding?
   - How will this help you to better assess students?
   - How will this information help you in planning lessons?

3. The Effective Teaching Practices describe specific actions that teachers must consider in planning and implementing lessons and assessing student performance.

   - How are the practices connected? Work with colleagues to plan a lesson that employs all of these practices.
   - How can you modify a traditional task so that it promotes reasoning and problem solving?
   - What representations will help students more deeply understand the concept?
   - How will you connect conceptual understanding to build procedural fluency?
   - What kinds of information will you look for to help inform your instruction?

   (For more information on the Effective Teaching Practices, go to www.nctm.org.)

## Part 1

Ratios and Proportional Relationships

Ratios and Proportional Relationships

Domain Overview

GRADE 6

Sixth graders are introduced to ratio, a relationship or comparison of two quantities or measures. Students represent ratios in various forms and compare types of ratios. At this level, they use reasoning about multiplication and division to solve ratio and rate problems about quantities. Students learn how and where ratios and rates are used in the real world.

GRADE 7

Continuing to develop an understanding of operations with rational numbers, seventh graders describe situations in which opposite quantities combine to make zero and determine the absolute value for a given number. Students estimate solutions, then add, subtract, multiply, and divide integers in the context of real-world problems. Given a real-world context, students simplify an expression using four integer operations and the order of operations.

6	7	
✓	✓	Common objects such as tennis shoes, cereal boxes, etc.
	✓	Copies of restaurant menus
✓		Counters (two-color, chips, etc.)
✓	✓	Graph paper
✓		Newspapers or grocery ads
✓		Percent wheel

KEY VOCABULARY

6	7	
✓	✓	**commission** a percentage of sales paid to a salesperson
✓		**complex fraction** a fraction with a fraction in the numerator and/or a fraction in the denominator
✓	✓	**constant of proportionality** same as unit rate
	✓	**coordinate plane** a plane formed by the intersection of a horizontal number line (called the x-axis) with a vertical number line (called the y-axis). The number lines intersect at their zero points, called the origin
	✓	**covariance** a measurement of how related the variances are between two variables. The extent to which any two random variables change together or vary together.
✓	✓	**discount** amount a store takes off of the original price of an item. It is usually expressed as a percent or fraction.
✓		**double number lines** two number lines used when quantities have different units to easily see there are numerous pairs of numbers in the same ratio
✓	✓	**equation** a mathematical statement of the equality of two mathematical expressions. An equation uses a sign stating two things are equal (=).
✓		**equivalent ratios** ratios that have the same value
✓		**gratuity** tip
✓	✓	**markdown** a reduction in price
✓	✓	**markup** the difference between the wholesale price and the selling price
✓	✓	**origin** on a coordinate plane, the point (0, 0)
✓	✓	**percent** a ratio per 100 such as 25% is 25 parts of 100

(Continued)

(Continued)

6	7	
✓	✓	**percent error** the ratio of the error compared to the exact value. For example, my estimate was off by 7. The exact value was 35, so the percent error is $\frac{7}{35} \times 100\% = 20\%$.
✓	✓	**percent increase/decrease** the amount of increase or decrease expressed as a percent of the original amount
✓	✓	**proportion** two equal ratios
✓	✓	**proportional reasoning** multiplicative reasoning as opposed to additive reasoning. It is often used when finding the better buy, sharing two items with three students, adjusting calculations of travel time with different speeds, or calculating a sale price when everything is 40% off.
✓		**rate** ratio that compares two quantities of different units such as 3 ft per second
✓	✓	**ratio** comparison of two quantities
✓		**ratio language** language used to describe a ratio relationship in number or quantity between two things such as *"For every vote candidate A received, candidate C received nearly three votes"*
	✓	**ratio table** a table that shows the relationships between different ratios and/or a comparison of two or more quantities
✓	✓	**simple interest** the formula is $I = prt$, where I is interest, p is principle, r is rate, and t is time
✓		**simplify a ratio** divide each number in the ratio by its greatest common factor; $\frac{2}{6}$ simplifies to $\frac{1}{3}$ by dividing 2 and 6 by 2
✓		**tape diagram** a drawing that looks like a segment of tape, used to illustrate number relationships; Also known as a strip diagram, bar model, fraction strip, or length model
✓	✓	**unit rate** ratio comparing an amount to one

Notes

Ratios and Proportional Relationships
6.RP.A*

Cluster A

Understand ratio concepts and use ratio reasoning to solve problems.

STANDARD 1

6.RP.A.1: Understand the concept of a ratio and use ratio language to describe a ratio relationship between two quantities. *For example, "The ratio of wings to beaks in the bird house at the zoo was 2:1, because for every 2 wings there was 1 beak." "For every vote candidate A received, candidate C received nearly three votes."*

STANDARD 2

6.RP.A.2: Understand the concept of a unit rate *a/b* associated with a ratio *a:b* with *b* ≠ 0, and use rate language in the context of a ratio relationship. *For example, "This recipe has a ratio of 3 cups of flour to 4 cups of sugar, so there is $\frac{3}{4}$ cup of flour for each cup of sugar." "We paid $75 for 15 hamburgers, which is a rate of $5 per hamburger."*[1]

[1]Expectations for unit rates in this grade are limited to non-complex fractions.

STANDARD 3

6.RP.A.3: Use ratio and rate reasoning to solve real-world and mathematical problems, e.g., by reasoning about tables of equivalent ratios, tape diagrams, double number line diagrams, or equations.

a. Make tables of equivalent ratios relating quantities with whole-number measurements, find missing values in the tables, and plot the pairs of values on the coordinate plane. Use tables to compare ratios.

b. Solve unit rate problems including those involving unit pricing and constant speed. *For example, if it took 7 hours to mow 4 lawns, then at that rate, how many lawns could be mowed in 35 hours? At what rate were lawns being mowed?*

c. Find a percent of a quantity as a rate per 100 (e.g., 30% of a quantity means $\frac{30}{100}$ times the quantity); solve problems involving finding the whole, given a part and the percent.

d. Use ratio reasoning to convert measurement units; manipulate and transform units appropriately when multiplying or dividing quantities.

*Major cluster

Ratios and Proportional Relationships   6.RP.A

Cluster A: Understand ratio concepts and use ratio reasoning to solve problems.
Grade 6 Overview

The focus for this cluster is the study of ratio concepts and the use of proportional reasoning to solve problems. Students learn how ratios and rates are used to compare two quantities or values and how to model and represent them. Sixth graders find out how ratios are used in real-world situations and discover solutions to percent problems using ratio tables, tape diagrams, and double number lines. Students also convert between standard units of measure.

Standards for Mathematical Practice
SFMP 1. Make sense of problems and persevere in solving them.

Sixth graders interpret and solve ratio problems.

SFMP 2. Reason abstractly and quantitatively.

Students solve problems by analyzing and comparing ratios and unit rates in tables, equations, and graphs.

SFMP 4. Model with mathematics.

Students model real-life situations with mathematics and model ratio problem situations symbolically.

SFMP 6. Attend to precision.

Students communicate precisely with others and use clear mathematical language when describing a ratio relationship between quantities.

SFMP 7. Look for and make use of structure.

Sixth graders begin to make connections between covariance, rates, and representations showing the relationships between quantities.

Related Content Standards

4.OA.2   5.NF.3   5.G.1   5.G.2   5.MD.1   6.EE.9   7.RP.A.1

Notes

Understand the concept of a ratio and use ratio language to describe a ratio relationship between two quantities. For example, "The ratio of wings to beaks in the bird house at the zoo was 2:1, because for every 2 wings there was 1 beak." "For every vote candidate A received, candidate C received nearly three votes."

In this standard, students learn to compare two quantities or measures such as 6:1 or 10:2. These comparisons are called ratios. Students discover that ratios can be written and described in different ways. For instance, 6:1 uses a colon to separate values. Ratios can also be stated with words such as 6 to 1, or as a fraction such as $\frac{6}{1}$. Standard 1 focuses on understanding the concept of a ratio, however, students should use ratio language to describe real-world experiences and use their understanding for decision making.

What the TEACHER does:

- Help students discover that a ratio is a relationship or comparison of two quantities or measures. Ratios compare two measures of the same types of things such as the number of one color of socks to another color of socks *or* two different things such as the number of squirrels to birds in the park. Ratios compare parts to a whole (part:whole) such as 10 of our 25 students take music lessons. Ratios can also compare a part of one whole to another part of the same whole (part:part) such as the ratio of white socks in the drawer to black socks in the drawer is 4:6. Ratios are expressed or written as *a* to *b*, *a:b*, or $\frac{a}{b}$.

- Compare and model ratios with real-world things such as pants to shirts or hot dogs to buns. Ratios can be stated as the comparison of 10 pairs of pants to 18 shirts and can be written as $\frac{10}{8}$, 10 to 18, or 10:18 and simplified to, $\frac{5}{9}$, 5 to 9, or 5:9. Ensure that students understand how the simplified values relate to the original numbers.

- Ask students to create or find simple real-world problems to use in their learning such as, *"There are 2 Thoroughbred horses and 6 Appaloosa horses in the field. As a ratio of Thoroughbreds to Appaloosas it is:* $\frac{2}{6}$ *or 2 to 6 or 2:6 or simplified as* $\frac{1}{3}$, *1 to 3, or 1:3. Or, there are 14 girls and 18 boys in our math class. As a ratio of girls to boys it is:* $\frac{14}{18}$, *14 to 18, or 14:18 or simplified as* $\frac{7}{9}$, *7 to 9, or 7:9."* Invite students to share their real-world examples of ratios and use ratio language to describe their findings such as, *"for every vote candidate A received, candidate C received nearly three votes."* The problems students select or write can also be used as cyclical reviews with distributed practice throughout the school year.

- Focus on the following vocabulary terms: *ratio, compare,* and *simplify.*

What the STUDENTS do:

- Understand that a ratio is a comparison between quantities.

- Determine when a ratio is describing part-to-part or part-to-whole comparison.

- Describe ratio relationships between two quantities using ratio language.

- Use the different ratio formats interchangeably (4:5, 4 to 5, $\frac{4}{5}$).

Addressing Student Misconceptions and Common Errors

Some sixth graders may confuse the order of the quantities such as when asked to write the ratio of boys to girls in the sentence, *"There are 14 girls and 18 boys in our math class."* Instead of writing 18:14, some students may write 14:18. Other students may not recognize the difference between a part-to-part ratio and a part-to-whole ratio such as, *"There are 14 girls compared to 18 boys in the class (14:18 part-to-part); however, 14 of the 32 students in our class are girls (14:32 part-to-whole)."* To address these common misconceptions, ask students to label the quantities they are comparing such as 14 girls/18 boys.

STANDARD 2 (6.RP.A.2)

Understand the concept of a unit rate a/b associated with a ratio a:b with b ≠ 0, and use rate language in the context of a ratio relationship. For example, "This recipe has a ratio of 3 cups of flour to 4 cups of sugar, so there is $\frac{3}{4}$ cup of flour for each cup of sugar." "We paid $75 for 15 hamburgers, which is a rate of $5 per hamburger."[1]

[1]Expectations for unit rates in this grade are limited to non-complex fractions.

This standard focuses student learning on the concept of a unit rate as a special kind of ratio. Students compare different units of measure such as the amount of money earned to the hours worked while babysitting and calculate unit rates by setting up ratios and simplifying them. Students understand a situation in ratio form and write the unit that describes the situation using appropriate rate language with words such as *per* and symbols such as / to compare different units or measures.

What the TEACHER does:

- Begin by exploring the difference between a ratio and a rate. Rate is a special ratio that compares two quantities with different units of measure. Share multiple examples for students to make sense of the concept for rate such as, "*LaShanda babysat for $35 for 7 hours.*" Or, "*Dad's new truck got 400 miles on 20 gallons of gas.*" Then explore the unit rate that expresses a ratio as part-to-one. Generate examples such as "*LaShanda is paid a unit rate of $5 per 1 hour for babysitting (5:1)*" and "*My dad's new truck gets 20 miles per gallon of gas (20:1).*"

- Ask students to locate and share real-world examples of cost per item or distance per time in newspapers, ads, or other media. (Note that in sixth grade, students do not work with unit rates expressed as complex fractions. Both the numerator and denominator of the original ratio will be whole numbers.)

- Model how to convert rates from fraction form to word form using per, each, or @ such as 360 miles/12 gallons of gas = 30 miles per gallon of gas. Allow students to talk with each other and their teacher to make sense of what they are learning and then write and share several rate conversion examples of their own.

- Focus on the following vocabulary terms: *ratios, rates, unit rates, compare,* and *per/@*. Math journals or exit slips at the end of a math class with writing prompts such as, "*An example of a ratio and a problem that goes with it is. . . .*" provide closure.

- Provide cyclical, distributed practice over time to continually review simple unit rate problems.

What the STUDENTS do:

- Understand rate as a ratio that compares two quantities with different units of measure.

- Understand that unit rates are the ratio of two measurements or quantities in which the second term means "one" such as 60 miles per one hour.

- Interpret rate language with the @ symbol or with the words *per* and/or *each*.

- Solve unit rate problems.

Addressing Student Misconceptions and Common Errors

Students often confuse the terms *ratio, rate,* and *unit rate*. Try using a paper foldable with vocabulary definitions to help students with these confusing terms. To make the foldable, divide an $8\frac{1}{2} \times 11$-inch sheet of blank paper in half horizontally. Then fold it into thirds as if a letter is being folded to fit an envelope. Unfold and write a term on each of the sections. On the inside of the foldable, write the definitions that match each term. Students may want to cut on the vertical fold lines to flip up each section to practice the definitions.

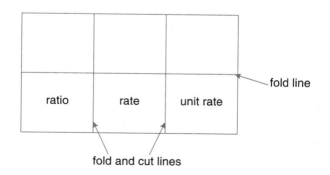

Use ratio and rate reasoning to solve real-world and mathematical problems, e.g., by reasoning about tables of equivalent ratios, tape diagrams, double number line diagrams, or equations.

   a. *Make tables of equivalent ratios relating quantities with whole-number measurements, find missing values in the tables, and plot the pairs of values on the coordinate plane. Use tables to compare ratios.*

   b. *Solve unit rate problems including those involving unit pricing and constant speed.* For example, if it took 7 hours to mow 4 lawns, then at that rate, how many lawns could be mowed in 35 hours? At what rate were lawns being mowed?

   c. *Find a* **percent** *of a quantity as a rate per 100 (e.g., 30% of a quantity means $\frac{30}{100}$ times the quantity); solve problems involving finding the whole, given a part and the percent.*

   d. *Use ratio reasoning to convert measurement units; manipulate and transform units appropriately when multiplying or dividing quantities.*

In these standards, students use reasoning about multiplication and division to solve a variety of ratio and rate problems about quantities. They make tables of equivalent ratios relating quantities with whole-number measurements, find missing values in the tables, and plot the pairs of values on the coordinate plane. They use tables to compare ratios and solve unit rate and constant speed problems. Problems involving finding the whole given a part and the percent, such as 20% of a quantity means $\frac{20}{100}$, are also a focus. For these standards, students can use equivalent ratio tables, tape diagrams, double number lines, or equations. Students connect ratios and fractions.

What the TEACHER does:

- Explore ratios and rates used in ratio tables and graphs to solve problems. Pose a ratio situation problem with students such as "*3 CDs cost $45. What would 8 CDs cost? How many CDs can be purchased for $150.00?*" To solve the problem, students can use ratios, unit rates, and multiplicative reasoning by creating and filling in the missing values on a chart. They should note that if three CDs cost $45, one CD will cost $15. Every CD purchased is an additional $15. $15 times the number of CDs = the cost. They write an equation such as C = $15n.

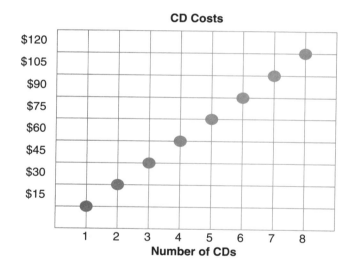

# of CDs	Cost
3	$45
8	??

- Ask students to plot the points on a coordinate plane and draw conclusions about what is happening with the problem above. Students should reason that for every one movement to the right on the x-axis, the y-axis increases to 15x. Also, for every one movement to the left on the x-axis, the y-axis decreases by 15.

- Investigate unit rate problems, including unit pricing such as, "*Quick Stop has 12-oz. drinks for $.99. Stop Here has 16-oz. drinks for $1.19. Which drink costs the least per ounce?*" Assign students to create ratio and rate reasoning examples to compare and solve real-world problems. Students could use newspapers, store ads, or online ads to find the examples and make the comparisons. Ask students to use reasoning to determine the better buys.

- Explore finding a percent of a quantity as a rate per 100 such as 40% of a quantity means $\frac{40}{100}$ times the quantity. Noting that a percent is a rate per 100, model how a

(continued)

What the TEACHER does (continued):

percent can be represented with a hundreds grid by coloring in 40 units. Have students write this as a fraction ($\frac{40}{100}$), a decimal (0.40), and a percent (40%). Consider using a percent wheel (see Reproducible 1) or use double number lines and tape diagrams in which the whole is 100 to find the rate per hundred.

- Solve problems involving finding the whole, given a part and the percent such as, "*What is 40% of 60? 80% of what number is 300? Or 50 is 30% of what number?*"

- Examine the process of how to use ratio reasoning to convert measurement units such as, "*How many centimeters are in 5 feet?*" Use the information that 1 inch ≈ 2.54 cm. Represent the conversion of 12 inches = 1 ft as a conversion factor in ratio form, $\frac{12 \text{ inches}}{1 \text{ foot}}$.

  Then multiply $\frac{12 \text{ inches}}{1 \text{ foot}} \times \frac{5 \text{ ft}}{1} = 60$ inches.

  Then 60 inches $\times \frac{2.54 \text{ cm}}{1 \text{ inch}} = 152.4$ cm.

(Note that conversions can be made between units within a measurement system such as inches to feet or between systems such as miles to centimeters.)

- Allow students to talk with each other and their teacher to make sense of what they are learning.

- Focus on the following vocabulary terms: *ratios, rates, unit rates, equivalent ratios, percents, ratio tables,* and *tape diagrams.*

- Provide cyclical, distributed practice over time to continually practice unit rate problems.

What the STUDENTS do:

- Create and interpret a table of equivalent ratios.
- Plot pairs of values from a table to a coordinate plane.
- Use a table to compare ratios and find missing values using ratios.
- Explain the difference between a ratio and a unit rate.
- Understand that rate problems compare two different units, such as revolutions per minute.
- Solve real-world problems using ratios and rates.
- Reason to determine the better buy.
- Write a percent as a rate over 100, including percents greater than 100 and less than 1.
- Find the percent of a number using rate methods.
- Represent the relationship of part to whole to describe percents using models.
- Convert units by multiplication or division.

Addressing Student Misconceptions and Common Errors

Some sixth graders misunderstand and believe that a percent is always a natural number less than or equal to 100. To help with this misconception, provide examples of percent amounts that are greater than 100% and percent amounts that are less than 1%. Try using a percent wheel for developing this understanding. See Reproducible 1.

Notes

Ratios and Proportional Relationships

Cluster A: Understand ratio concepts and use ratio reasoning to solve problems.

Standard: 6.RP.A.1. *Understand the concept of a ratio and use ratio language to describe a ratio relationship between two quantities.* For example, "The ratio of wings to beaks in the bird house at the zoo was 2:1, because for every 2 wings there was 1 beak." "For every vote candidate A received, candidate C received nearly three votes."

Standards for Mathematical Practice:

SFMP 2. Reason abstractly and quantitatively.

Students solve problems by analyzing and comparing ratios and unit rates in tables, equations, and graphs.

SFMP 4. Model with mathematics.

Students model real-life situations with mathematics and model ratio problem situations symbolically.

SFMP 6. Attend to precision.

Students communicate precisely with others and use clear mathematical language when describing a ratio relationship between quantities.

Goal:

Students use real-world objects to compare two quantities such as the number of red candy pieces to the number of green candy pieces in the same bag (part to part) and the number of parts to a whole such as the number of red candy pieces compared to the total number of candy pieces in the entire bag (part to whole).

Planning:

Materials: plastic bags with approximately 35–40 pieces of M & M's™ candies or 1-inch color tiles, paper and pencil to write the ratios

Sample Activity

- Give each student a bag of M & M's™ to compare and model ratios. Divide students into partner pairs. Ask them to write a ratio comparing the number of M & M's™ they have to the number their partner has. Students will count and compare the number of M & M's™ each have in their own bags and then write the comparison such as $\frac{36}{40}$ or 36:40. Facilitate a discussion about how they just compared a whole to a whole.

- Next, ask students to compare the number of red M & M's™ in their bags to the number of brown M & M's™. Students will count and record comparisons such as 8 red/14 brown or 8:14. Facilitate a discussion about how this ratio compares a part of one whole to another part of the same whole (part to part). Ask students to create their own part to part ratios with their M & M's™ and record.

- Ask students to count the number of yellow M & M's™ and compare that number to the entire number of M & M's™ in the bag, such as 7 yellow compared to all 36 in the bag. Have students record the ratio such as $\frac{7 \text{ yellow}}{36 \text{ bag}}$ or 7:36. Facilitate a discussion leading students to reason that the ratio they just created is a part:whole ratio. This can be done by reviewing the other types of ratios created earlier in this lesson.

Questions/Prompts:

- Ask students to explain the comparisons of 8 red compared to 14 brown ($\frac{8}{14}$ and 8:14 vs. $\frac{14}{8}$ and 14:8).

- Ask students to compare other colors to show the relationship written as a ratio.

- Ask students to explain part-to-part versus part-to-whole ratios.

Differentiating Instruction:

Struggling Students: Some students may confuse the order of the quantities and may need to label, such as 8 red/14 brown or 14 brown/8 red. Have the students record the color order you request before they make the ratio. This will help them understand that the order matters.

Extension: Try other ratio scenarios. Direct students to look around the classroom to find the ratio of boys to the total number of students in the classroom. Have them compare the number of boys to the number of girls. Ask them to compare the number of students in their classroom to the entire sixth grade or find the ratio of sixth graders to seventh graders.

Notes

PLANNING PAGE

Ratios and Proportional Relationships

Cluster A: Understand ratio concepts and use ratio reasoning to solve problems.

Standard:

Standards for Mathematical Practice:

Goal:

Planning:

Materials:

Sample Activity:

Questions/Prompts:

Differentiating Instruction:

Struggling Students:

Extension:

Notes

Ratios and Proportional Relationships
7.RP.A*

Analyze proportional relationships and use them to solve real-world and mathematical problems.

STANDARD 1   **7.RP.A.1:** Compute unit rates associated with ratios of fractions, including ratios of lengths, areas and other quantities measured in like or different units. *For example, if a person walks $\frac{1}{2}$ mile in each $\frac{1}{4}$ hour, compute the unit rate as the complex fraction $\frac{\frac{1}{2}}{\frac{1}{4}}$ miles per hour, equivalently 2 miles per hour.*

STANDARD 2   **7.RP.A.2:** Recognize and represent proportional relationships between quantities.

   a. Decide whether two quantities are in a proportional relationship, e.g., by testing for equivalent ratios in a table or graphing on a coordinate plane and observing whether the graph is a straight line through the origin.

   b. Identify the constant of proportionality (unit rate) in tables, graphs, equations, diagrams, and verbal descriptions of proportional relationships.

   c. Represent proportional relationships by equations. *For example, if total cost* t *is proportional to the number* n *of items purchased at a constant price* p, *the relationship between the total cost and the number of items can be expressed as* t = pn.

   d. Explain what a point (x, y) on the graph of a proportional relationship means in terms of the situation, with special attention to the points $(0, 0)$ and $(1, r)$ where r is the unit rate.

STANDARD 3   **7.RP.A.3:** Use proportional relationships to solve multi-step ratio and percent problems. *Examples: simple interest, tax, markups and markdowns, gratuities and commissions, fees, percent increase and decrease, percent error.*

*Major cluster

Ratios and Proportional Relationships   7.RP.A

Cluster A: Analyze proportional relationships and use them to solve real-world and mathematical problems.
Grade 7 Overview

These standards extend what students learned in Grade 6 about ratios to analyzing proportions and proportional relationships. Students calculate unit rates with complex fractions and move to recognizing and representing proportional relationships in equations and on graphs. These skills and understandings are used to solve multi-step ratio and percent problems involving real-world scenarios such as interest, tax, shopping sales, and so on.

Standards for Mathematical Practice
SFMP 1. Make sense of problems and persevere in solving them.

Students solve multi-step ratio and real-world percent problems.

SFMP 3. Construct viable arguments and critique the reasoning of others.

Students recognize proportional relationships from non-proportional ones and discuss their reasoning with others.

SFMP 4. Model with mathematics.

Students learn to represent proportional relationships as tables, graphs, verbal descriptions, diagrams, and equations.

SFMP 6. Attend to precision.

Students use units in their ratios requiring them to attend to the units such as 8 miles in 4 hours is a rate of 2 miles per hour.

Related Content Standards

6.RP.A.2   7.EE.A.2   8.EE.B.5

Notes

Compute unit rates associated with ratios of fractions, including ratios of lengths, areas and other quantities measured in like or different units. For example, if a person walks $\frac{1}{2}$ mile in each $\frac{1}{4}$ hour, compute the unit rate as the complex fraction $\frac{\frac{1}{2}}{\frac{1}{4}}$ miles per hour, equivalently 2 miles per hour.

This standard focuses on computing unit rates using ratios of fractions known as complex fractions. In a complex fraction, the numerator, denominator, or both are fractions. In the standard, $\frac{\frac{1}{2}}{\frac{1}{4}}$ is an example of a complex fraction. Complex fractions can be interpreted as division statements. For example, $\frac{\frac{1}{2}}{\frac{1}{4}}$ can be thought of as $\frac{1}{2} \div \frac{1}{4}$. Applications include situations where the quantities are measured in different units such as miles per hour, pounds per square foot, feet per second, and so on.

What the TEACHER does:

- Explore unit rates with ratios of fractions and compare them to unit rates with whole numbers from Grade 6.

- Treat complex fractions as division of fractions.

- Set up error analysis scenarios where students can identify errors in computing unit rates with complex fractions. For example, Homer calculated that if a person walks $\frac{1}{2}$ mile every $\frac{1}{4}$ hour, the unit rate is 2 miles. However, Homer made an error. Find his error, correct it, and explain to Homer why 2 miles is not the correct answer.

- Provide opportunities for students to compute the unit rates in real-world problems.

What the STUDENTS do:

- Discover that the structure of computing unit rates with whole numbers is the same concept as unit rates with ratios of fractions.

- Compute unit rates in real-world problems that involve complex fractions.

- In writing, explain the errors that can be made when computing unit rates with complex fractions and unlike units.

Addressing Student Misconceptions and Common Errors

It is not uncommon to find seventh-grade students who are not fluent with fraction division. Sometimes the format of a complex fraction confuses them when they are used to seeing fraction division written horizontally as $\frac{1}{2} \div \frac{1}{4}$. Discuss how the division bar in the complex fraction means the same as the symbol ÷.

For students having difficulty understanding unit rate and those having trouble with different units such as miles per hour, pictures and diagrams may help. Use the example from this standard: *If a person walks $\frac{1}{2}$ mile in each $\frac{1}{4}$ hour, compute the unit rate as the complex fraction $\frac{\frac{1}{2}}{\frac{1}{4}}$ miles per hour, equivalently 2 miles per hour.* Model with a diagram as shown. The bar represents 1 hour broken into $\frac{1}{4}$ hour segments.

$\frac{1}{4}$ hour	$\frac{1}{4}$ hour	$\frac{1}{4}$ hour	$\frac{1}{4}$ hour
$\frac{1}{2}$ mile	$\frac{1}{2}$ mile	$\frac{1}{2}$ mile	$\frac{1}{2}$ mile

From this diagram, students can see that the word problem is showing $\frac{1}{2}$ mile every $\frac{1}{4}$ hour.

STANDARD 2 (7.RP.A.2)

Recognize and represent proportional relationships between quantities.

> a. *Decide whether two quantities are in a proportional relationship, e.g., by testing for equivalent ratios in a table or graphing on a coordinate plane and observing whether the graph is a straight line through the origin.*

Sections a–d of 7.RP.A.2 break down the standard to give guidance on ways to recognize and represent proportional relationships.

This standard emphasizes two methods for deciding whether a proportional relationship exists. One method is to use equivalent ratios in a table. If the ratios are equivalent, then you have a proportional relationship such as:

# of people in a room	1	2	3	4	5
# of hands in the room	2	4	6	8	?

The other method is to graph the relationship on a coordinate plane and observe whether the graph is a straight line that goes through the origin. Note that computation using cross-multiplication is not a part of this standard.

What the TEACHER does:

- Explore proportional reasoning scenarios with students to be sure they understand the meaning of proportional relationships in context before using the tables or graphs. While some number combinations may be proportional, the real-world example attached to the numbers may not be. Use examples and non-examples for students to identify and compare. An example is: "*2 music downloads cost $1.98; therefore, 4 music downloads cost $3.96.*" A non-example is: "*Three boys can run a mile in 10 minutes; therefore, 6 boys can run a mile in 20 minutes.*"

- Ask students to write their own examples and non-examples of proportional relationships. Student work can be shared and discussed.

- Discuss equivalent ratios with the students. Ask them to suggest some equivalent pairs. Relate to equivalent fractions. Display the pairs as the students suggest them in the form $\frac{a}{b} = \frac{c}{d}$, where $b \neq 0$ and $d \neq 0$. Define two equivalent ratios as a proportion.

- Pose examples of proportions written with the quantities in different positions. Encourage students to decide if there is more than one correct way to set up a proportion. For example: "*Set up a proportion showing that 3 out of 15 students are girls is the same ratio as 1 out of 5 students are girls.*"

$$\frac{3}{15} = \frac{1}{5} \text{ or } \frac{15}{3} = \frac{5}{1} \text{ or } \frac{1}{3} = \frac{5}{15} \text{ or } \frac{3}{1} = \frac{15}{5}$$

Ask students to explain how they know $\frac{15}{1} = \frac{5}{3}$ is not a correct proportion for the example.

- Provide examples of equivalent and non-equivalent ratios to students for them to test with a table to decide if they are proportions. Conversely, present students with a table for a context and ask them to determine if all of the entries in the table are proportional.

- Graph two ratios on a coordinate plane from a proportional scenario and look for a straight line that goes through the origin to determine if the two ratios are proportional. For example: "*Maria sells necklaces and makes a profit of $6 for each necklace. How much money does she make for selling 3 necklaces?*"

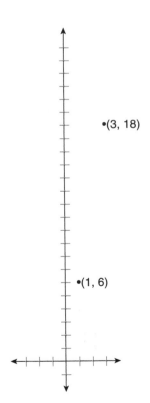

- Pose the task to students: Select other points on the graphed line and determine if they are also proportional.

What the STUDENTS do:

- Sort real-world examples of proportional relationships from non-examples. Students can create their own examples to demonstrate that they understand the concept of proportional relationships when there is a context attached.

- Communicate orally and/or in writing that a proportion is a statement of two equivalent ratios. Students apply what they know about equivalent fractions to equivalent ratios.

- Model proportional relationships by creating tables; determine if a proportional relationship exists from a given table.

- Model relationships on graphs to determine if they are proportional.

- Test their hypotheses about whether a proportional relationship exists between any two points on the lines graphed. Students may draw the conclusion that all points on the line are proportional to all other points on the line by relying on tables, verbal statements, or logical arguments to draw the conclusion.

Addressing Student Misconceptions and Common Errors

While graphing, students may need to be reminded that the same types of quantities need to be graphed on the same axis. For example, when checking to determine if 10 cans of soda for $2 is proportional to 50 cans of soda for $10, the cans of soda must both be represented on the same axis and the dollar amounts must be on the other axis. Ensure students are using graph paper or graphing calculators for all graphing. Remind them to label the axes.

Notes

b. *Identify the constant of proportionality (unit rate) in tables, graphs, equations, diagrams, and verbal descriptions of proportional relationships.*

This standard focuses on proportional relationships that can be represented as tables, graphs, equations, diagrams, and verbal descriptions. Students have already seen tables, graphs, and verbal descriptions. The unit rate on a graph is the point where $x = 1$. In an equation, it is the slope represented by the coefficient, m, in the formula $y = mx + b$. The terms *unit rate, constant of proportionality*, and *slope* are equivalent. Note that students are only required to read and interpret equations in this standard.

What the TEACHER does:

- Facilitate a discussion about representations of proportional relationships using a real-world scenario. For example, beginning with the verbal description: Mark was looking to fertilize his lawn, which is 432 sq. ft. He read the packages of 5 different fertilizer bags to see how much should be used. Bag A stated 2 ounces per 4 square feet, Bag B stated 4 ounces per 8 square feet, Bag C stated 1.5 ounces per 3 square feet, and Bag D stated 6 ounces per 12 square feet. Are these rates proportional? If yes, what is the unit rate? How much fertilizer does Mark need for his lawn?

- Using a real-world context have students determine if the relationship is proportional using graphs and/or tables. If it is proportional, facilitate a discussion with the class on the unit rate.

- Share a verbal description of a proportional relationship and ask students to interpret it with a diagram such as bars. Encourage students to write how they interpreted the proportional relationship.

- Introduce equations as a statement of the proportional relationship. For the fertilizer story the equation is $f = 2z$, where f is the amount of fertilizer needed and z is the size of the lawn in square feet.

- Provide students with a real-world proportional relationship expressed in a verbal description, graph, table, and equation. Challenge students to work with a partner to compare how the unit rate is expressed in each representation. Share student discoveries in a large class discussion.

What the STUDENTS do:

- Model proportional relationships several different ways.

- Translate a proportional relationship from a verbal description into a diagram and explain in writing how the diagram shows a proportional relationship.

- Determine the unit rate from equations, graphs, tables, diagrams, and verbal descriptions of proportional relationships.

- Discover that the unit rate (constant of proportionality) is the numerical coefficient in the equation of a proportional relationship.

Addressing Student Misconceptions and Common Errors

Finding the unit rate from a graph can be confusing. Some students cannot remember if the unit rate is the $(1, y)$ or $(x, 1)$ point. It is helpful to have a familiar unit rate students can recite such as 1 CD for $11.99 that helps them remember the x, which is first in a coordinate pair, is the 1 and the y is the unit rate.

Notes

c. *Represent proportional relationships by equations.* For example, if total cost *t* is proportional to the number *n* of items purchased at a constant price *p*, the relationship between the total cost and the number of items can be expressed as $t = pn$.

In the previous standard students read equations to find the unit rates. In this standard students are given verbal descriptions of proportional relationships and are expected to create the equations in the form $y = mx$. For example, in Town C if you are caught speeding, you receive a traffic ticket. The penalty is $25 for every mile over the speed limit. What is the equation if *p* represents the penalty and *m* represents the number of miles over the speed limit? The equation is $p = 25m$.

What the TEACHER does:

- Provide students with real-world proportional reasoning problems. Ask students to represent the stories as tables and graphs. Using the student-generated graphs and tables, create equations that model the proportional relationship.

- Provide students with real-world proportional relationship problems presented as tables, graphs, and verbal descriptions. Have students write equations to model those relationships.

- Provide opportunities for students to write about how they create equations that model proportional relationships. Some suggestions are exit slips, entrance slips, letters, and journals.

What the STUDENTS do:

- Model proportional relationships presented as tables, verbal descriptions, and graphs in equation form.

- Justify in writing the reasoning used in creating an equation for a given proportional relationship expressed verbally.

Addressing Student Misconceptions and Common Errors

Some students confuse the variables in equations when they try to express the proportional relationship. It can be helpful to use letters closely representing what the variables stand for such as using *f* for fertilizer instead of *x*.

Notes
_____
_____
_____
_____
_____
_____
_____
_____
_____
_____
_____
_____

d. *Explain what a point (x, y) on the graph of a proportional relationship means in terms of the situation, with special attention to the points (0, 0) and (1, r) where r is the unit rate.*

An example of a proportional situation is: The scale on a map suggests that 1 centimeter represents an actual distance of 4 kilometers. The map distance between two towns is 8 centimeters. What is the actual distance? The graph of this relationship is represented as:

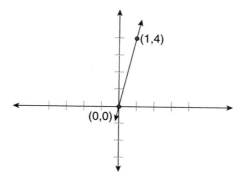

Note the points (0,0) and (1,4). The 4 is the unit rate or slope of the line for the equation $d = 4c$, where d is total distance and c is the number of centimeters.

What the TEACHER does:

- Present students with a verbal description of a proportional relationship and build the graphical representation with the students. Be sure students give input on the labels for the x- and y-axes. Facilitate a discussion about the graph with students asking them for the meaning of individual points and asking students to justify their responses.

- Have students compare graphs that show proportional relationships and talk to a partner about what they notice.

- Focus on points $(0, 0)$ and $(1, r)$, the origin and the unit rate, respectively.

- Use points that are not whole numbers and points where students need to estimate the coordinates.

What the STUDENTS do:

- Explain the meaning of a point on a graph in the context of the situation. Students should be able to explain examples with words such as, *"Point (5, 7) is the point that represents 5 health bars for $7.00"* or *"(1, 10) represents the unit rate (constant of proportionality), meaning 1 teacher for every 10 students at the school."*

- Discover that graphed proportional relationships are straight lines.

Addressing Student Misconceptions and Common Errors

When finding points on a line that represents a real-world proportional relationship, students may think that the line stops at the origin. The teacher should show that the line continues into Quadrant III but that the points are not appropriate for the real-world situation. For example, in a proportional relationship between the number of teachers and the number of students at a grade level, it does not make sense to have −3 teachers.

> *Notes*

Use proportional relationships to solve multi-step ratio and percent problems. Examples: simple interest, tax, markups and markdowns, gratuities and commissions, fees, percent increase and decrease, percent error.

In this standard students solve problems involving proportional relationships. Students set up and solve proportions using cross-multiplication. For example: *"Directions to make a tablecloth call for $\frac{3}{4}$ yard of ribbon for every 2 yards of fabric. If you increase the amount of fabric used to 3 yards, how much ribbon will be needed?"* The proportion is $\frac{\frac{3}{4}}{2} = \frac{x}{3}$. To cross-multiply:

$$3 \cdot \frac{3}{4} = 2x$$

Problems for this standard should be multi-step and include contexts with simple interest, tax, tips, commissions, percent error, percent increase/decrease, discounts, fees, markups, markdowns, discount, sales, and/or original prices.

To calculate a percent increase from 2 to 10, find the difference between the two numbers, in this case, $10 - 2 = 8$. Take the difference, 8, and divide by the original number: $\frac{8}{2} = 4$. Multiply the quotient by 100: $4 \times 100 = 400\%$.

What the TEACHER does:

- Focus time on the vocabulary for this standard. Paper foldables, word walls, graphic organizers, using words in context, and writing stories all give students a chance to clarify the meaning of these terms, which they may encounter in daily life but not fully understand. Bring in items familiar to students such as tennis shoes, a six-pack of soda, and so on and use them to model situations that use the vocabulary. Vocabulary should include simple interest, tax, tip/gratuity, discount, commission, fees, sale, markup, markdown, and original price.

- Use cross-multiplication to solve problems involving proportional relationships. Use numbers in your problems that do not lend themselves easily to mental arithmetic.

- Begin with single-step problems and move to multi-step using a wide variety of contexts. Make use of everyday examples such as finding sales online, in print media, and on TV.

- Ask students to write problems that can be solved with setting up proportions prompted by media ads.

- Introduce students to percent increase/decrease and percent error problems. Encourage students, through questioning, to discover the similarities among the formulas for these concepts.

What the STUDENTS do:

- Explore use of the vocabulary words in this standard by finding examples in the media and explain how they are used in each situation.

- Solve problems involving proportions using cross-multiplication.

- Solve problems involving percent error and percent increase/decrease.

- Use the structure of percent error and percent increase/decrease problems to explain how the formulas for these concepts are similar.

Addressing Student Misconceptions and Common Errors

Students may have misconceptions about the vocabulary commonly used in the media such as sale, discount, and tax. It is important to discuss what students already know about these words in order to correct any pre-existing misconceptions. For individuals with difficulties with particular words, use graphic organizers such as the Frayer model (see Reproducible 2). Acting out situations can help students remember certain steps. For example, acting out shopping for a pair of tennis shoes and a tennis racket and paying tax at the register will help students remember that tax is calculated on the cost of the total bill where the items bought need to be added up before tax is calculated.

Ratios and Proportional Relationships

Cluster A: Analyze proportional relationships and use them to solve real-world and mathematical problems.

Standard: 7.RP.A.3. *Use proportional relationships to solve multi-step ratio and percent problems.* Examples: simple interest, tax, markups and markdowns, gratuities and commissions, fees, percent increase and decrease, percent error.

Standards for Mathematical Practice:

SFMP 1. Make sense of problems and persevere in solving them.
Students solve multi-step problems involving percents.

SFMP 6. Attend to precision.
Students check answers to see if they are reasonable.

Goal:
Students demonstrate understanding of the vocabulary tax and tip (gratuity) while solving multi-step problems.

Planning:

Materials: paper and pencil, copies of restaurant menus

Sample Activity:

- Provide groups of students with a menu and the following problem:

**Route 15 Lunch Market
Take-Out Menu**

Pulled Pork Sandwich	$4.49
Hamburger	$3.39
Cheeseburger	$3.99
Chicken Sandwich	$4.49
Fish Sandwich	$4.49
Hot Dog	$1.99

Add fries and a 12-oz.
drink for $1.99 more!

Image courtesy of clipart.com.

Your group decides to keep working through lunch today so you will order lunch from the Route 15 Lunch Market.

Use the take-out menu to figure out:

a. What you want to order

b. How much the food will cost

c. How much tax will be added to the bill at a rate of 5.5%

d. What percent tip you will leave and then calculate the tip

e. Your total cost for lunch, including tax and tip

Remember to write everything down clearly, step by step, so that the waitress at the restaurant can fill your order accurately.

Questions/Prompts:

- Are students overwhelmed by the number of steps? Suggest they make a list of each part of the problem.

- Are students confused about whether they compute tax or tip first? Ask questions for students to reason if it makes sense to pay a tip on the tax.

- Is the order illegible? Ask students to read what they wrote to you. Point out that if you cannot read it, neither can the workers at the restaurant. Suggest ways to improve the clarity. Provide graph paper for groups that may need it to keep numbers lined up.

- Ask, *"Does your answer make sense?"*

Differentiating Instruction:

Struggling Students: For students struggling with the number of steps, break the problem down into steps. Write each step on an index card. Ask the students to order the steps so they can discuss what should come first before they tackle the problem.

Extension: Ask students to create their own word problems from the menu for their classmates.

Notes

Ratios and Proportional Relationships

Cluster A: Analyze proportional relationships and use them to solve real-world and mathematical problems.

Standard:

Standards for Mathematical Practice:

Goal:

Planning:

Materials:

Sample Activity:

Questions/Prompts:

Differentiating Instruction:

Struggling Students:

Extension:

Reflection Questions: Ratios and Proportional Relationships

1. The domain *Ratios and Proportional Relationships* appears in Grades 6 and 7 only. What ideas from Grades K–5 prepare students for the study of ratios and proportional reasoning?

2. This domain has several big ideas. Select one main idea and trace its development through Grades 6–7.

3. What big ideas from this domain are foundational for the functions domain in Grade 8?

## Part 2

The Number System

The Number System

Domain Overview

GRADE 6

Sixth graders continue their previous understanding of the meaning of fractions, the meanings of multiplication and division, and the relationship between multiplication and division to explain why the procedures for dividing fractions make sense. Students use visual models and equations to divide whole numbers by fractions and fractions by fractions to solve word problems. Students work with the system of rational numbers, including negative rational numbers. Sixth graders focus on the order and absolute value of rational numbers and location of points in all four quadrants of the coordinate plane.

GRADE 7

Seventh graders develop an understanding of number, recognizing fractions, decimals, and percents as different representations of rational numbers. Students extend addition, subtraction, multiplication, and division to all rational numbers and explain and interpret the rules for adding, subtracting, multiplying, and dividing with negative numbers. Seventh graders solve real-world and mathematical problems involving all four operations with rational numbers.

GRADE 8

Eighth graders learn to distinguish between rational and irrational numbers. Building on seventh grade understanding, students recognize that the decimal equivalent of a fraction will either terminate or repeat and they convert repeating decimals into their fraction equivalents. Finally, eighth graders use rational approximations of irrational numbers to compare the size of irrational numbers, locate them approximately on a number line, and estimate the value of expressions.

6	7	8	
✓			Adding machine tape (optional, used to create number lines)
	✓		Algeblocks™ or Algebra Tiles™
✓			Coordinate grids
✓			Decimal blocks
✓			Factor trees
✓	✓	✓	Number lines
✓			Pattern blocks
✓	✓		Two-color counters

KEY VOCABULARY

6	7	8	
✓	✓		**absolute value** distance from 0 on a number line
	✓		**additive inverse** a number that, when added to another number, gives a sum of zero
✓			**algorithm** a set of steps used to solve a mathematical computation such as long division
✓			**common factor** a factor that two or more numbers have in common
	✓		**complex fraction** a fraction with a fraction in the numerator and/or a fraction in the denominator
✓			**coordinate plane** a plane formed by the intersection of a horizontal number line (called the x-axis) with a vertical number line called the y-axis. The number lines intersect at their zero points called the origin.
✓			**coordinates** set of numbers, or a single number, that locates a point on a line, on a plane, or in space
✓			**denominator** the bottom number of a fraction that shows how many equal parts the whole is divided into
✓			**distributive property** the property that states that multiplying a sum by a number is the same as multiplying each addend by the number and then adding the products. The distributive property is $a \times (b + c) = (a \times b) + (a \times c)$.
✓			**dividend** the number to be divided
✓			**divisor** the number that divides the dividend in a division problem

(Continued)

KEY VOCABULARY

6	7	8	
✓			**factors** numbers that divide without remainders into the number such as 2 and 3 are factors of 6
✓			**greatest common factor (GCF)** the largest factor that two or more numbers have in common
✓	✓	✓	**integers** the whole numbers and their opposites
✓		✓	**irrational numbers** non-repeating, non-terminating decimals
✓			**least common multiple (LCM)** the smallest multiple that two or more numbers have in common
✓			**multiplicative inverse** another name for reciprocal. When you multiply a number by its "multiplicative inverse," you get 1. Example: $6 \times \frac{1}{6} = 1$.
✓			**multi-digit** more than one digit
✓			**multiple** the result of multiplying a number by an integer such as 15 is a multiple of 3, as $3 \times 5 = 15$
✓			**numerator** the top number in a fraction. In the fraction $\frac{3}{8}$, 3 is the numerator that tells how many of 8 parts.
✓			**ordered pairs** a pair of numbers used to show the position on a graph, where the "x" (horizontal) value is first, and the "y" (vertical) value is second
✓			**prime factorization** determining which prime numbers multiply together to make the original number
✓			**quadrant** the x- and y-axes divide the coordinate plane into four sections labeled, counterclockwise, I, II, III, and IV, with Quadrant I having all points with positive x and y coordinates
✓			**quotient** the number obtained by dividing one quantity by another
	✓	✓	**rational numbers** repeating or terminating decimals; any decimal that can be written in fraction form
	✓	✓	**repeating decimal** a decimal in which, after a certain point, one digit or a set of digits repeat themselves an infinite number of times. Repeating digits are designated with a bar above them.
✓	✓		**signed numbers** positive and negative numbers
	✓	✓	**terminating decimal** decimal form of a rational number that ends in 0

The Number System
6.NS.A*

Apply and extend previous understandings of multiplication and division to divide fractions by fractions.

STANDARD 1

6.NS.A.1: Interpret and compute quotients of fractions, and solve word problems involving division of fractions by fractions, e.g., by using visual fraction models and equations to represent the problem. For example, create a story context for $\frac{2}{3} \div \frac{3}{4}$ and use a visual fraction model to show the quotient; use the relationship between multiplication and division to explain that $\frac{2}{3} \div \frac{3}{4} = \frac{8}{9}$ because $\frac{3}{4}$ of $\frac{8}{9}$ is $\frac{2}{3}$. (In general, $\frac{a}{b} \div \frac{c}{d} = \frac{ad}{bc}$.) How much chocolate will each person get if 3 people share $\frac{1}{2}$ lb of chocolate equally? How many $\frac{3}{4}$ -cup servings are in $\frac{2}{3}$ of a cup of yogurt? How wide is a rectangular strip of land with length $\frac{3}{4}$ mi and area $\frac{1}{2}$ square mi?

*Major cluster

The Number System   6.NS.A

Cluster A: Apply and extend previous understandings of multiplication and division to divide fractions by fractions.

Grade 6 Overview

This cluster focuses on the use of visual fraction models and equations to divide whole numbers by fractions and fractions by fractions. Sixth graders interpret the meaning of fractions, the meanings of multiplication and division, and the relationship between multiplication and division to understand and explain why the procedures for dividing fractions make sense.

Standards for Mathematical Practice

SFMP 1. Make sense of problems and persevere in solving them.

Sixth graders interpret and make sense of a problem involving division of fractions.

SFMP 2. Reason abstractly and quantitatively.

Students use the meaning of fractions, the meanings of multiplication and division, and the relationship between multiplication and division to understand and explain why the procedures for dividing fractions make sense.

SFMP 4. Model with mathematics.

Sixth graders use manipulatives to model everyday problems with fractions.

SFMP 6. Attend to precision.

Students communicate precisely with others and use clear mathematical language when discussing the understanding and procedure for dividing fractions.

Related Content Standards

5.NF.B.3   5.NF.B.4   5.NF.B.7.a   5.NF.B.7.b   5.NF.B.7.c   7.NS.A.2

Interpret and compute quotients of fractions, and solve word problems involving division of fractions by fractions, e.g., by using visual fraction models and equations to represent the problem. For example, create a story context for $\frac{2}{3} \div \frac{3}{4}$ and use a visual fraction model to show the quotient; use the relationship between multiplication and division to explain that $\frac{2}{3} \div \frac{3}{4} = \frac{8}{9}$ because $\frac{3}{4}$ of $\frac{8}{9}$ is $\frac{2}{3}$. (In general, $\frac{a}{b} \div \frac{c}{d} = \frac{ad}{bc}$.) How much chocolate will each person get if 3 people share $\frac{1}{2}$ lb of chocolate equally? How many $\frac{3}{4}$-cup servings are in $\frac{2}{3}$ of a cup of yogurt? How wide is a rectangular strip of land with length $\frac{3}{4}$ mi and area $\frac{1}{2}$ square mi?

This standard emphasizes the use of fraction models including manipulatives and visual diagrams to interpret, represent, and solve word problems with division of fractions. Students write equations to show how word problems are solved. Sixth graders interpret the meaning of fractions, the meanings of multiplication and division, and the relationship between multiplication and division to understand and explain why the procedures for dividing fractions make sense. What they are actually doing is working with a complex fraction. In the example $\frac{2}{3} \div \frac{3}{4}$, $\frac{2}{3}$ *is the numerator and* $\frac{3}{4}$ *is the denominator as* $\dfrac{\frac{2}{3}}{\frac{3}{4}}$.

What the TEACHER does:

- Begin teaching division of fractions with a concrete hands-on model such as pattern blocks that students can touch and move. Provide a yellow hexagon, a red trapezoid, a blue rhombus, and green triangles to each group of four students. Ask the students to solve the problem $\frac{1}{2} \div \frac{1}{6}$.

  Use a pattern block's red trapezoid to show $\frac{1}{2}$.

  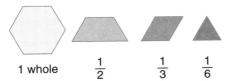

  Ask students how many $\frac{1}{6}$s fit on the red trapezoid. Ask students to show $\frac{1}{2} \div \frac{1}{6} = 3$.

- Continue with additional visual drawings to help students understand quotients of fractions by building from familiar scenarios. For example, 3 people share $\frac{1}{2}$ of a cake. How many pieces does each person get? Ask students to draw a diagram to show each person gets $\frac{1}{6}$ of the cake.

   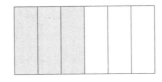

- Ask students, "*In the equation* $\frac{1}{2} \div \frac{1}{6}$, *why does the 3 make sense as the answer when it is so much bigger than* $\frac{1}{2}$ *or* $\frac{1}{6}$?" (Answer: 3 tells you how many $\frac{1}{6}$s make $\frac{1}{2}$.)

- Present word problems for students to solve such as, "*I have* $\frac{2}{3}$ *of a yard of fabric and want to make pencil bags that are* $\frac{1}{6}$ *of a yard each. How many can I make?*" Have students create number line drawings to illustrate $\frac{2}{3} \div \frac{1}{6} = $.

  o Students should start with a number line divided into thirds.

  o Divide each third into halves to create sixths.

  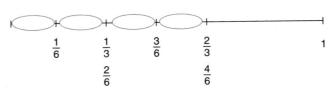

  o Each circled part represents $\frac{1}{6}$. There are 4 sixths in $\frac{2}{3}$. I can make 4 pencil bags.

  (continued)

What the TEACHER does (continued):

- Lead students from using manipulatives and diagrams for dividing fractions to computing answers procedurally using the multiplicative inverse, which is a synonym for "reciprocal." With the "number" x, its reciprocal (or multiplicative inverse) is $\frac{1}{x}$. Try the following problems:
  - "You have $\frac{5}{8}$ pound of nuts. You decide to share a $\frac{1}{4}$ of a pound with each of your friends. How many friends can you share the nuts with?"
  - "You have a $\frac{3}{4}$-acre lot. You must divide it into $\frac{3}{8}$-acre lots. How many lots will you create?"

- Incorporate the following vocabulary terms into instruction about division of fractions: *numerator, denominator, reciprocal, quotient, multiplicative inverse.*

- Ensure students have opportunities to talk with the teacher and each other to make sense of what they are learning about division of fractions. Talk about the relationship between multiplication and division, specifically explaining that $\frac{2}{3} \div \frac{3}{4} = \frac{8}{9}$ because $\frac{3}{4}$ of $\frac{8}{9}$ is $\frac{2}{3}$.

What the STUDENTS do:

- Model division of fractions with manipulatives, visual diagrams (bar models, number lines), and word problems.

- Divide fractions procedurally using the multiplicative inverse.

- Interpret what the quotient represents in mathematical and real-world problems.

- Understand that multiplication and division are inverse operations.

Addressing Student Misconceptions and Common Errors

Sixth graders may incorrectly model division of fractions. Some students may think dividing *by* $\frac{1}{2}$ is the same as dividing *in* half. Dividing *by* $\frac{1}{2}$ means to find how many one halves there are in a quantity. Dividing *in* half means to take quantity and divide it into two equal parts. To address the misconception, ask them to demonstrate two examples, one that shows dividing by $\frac{1}{2}$ and another that shows dividing in half. For example, 9 divided by $\frac{1}{2}$ equals 18 and 9 divided in half equals $4\frac{1}{2}$.

Notes

The Number System
6.NS.B

Compute fluently with multi-digit numbers and find common factors and multiples.

STANDARD 2   **6.NS.B.2:** Fluently divide multi-digit numbers using the standard algorithm.

STANDARD 3   **6.NS.B.3:** Fluently add, subtract, multiply, and divide multi-digit decimals using the standard algorithm for each operation.

STANDARD 4   **6NS.B.4:** Find the greatest common factor of two whole numbers less than or equal to 100 and the least common multiple of two whole numbers less than or equal to 12. Use the distributive property to express a sum of two whole numbers 1–100 with a common factor as a multiple of a sum of two whole numbers with no common factor. *For example, express 36 + 8 as 4(9 + 2).*

The Number System   6.NS.B

Cluster B: Compute fluently with multi-digit numbers and find common factors and multiples.
Grade 6 Overview

Fluency and accuracy with multi-digit addition, subtraction, and division is the focus for this cluster along with a spotlight on greatest common factors and least common multiples. The cluster also builds on previous learning of the multiplicative structure as well as prime and composite numbers.

Standards for Mathematical Practice
SFMP 2. Reason abstractly and quantitatively.

Students are able to understand the meaning of a division problem.

SFMP 7. Look for and make use of structure.

Sixth graders apply division algorithms to divide multi-digit numbers.

SFMP 8. Look for and express regularity in repeated reasoning.

Students consider the reasonableness of an estimated quotient.

Related Content Standards

5.NBT.B.6   5 NBT.B.7   7.NS.A.2.b   7.NS.A.2.c   7.NS.A.2.d   7.NS.A.3

Notes

STANDARD 2 (6.NS.B.2)

Fluently divide multi-digit numbers using the standard algorithm.

The focus for this standard is using the traditional, standard algorithm for long division. However, major emphasis is placed on the meaning of division and the understanding of place value of multi-digit numbers when dividing fluently. Fluently dividing multi-digit numbers means dividing quickly and accurately. To have fluency, students need sufficient, on-going practice with long division.

What the TEACHER does:

- Pose a problem-solving situation to focus on the understanding and meaning of division such as, *"Sam wants to purchase a new smart phone for $168. He earns $12 an hour for mowing lawns. How many hours will he need to mow lawns to have enough money for his phone?"*

- Explore division with a variety of models that are used as a tool for division such as the area model or partial quotients model. Students describe their understanding of place value as they divide such as when dividing 7,964 by 44. In this example, as students write a 1 in the quotient, they should say, *"There are 100 forty-fours in 7964."*

Students write:	Students think:
$$\begin{array}{r} 100 \\ 44\overline{)7964} \end{array}$$	There are 100 forty-fours in 7964.
$$\begin{array}{r} 100 \\ 44\overline{)7964} \\ -4400 \\ \hline 3564 \end{array}$$	100 times 44 is 4400. 7964 minus 4400 is 3564. $$\begin{array}{r} 180 \\ 44\overline{)7964} \\ -4400 \\ \hline 3564 \end{array}$$ There are 80 forty-fours in 3564. $$\begin{array}{r} -3520 \\ \hline 44 \end{array}$$
$$\begin{array}{r} 181 \\ 44\overline{)7964} \\ -4400 \\ \hline 3564 \\ -3520 \\ \hline 44 \\ -\ \ 44 \end{array}$$	There is 1 forty-four in 44. 1 times 44 is equal to 44.

- Investigate mental math to quickly estimate the quotient of a division problem. Try using compatible numbers to make the estimation much easier. The division problem 73 divided by 23 could be thought of as 75 divided by 25. Explore with additional division problems using compatible numbers to estimate the reasonableness of answers.

- Model the following vocabulary terms associated with multi-digit division: *division, dividend, divisor, quotient,* and *algorithm.*

- Provide cyclical, distributed practice over time to continually review multi-digit division throughout the year as fluency develops over time. Allow students to practice in a variety of ways including pencil-and-paper algorithms, mental math, and with problem-solving situations.

What the STUDENTS do:

- Communicate the meaning of division using precise mathematical vocabulary.

- Understand place value of multi-digit numbers and use it when dividing.

- Know division is the inverse of multiplication.

- Develop fluency with the traditional, standard algorithm for division of multi-digit whole numbers.

- Use compatible numbers to estimate the reasonableness of answers.

Addressing Student Misconceptions and Common Errors

For some students, the traditional standard division algorithm is difficult simply because of the many steps involved in the procedure. Some sixth graders may focus on individual digits when dividing rather than thinking about the whole number. Others may ignore place value and get an incorrect answer. To help students, remind them to describe both the place value as they divide and place value of the digits in the quotients. Ask them to show the steps of division, one at a time. Provide graph paper to keep the work legible.

Fluently add, subtract, multiply, and divide multi-digit decimals using the standard algorithm for each operation.

This standard requires students to extend the models and strategies for the four operations previously developed for whole numbers in Grades 1–5 to decimals. Emphasis for addition, subtraction, multiplication, and division of multi-digit decimals is on using standard algorithms. Students estimate answers and self-correct errors in computation if needed. Fluently adding, subtracting, multiplying, and dividing multi-digit decimals means students can find a sum, difference, product, or quotient quickly and accurately. To obtain fluency, students need sufficient, on-going practice for each operation.

What the TEACHER does:

- Model estimating the sum, difference, product, or quotient from the problems before performing the operation.

- Explore estimating the sum and then finding the exact sum for adding decimals. For example, to estimate 15.2 and 7.65, an estimate of the sum could be 15 + 7 or 22. Expect that students know if their estimate is too high or too low. Ask students to reason, *"Why does it make sense that your answer must be larger than 22?"* Teach students to use their estimates to self-correct any errors in their computation.

- Practice previous understanding related to the patterns involved when multiplying and dividing by powers of 10 to develop fluency with operations with multi-digit decimals.

- Ensure that students understand the role of place value in the operations of addition, subtraction, multiplication, and division. Use decimal blocks to review place value if needed.

- Focus on the following vocabulary terms associated with decimal computation: *estimate, multi-digit decimals,* and *algorithm.*

- Provide cyclical, distributed practice over time to continually practice multi-digit decimal computation throughout the year as fluency develops over time. Allow students to practice in a variety of ways, including pencil-and-paper algorithms, mental math, and with problem-solving situations.

What the STUDENTS do:

- Understand decimal place values.

- Know basic facts for addition, subtraction, multiplication, and division.

- Add, subtract, multiply, and divide multi-digit decimals using the standard algorithms.

- Use vocabulary associated with multi-digit computation with multi-digit decimals both orally and in writing.

Addressing Student Misconceptions and Common Errors

Some students may not remember to use the concept of place value when adding tenths to hundredths. For example, when adding five-tenths to eighty-five hundredths, some students may not realize the answer is one whole and thirty-five hundredths. To help with this misconception, try using decimal blocks or drawing a picture to show how the decimals have been added. Adding a zero to 0.5 to write 0.50 before adding it to 0.85 helps students focus on the place values.

Notes

STANDARD 4 (6.NS.B.4)

Find the greatest common factor of two whole numbers less than or equal to 100 and the least common multiple of two whole numbers less than or equal to 12. Use the distributive property to express a sum of two whole numbers 1–100 with a common factor as a multiple of a sum of two whole numbers with no common factor. For example, express 36 + 8 as 4(9 + 2).

The emphasis for this standard is finding factors and multiples of a given number(s). Students need to know that numbers being multiplied are the factors, and the product is the multiple. Explore two different methods for factoring.

Introduce the distributive property as an application of factors. When you add two numbers that have a common factor such as 36 and 8, you can remove the greatest common factor, 4, and distribute it to the remaining factors, such as: 36 + 8 = (4 × 9) + (4 × 2) = 4(9 + 2).

What the TEACHER does:

- Explore finding the greatest common factor (GCF) of two whole numbers less than or equal to 100. The greatest common factor is the largest number that is a factor of two whole numbers. For example, 30 and 18 can be found first by

  o Listing the factors of 30 (1, 2, 3, 5, **6**, 10, 15, 30)
  o Listing the factors of 18 (1, 2, 3, **6**, 9, 18) and noticing the largest number in each list is the greatest common factor (6)

  Examine another way for students to find the GCF. List the prime factors of two numbers and then multiply the common factors. For example, 40 = (2 · 2 · 2 · 5) and 16 = (2 · 2 · 2 · 2), and then multiply prime common factors (2 · 2 · 2 = 8).

- Ensure students understand the process of prime factorization. Prime factorization is finding which prime numbers multiply together to make the original number such as the number 24 can be written as a product of prime numbers: 24 = 2 × 2 × 2 × 3. This is called the prime factorization of 24. Model prime factorization for numbers 1–100 using factor trees.

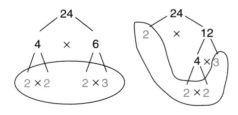

Both factor tree examples have the same prime factorization.

- Investigate the distributive property using sums and its use in adding numbers 1–100 with a common factor. For example, 20 + 24 = 4(5 + 6). Use a common factor and the distributive property to find the sum of 36 and 8.

$$36 + 8 = 4(9) + 4(2)$$
$$44 = 4(9 + 2)$$
$$44 = 4(11)$$
$$44 = 44$$

- Emphasize the least common multiple as it relates to this standard. The least common multiple (LCM) of two numbers is the smallest number (not zero) that is a multiple of both. For example, for 3 and 4, first list the multiples of each to discover the smallest number that is a multiple of both is 12.

  Multiples of 3: 3, 6, 9, <u>12</u>, 15, 18, 21, 24 . . .

  Multiples of 4: 4, 8, <u>12</u>, 16, 20, 14, 28 . . .

  The LCM of 3 and 4 is <u>12</u>

- Pose questions such as, "*What is the least common multiple (LCM) of 10 and 6? How can you use multiple lists or the prime factorizations to find the LCM?*"

- Focus on the following vocabulary terms: *distributive property, factor, greatest common factor (GCF), least common multiple (LCM), multiple, prime factorization,* and *factor trees.*

- Present problem-solving situations to the students to apply their knowledge. A great example is the famous hotdog/bun problem. "*Hot dogs come in a package of 8 and buns in a package of 12. How many packages of hot dogs and packages of buns would you need to purchase to have an equal number of hot dogs and buns?*"

- Ensure students have opportunities to talk with the teacher and each other to make sense of what they are learning about common factors and common multiples using precise mathematical vocabulary.

What the STUDENTS do:

- Understand that a factor is a whole number that divides without a remainder into another number.
- Understand that a multiple is a whole number that is a product of the whole number and any other factor.
- Calculate GCF and LCM for given sets of numbers.

- Apply knowledge of factors and multiples to problem solving.
- Communicate, using precise mathematical language, how the distributive property makes use of factors and multiples.

Addressing Student Misconceptions and Common Errors

Some students may confuse the concepts of factors and multiples. To help with this, use the vocabulary of factors and multiples when working with multiplication and division such as the numbers being multiplied are the factors; the product is the multiple. Paper foldables with vocabulary definitions or mathematics games may also help students practice confusing vocabulary terms.

Notes

The Number System
6.NS.C*

Apply and extend previous understandings of numbers to the system of rational numbers.

STANDARD 5

6.NS.C.5: Understand that positive and negative numbers are used together to describe quantities having opposite directions or values (e.g., temperature above/below zero, elevation above/below sea level, credits/debits, positive/negative electric charge); use positive and negative numbers to represent quantities in real-world contexts, explaining the meaning of 0 in each situation.

STANDARD 6

6.NS.C.6: Understand a rational number as a point on the number line. Extend number line diagrams and coordinate axes familiar from previous grades to represent points on the line and in the plane with negative number coordinates.

   a. Recognize opposite signs of numbers as indicating locations on opposite sides of 0 on the number line; recognize that the opposite of the opposite of a number is the number itself, e.g., –(–3) = 3, and that 0 is its own opposite.
   b. Understand signs of numbers in ordered pairs as indicating locations in quadrants of the coordinate plane; recognize that when two ordered pairs differ only by signs, the locations of the points are related by reflections across one or both axes.
   c. Find and position integers and other rational numbers on a horizontal or vertical number line diagram; find and position pairs of integers and other rational numbers on a coordinate plane.

STANDARD 7

6.NS.C.7: Understand ordering and absolute value of rational numbers.

   a. Interpret statements of inequality as statements about the relative position of two numbers on a number line diagram. *For example, interpret –3 > –7 as a statement that –3 is located to the right of –7 on a number line oriented from left to right.*
   b. Write, interpret, and explain statements of order for rational numbers in real-world contexts. *For example, write –3 °C > –7 °C to express the fact that –3 °C is warmer than –7 °C.*
   c. Understand the absolute value of a rational number as its distance from 0 on the number line; interpret absolute value as magnitude for a positive or negative quantity in a real-world situation. *For example, for an account balance of –30 dollars, write |–30| = 30 to describe the size of the debt in dollars.*
   d. Distinguish comparisons of absolute value from statements about order. *For example, recognize that an account balance less than –30 dollars represents a debt greater than 30 dollars.*

STANDARD 8

6.NS.C.8: Solve real-world and mathematical problems by graphing points in all four quadrants of the coordinate plane. Include use of coordinates and absolute value to find distances between points with the same first coordinate or the same second coordinate.

*Major cluster

The Number System 6.NS.C

Cluster C: Apply and extend previous understandings of numbers to the system of rational numbers.
Grade 6 Overview

At this level, students use fractions, decimals, and integers to represent real-world situations. They extend the number line to represent *all* rational numbers and recognize that number lines may be either horizontal or vertical which helps sixth graders move from number lines to coordinate grids. The focus of this cluster is to learn about negative numbers, their relationship to positive numbers, and the meaning and uses of absolute value. Cluster C lays the foundation for working with rational numbers, algebraic expressions and equations, functions, and the coordinate plane in seventh and eighth grades.

Standards for Mathematical Practice
SFMP 1. Make sense of problems and persevere in solving them.

Students relate the concepts of positive and negative numbers to real-world applications.

SFMP 2. Reason abstractly and quantitatively.

Students attend the meaning of quantities, not just how to compute them.

SFMP 4. Model with mathematics.

Students describe a real-world scenario with number lines and coordinate grids and interpret the results.

Related Content Standards

7.NS.A.1.b   7.NS.A.1.c

Notes

STANDARD 5 (6.NS.C.5)

Understand that positive and negative numbers are used together to describe quantities having opposite directions or values (e.g., temperature above/below zero, elevation above/below sea level, credits/debits, positive/negative electric charge); use positive and negative numbers to represent quantities in real-world contexts, explaining the meaning of 0 in each situation.

In this standard, students investigate positive and negative numbers (integers) in real-world scenarios as being opposite values or opposite directions such as 10° below zero (−10) and 10° above zero (+10). They use vertical and horizontal number lines to show all rational numbers and must explain that the meaning of zero is determined by the real-world context.

What the TEACHER does:

- Explore with multiple examples and experiences using positive and negative integers to represent real-world situations such as a bank account with credits and debits, temperature, and above and below sea level.

- Investigate the use of both vertical and horizontal number lines to illustrate examples such as, *"Our football team lost 7 yards on the first down."* Or, *"It is freezing outside today and is 10 degrees below zero."* Or, *"The bank statement for the middle school football team has a balance of $4,026. The coach bought new equipment for the team for a total of $4,400. How much money should the coach deposit into the football account in order to stop the account from being overdrawn?"*

- Have students create their own examples to show on their number lines and explain the meaning of 0 in each situation.

- Pose questions such as, *"When you look at the number line, what do you notice about the location of the negative numbers?"* which will lead students to discover that all negative numbers are less than zero.

What the STUDENTS do:

- Understand that zero represents a position on the number line.

- Discover that every negative integer is less than zero.

- Understand that the meaning of zero is determined by the real-world context. For example, on a Celsius thermometer, everything below zero is negative, and everything above zero is positive.

- Represent real-world scenarios such as bank account balances, temperature, and sea level with integers.

- Use precise mathematical vocabulary to discuss positive and negative numbers.

Addressing Student Misconceptions and Common Errors

Some sixth graders may believe the greater the magnitude of a negative number, the greater the number. To help with this misconception, continue to use the number line. Have the students trace a horizontal number line with a finger starting at a positive number such as 10 and moving left one number at a time. Ask the student each time the finger moves one number left if the number is getting larger or smaller. Continue across 0. By then, a pattern of numbers getting smaller as you move left on the number line should be established.

Notes

STANDARD 6 (6.NS.C.6)

Understand a rational number as a point on the number line. Extend number line diagrams and coordinate axes familiar from previous grades to represent points on the line and in the plane with negative number coordinates.

   a. *Recognize opposite signs of numbers as indicating locations on opposite sides of 0 on the number line; recognize that the opposite of the opposite of a number is the number itself, e.g., −(−3) = 3, and that 0 is its own opposite.*

   b. *Understand signs of numbers in ordered pairs as indicating locations in quadrants of the coordinate plane; recognize that when two ordered pairs differ only by signs, the locations of the points are related by reflections across one or both axes.*

   c. *Find and position integers and other rational numbers on a horizontal or vertical number line diagram; find and position pairs of integers and other rational numbers on a coordinate plane.*

The heart of this standard focuses on previous understanding with the use of both horizontal and vertical number lines. Students extend graphing points and reflecting across zero on a number line to graphing and reflecting points across axes on a coordinate grid. They identify and plot coordinates in all four quadrants of a coordinate plane.

What the TEACHER does:

- Facilitate a discussion around a number line that allows students to discover that a number and its opposite are equidistant from zero. The opposite sign (−) shifts the number to the opposite side of 0 such as −5 is stated as "the opposite of 5," which is negative 5. Remind students that zero is its own opposite, and the opposite of the opposite of a number is the number itself, such as −(−5) =5.

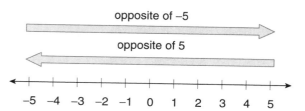

- Plan an activity for students to place numbers on a number line such as −3.5, 1, 4.2, −5, $\frac{9}{2}$ and justify their order.

  Then, students can make statements about the relationships between the numbers.

- Help students relate graphing points and reflecting across zero on a number line to graphing and reflecting points across axes on a coordinate grid. As the *x*-axis and *y*-axis are extended to include negatives, help students recognize the point where the *x*-axis and *y*-axis intersect as the origin, to identify the four quadrants, and to identify the quadrant for an ordered pair based on the signs of the coordinates, such as Quadrant I (+,+), Quadrant II (−,+), Quadrant III (−,−), and Quadrant IV (+, −).

- Plan an activity for students to discover the relationship between two ordered pairs differing only by signs as reflections across one or both axes. Have them plot the ordered pairs (−4, 5) and (−4, −5), to discover the *y*-coordinates differ only by signs, which represents a reflection across the *x*-axis. Students should explain why a change in the *x*-coordinates from (−4, 5) to (4, 5) represents a reflection across the *y*-axis. When the signs of both

coordinates change [(4, −5) changes to (−4, 5)], the ordered pair has been reflected across both axes.

- Emphasize the following vocabulary terms: *rational numbers*, *opposites*, *origin*, *quadrants*, *coordinate plane*, *ordered pairs*, x-*axis*, y-*axis*, and *coordinates*.

- Ensure students have opportunities to talk with the teacher and each other to make sense of what they are learning about recognizing opposite signs of numbers; recognizing that when two ordered pairs differ only by signs, the locations of the points are related by reflections across one or both axes; finding and positioning integers and other rational numbers on a horizontal or vertical number line diagram; and finding and positioning pairs of integers and other rational numbers on a coordinate plane.

What the STUDENTS do:

- Understand the meaning of the term *opposite* and plot opposites on a number line.

- Reason that the opposite of the opposite of the number is the number itself (e.g., −(−3)), and zero is its own opposite.

- Describe quantities having opposite values.

- Use vertical and horizontal number lines to show integers.

- Plot integers on the number line and coordinates in all four quadrants of a coordinate plane.

- Understand that the signs of numbers in ordered pairs represent a singular location on the coordinate plane.

- Understand that an ordered pair is composed of two parts: The first coordinate refers to the *x*-axis, and the second coordinate refers to the *y*-axis.

- Recognize the signs of all ordered pairs on the coordinate plane: Quadrant I (+,+), Quadrant II (−,+), Quadrant III (−,−), and Quadrant IV (+, −).

- Understand that changing the sign of one or both numbers in the ordered pair will create a reflection of the point.

- Find reflection points across axes.

Some sixth graders do not understand that negative signs change a number to the same distance on the opposite side of 0. Use a tool such as a ruler to measure the distance to prove this is true. Some students confuse quadrant labels I through IV going counterclockwise. When introducing the quadrants, have students write the quadrant numbers in the quadrants to help them remember. Some learners may confuse (3, 2) and (−3, 2), thinking both ordered pairs look the same. Using paper folding or mirrors may help the students understand the connection between signs on coordinates and their reflections across the axes.

Notes

STANDARD 7 (6.NS.C.7)

Understand ordering and absolute value of rational numbers.

a. *Interpret statements of inequality as statements about the relative position of two numbers on a number line diagram.* For example, interpret $-3 > -7$ as a statement that -3 is located to the right of -7 on a number line oriented from left to right.

b. *Write, interpret, and explain statements of order for rational numbers in real-world contexts.* For example, write -3 °C > -7 °C to express the fact that -3 °C is warmer than -7 °C.

c. *Understand the absolute value of a rational number as its distance from 0 on the number line; interpret absolute value as magnitude for a positive or negative quantity in a real-world situation.* For example, for an account balance of -30 dollars, write $|-30| = 30$ to describe the size of the debt in dollars.

d. *Distinguish comparisons of absolute value from statements about order.* For example, recognize that an account balance less than -30 dollars represents a debt greater than 30 dollars.

This standard focuses on understanding the ordering and the absolute value of rational numbers. Students explore the meaning of absolute value as the distance from zero on a number line. They learn that the value of -5 is less than -3 and that with negative numbers, as the absolute value increases, the value of the number decreases.

Students interpret that absolute value in a real-world scenario refers to magnitude. For example, in the case of a debt of -30 dollars, the absolute value, 30, is the magnitude or size of the debt. Emphasis in this standard is also placed on comparing rational numbers using inequality symbols.

What the TEACHER does:

- Use models such as number lines, thermometers, and checkbooks for profit/loss to focus instruction on ordering and inequalities.

  o Use number line models to order and locate integers and other rational numbers on the number line. Ask students to place the following numbers on the number line: -4.5, 2, 5.2, -5, $\frac{7}{2}$ and justify why they were placed in the specific locations.

  o Facilitate a discussion that uncovers the fact that as you move left on the number line, numbers get smaller. Use this knowledge to help students write inequalities such as $-3 < -2$.

  o Use thermometers to demonstrate inequalities. Then, provide real-world scenarios to help students make sense of what they are learning. For example, *"On Wednesday the temperature was -8 °F and on Thursday the temperature was -5 °F. Which day was colder? Model it on a horizontal number line, write an inequality, and explain how you know your answer is correct."*

  o Use profit/loss models. A positive number corresponds to a profit and a negative number corresponds to a loss. Provide real-world scenarios such as checkbook balances. *"My checkbook balance was $-\$10.40$. My friend's checkbook balance was $-\$8.50$. Write an inequality to show the relationship between the checkbook amounts. Who owes more?"*

- Have students create and write their own real-life scenarios using two rational numbers and share them with the class. For each scenario, have students write an inequality to represent the situation.

- Lead students to discover the absolute value or magnitude of a rational number as the distance from zero and recognize the symbols $|\ |$ as representing absolute value. For example, $|-5|$ means the distance -5 is from 0, which would be 5. $|5|$ means the distance 5 is from 0, which would also be 5. Focus understanding on the concept that as the negative number increases (moves to the left on a number line), the value of the number decreases such as -13 is less than -4 because -13 is located to the left of -4 on the number line. Since absolute value is the distance from zero, the absolute value (distance) of -13 is greater than -4. With negative numbers, as the absolute value increases, the value of the number decreases.

- Provide real-world scenarios where students use the absolute value of the numbers to answer the questions such as, *"Cecily has -30 dollars in her account. What does that mean?"* Answer: It means that Cecily is short or owes her bank 30 dollars.

- Emphasize the following vocabulary terms: *rational numbers, inequalities, value, greater than, >, and less than, <, greater than or equal to, ≥, less than or equal to, ≤, and absolute value.*

- Ensure that multiple experiences are provided for students to understand the relationships between numbers, absolute value, and statements about order.

What the STUDENTS do:

- Order rational numbers on a number line.
- Compare rational numbers using inequality symbols and justify orally and/or in writing the inequality symbol used.

(continued)

What the STUDENTS do (continued):

- Understand, compare, and interpret rational numbers found in real-world scenarios.

- Discover absolute value of a rational number as its distance from 0 on the number line.

- Model absolute value with number lines. Correctly use absolute value symbols.

- Interpret absolute value in real-world scenarios as magnitude.

- Understand that quantities could have a negative value based on the scenario such as debt.

- Explain, orally or in writing in journals or on exit slips, the reasoning that as the value on a negative rational number decreases, its absolute value (distance from zero) increases.

Addressing Student Misconceptions and Common Errors

Common misconceptions occur when students are unable to order rational numbers on the number line. Some students may incorrectly place $-1\frac{3}{4}$ between -1 and 0 instead of between -2 and -1. To address this, have students order the opposites. For example, if a student has difficulty placing $-1\frac{3}{4}$ on the number line, have the student place $+1\frac{3}{4}$. Discuss with the student how $1\frac{3}{4}$ came between 1 and 2. Then use that reasoning to help the student place $-1\frac{3}{4}$.

Notes

STANDARD 8 (6.NS.C.8)

Solve real-world and mathematical problems by graphing points in all four quadrants of the coordinate plane. Include use of coordinates and absolute value to find distances between points with the same first coordinate or the same second coordinate.

The focal point for Standard 8 is solving problems by graphing points in all four quadrants of the coordinate plane. Students learn that the distance from a point on a coordinate plane to an axis is an absolute value. The coordinate plane is used to represent real-world scenarios.

What the TEACHER does:

- Create a coordinate grid on the floor and ask sixth graders to stand on points or place objects on the points. Find the distance between students or objects. Make sure that the two points have either the same first coordinate or the same second coordinate. Lead students to conclude that when you are on the same x- or the same y-coordinate, you are on the same line.

- Provide a variety of simple word problem experiences for the students to model on a Cartesian plane such as, *"My house is at (−3, 5), the shopping mall is at (−4, −2), and the school is at (3, −1). What is the distance between my house and the shopping mall? The shopping mall and the school? Explain and show two different ways you used to find the different locations."*

What the STUDENTS do:

- Understand that a line segment from one coordinate pair to another represents a distance.

- Understand that if two coordinates have the same x- or y-value, they are on the same line.

- Understand that the distance from a point on a coordinate plane to an axis is an absolute value.

- Use the coordinate plane to represent real-world scenarios, such as streets of a map.

- Model solutions to real-world problems on a coordinate plane.

Addressing Student Misconceptions and Common Errors

Students may have procedural graphing misconceptions and may plot points in spaces rather than intersections. Some sixth graders count intervals on lines rather than x- or y-axes. Provide hands-on experiences for these learners. Have students plot real objects on a coordinate grid while you observe. Then, have them find the distance between the objects and explain how they found it.

Notes

The Number System

Cluster C: Apply and extend previous understandings of numbers to the system of rational numbers.

Standard: 6.NS.C.5. *Understand that positive and negative numbers are used together to describe quantities having opposite directions or values (e.g., temperature above/below zero, elevation above/below sea level, credits/ debits, positive/negative electric charge); use positive and negative numbers to represent quantities in real-world contexts, explaining the meaning of 0 in each situation.*

Standards for Mathematical Practice:

SFMP 2. Reason abstractly and quantitatively.

Students understand the meaning of quantities as they relate to the real world.

SFMP 4. Model with mathematics.

Sixth graders use number lines to visualize and explain real-world scenarios.

SFMP 6. Attend to precision.

Students represent answers depending on the phrasing of the question, the context of the word problem, or the real-world situation.

Goal:

Students use vertical number lines to model simple real-world scenarios.

Planning:

Materials: rolls of adding machine tape, paper and pencil to create number lines

Sample Activity:

- Have each student tear/rip three pieces of adding machine tape. The tape should be unrolled approximately 24–30 inches long (from the tip of the nose to the middle finger of the right hand).

- Ask students to draw a line on the adding machine tape stretching from end to end. Ask them to mark 0 in the middle of the tape with a horizontal line and then mark positive whole numbers above 0 and negative numbers below 0.

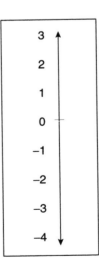

- Provide real-world scenarios such as, "*I have a friend that owes me $2. My friend does not have any money. My friend would need to give me $2 to pay me back. Using an arrow, show this on the number line and explain what 0 means in this scenario.*" With another number line, show the following scenario: "*A shark was spotted approximately 3 feet below sea level. Use a negative number to represent this and tell what 0 represents in the scenario.*" Continue with temperature scenarios and another number line such as, "*Today is a cold day with the thermometer registering at 0 degrees. The weatherman says the temperature will drop 4 more degrees overnight. Show this on your number line and explain what 0 means in this scenario.*"

Questions/Prompts:

- Are students able to explain the meaning of 0 in each situation?

- Are students able to explain positive and negative numbers to represent quantities in real-world scenarios?

Differentiating Instruction:

Struggling Students: Create a number line by taping it to the floor. Ask the students to "walk and talk" about each scenario. Listen to their thinking.

Extension: Ask students to create their own simple scenarios involving negative numbers and explain the meaning of 0 in each situation.

Notes

The Number System

Cluster A: Apply and extend previous understandings of multiplication and division to divide fractions by fractions.

Standard:

Standards for Mathematical Practice:

Goal:

Planning:

Materials:

Sample Activity:

Questions/Prompts:

Differentiating Instruction:

Struggling Students:

Extension:

The Number System

Cluster B: Compute fluently with multi-digit numbers and find common factors and multiples.

Standard:

Standards for Mathematical Practice:

Goal:

Planning:

Materials:

Sample Activity:

Questions/Prompts:

Differentiating Instruction:

Struggling Students:

Extension:

The Number System

Cluster C: Apply and extend previous understandings of numbers to the system of rational numbers.

Standard:

Standards for Mathematical Practice:

Goal:

Planning:

Materials:

Sample Activity:

Questions/Prompts:

Differentiating Instruction:

Struggling Students:

Extension:

Notes

The Number System
7.NS.A*

Apply and extend previous understandings of operations with fractions to add, subtract, multiply, and divide rational numbers.

STANDARD 1   **7.NS.A.1:** Apply and extend previous understandings of addition and subtraction to add and subtract rational numbers; represent addition and subtraction on a horizontal or vertical number line diagram.

   a. Describe situations in which opposite quantities combine to make 0. *For example, a hydrogen atom has a 0 charge because its two constituents are oppositely charged.*

   b. Understand $p + q$ as the number located a distance $|q|$ from p, in the positive or negative direction depending on whether q is positive or negative. Show that a number and its opposite have a sum of 0 (are additive inverses). Interpret sums of rational numbers by describing real-world contexts.

   c. Understand subtraction of rational numbers as adding the additive inverse, $p - q = p + (-q)$. Show that the distance between two rational numbers on the number line is the absolute value of their difference, and apply this principle in real-world contexts.

   d. Apply properties of operations as strategies to add and subtract rational numbers.

STANDARD 2   **7.NS.A.2:** Apply and extend previous understandings of multiplication and division of fractions to multiply and divide rational numbers.

   a. Understand that multiplication is extended from fractions to rational numbers by requiring that operations continue to satisfy the properties of operations, particularly the distributive property, leading to products such as $(-1)(-1)$ and the rules for multiplying signed numbers. Interpret products of rational numbers by describing real-world contexts.

   b. Understand that integers can be divided, provided that the divisor is not zero, and every quotient of integers (with non-zero divisor) is a rational number. If p and q are integers, then $-\frac{p}{q} = \frac{-p}{q} = \frac{p}{-q}$. Interpret quotients of rational numbers by describing real-world contexts.

   c. Apply properties of operations as strategies to multiply and divide rational numbers.

   d. Convert a rational number to a decimal using long division; know that the decimal form of a rational number terminates in 0s or eventually repeats.

STANDARD 3   **7.NS.A.3:** Solve real-world and mathematical problems involving the four operations with rational numbers.[1]

[1]Computations with rational numbers extend the rules for manipulating fractions to complex fractions.

*Major cluster

The Number System   7.NS.A

Cluster A: Apply and extend previous understandings of operations with fractions to add, subtract, multiply, and divide rational numbers.

Grade 7 Overview

This cluster is about understanding and computing with rational numbers. Rational numbers include integers, positive and negative fractions, and positive and negative decimals. Students learn how to add, subtract, multiply, and divide integers and apply properties of operations as strategies for each operation. Students journey from exploring the operations to formalizing rules. Students convert rational numbers to decimal form using division. The understanding of a rational number as one that terminates or repeats is covered in Grade 7 as preparation for the introduction of irrational numbers in Grade 8.

Standards for Mathematical Practice

SFMP 4. Model with mathematics.

Students use multiple strategies to demonstrate the same meaning of an operation which include modeling with manipulatives or on a number line.

SFMP 6. Attend to precision.

Students are working toward being independent thinkers by self-correcting any errors they find.

SFMP 7. Look for and make use of structure.

Students make use of what they already know about operations and their properties and extend that understanding to rational numbers.

SFMP 8. Look for and express regularity in repeated reasoning.

Students use several examples of integer multiplication to generalize a formal rule.

Related Content Standards

8.NS.A.1   6.NS.C.6   6.NS.C.7

Notes

Apply and extend previous understandings of addition and subtraction to add and subtract rational numbers; represent addition and subtraction on a horizontal or vertical number line diagram.

> a. *Describe situations in which opposite quantities combine to make 0. For example, a hydrogen atom has a 0 charge because its two constituents are oppositely charged.*

Students use real-world situations that model using opposite quantities to make zero. This prepares students for adding rational numbers with opposite signs such as $4 + (-4) = 0$. Examples can include temperature, elevation above and below sea level, owing money, and so on.

What the TEACHER does:

- Open a discussion for students to talk about positive and negatives in the real world such as temperature above and below zero, going up and down in an elevator, or owing money.

- Provide students with two color counters (or cubes or tiles), with one color representing positive and the other negative. An equal number of positive and negative counters represents zero. Challenge students to make zero multiple ways. This can also be done with Algeblocks™ or Algebra Tiles™.

- Model on a number line how a certain number of moves in a positive direction from zero combined with the same number of moves in the opposite direction ends at zero on the number line.

- Challenge students to write a real-world story where opposites make zero.

- Provide students with opportunities to write to clarify their understanding of the concept of making zero. Give a prompt for students to write about in their mathematics journals such as, *"What did you learn about positive, negative, and zero? Do you think this is always true? Explain."*

What the STUDENTS do:

- Consider real-world examples in terms as positive and negative such as 30 degrees below 0 is −30.

- Represent multiple "zeroes" by combining the same number of positive and negative counters.

- Model on a number line how a certain number of moves in a positive direction from zero combined with the same number of moves in the opposite direction ends at zero on the number line.

- Model positive and negative combining to make zero in real-world situations.

- Communicate understanding of positive, negative, and zero orally and in writing.

Addressing Student Misconceptions and Common Errors

Students may understand that one positive and one negative make zero but have difficulty understanding that this is also true for all equal amounts of positives and negatives such as five positives and five negatives. One way to make this clear is to start with one positive and one negative counter. As soon as the student establishes that this is zero, add another pair. When the student recognizes that you have just added another zero to the first zero, repeat. Repeat until the student has developed the concept.

Notes

b. *Understand p + q as the number located a distance |q| from p, in the positive or negative direction depending on whether q is positive or negative. Show that a number and its opposite have a sum of 0 (are additive inverses). Interpret sums of rational numbers by describing real-world contexts.*

This standard formalizes the concept of a positive and a negative making zero from the previous standard into written equations. For example, $4 + (-4) = 0$. The 4 and (-4) are opposites because they are equidistant from 0 on the number line in opposite directions. They are also additive inverses because their sum is 0. Be sure to include examples of fractions and decimals such as $-\frac{1}{2}$ and -4.72 so that students are working with all types of rational numbers. Addition of integers is modeled on a number line as in the following example: *"Jose has $6 and owes Steven $5. How much money will Jose have left when he pays Steven what he owes?"*

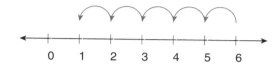

What the TEACHER does:

- Provide students with a mat that has one side labeled "positive" and the other side "negative" and ask students to show zero using their counters (or cubes, tiles, etc.). Define this concept as the additive inverse and ask students to show more examples of additive inverse in the form of $p + q = 0$.

Positive +	Negative −

- Challenge students to figure out the sum when five counters are placed on the positive side and four counters on the negative side. Repeat the challenge with different combinations that result in positive and negative sums. Ask students to explain how they arrived at their answers.

- Challenge students to find sums with more combinations of positive and negative integers using number lines. Let students justify their reasoning to classmates. Encourage them to use fractions and decimals also such as $-\frac{1}{2}$ or -4.5.

- Present equations to students in the form $p + q =$ and allow them to solve using number lines, counters, and/or rules they developed.

- Give an equation such as $-17 + 4 =$ and ask students to give a real-world scenario for the equation such as, *"I owe my friend $17. I pay him $4. How much do I still owe?"*

- Encourage a class discussion of any patterns/algorithms/rules students may have developed for adding rational numbers.

- Provide writing prompts such as, *"Give a real-world example of additive inverse."*

What the STUDENTS do:

- Demonstrate an understanding of additive inverse by developing examples.

- Model, using mats, number lines, counters, equations, and so on, different combinations of positive and negative integers and explain how they reason their solutions.

- Solve equations using number lines, counters, and/or rules the students may have developed for addition of rational numbers.

- Discover and apply formal rules for adding rational numbers with different signs.

- Communicate reasoning for addition through writing.

Addressing Student Misconceptions and Common Errors

Students who are not able to solve equations abstractly as quickly as others may need to use number lines and/or two-color counters for a longer period of time until they understand the concepts. Algebra Tiles™ and/or Algeblocks™ can also be used as models.

Notes

c. *Understand subtraction of rational numbers as adding the additive inverse, p – q = p + (–q). Show that the distance between two rational numbers on the number line is the absolute value of their difference, and apply this principle in real-world contexts.*

Subtraction of rational numbers can be thought of in terms of addition using the additive inverse (sometimes referred to as "the opposite"). For example, $6 - 7$ can be understood as $6 + (-7)$. The distance between two rational numbers on a number line is the same as the absolute value of the difference between the two numbers. For example, using a real-world context, if the temperature is –6 at 7 a.m. and +8 at noon, how many degrees has the temperature increased between 7 a.m. and noon? The difference between $-6 - 8 = -14$. $|-14| = 14$. Shown on a number line, the distance between –6 and 8 is 14.

What the TEACHER does:

- Provide students with examples of simple subtraction such as $6 - 5$ to model on the number line followed by its corresponding addition with an additive inverse such as $6 + (-5)$. Repeat with progressively more complex examples to model such as $-4.6 - 3$ followed by $-4.6 + (-3)$ and $2\frac{3}{4} - (-1)$ followed by $2\frac{3}{4} + (1)$.

- Supply students with opportunities to communicate what they are doing and reasoning orally and in writing. Examples can be talking to a partner or writing in a mathematics journal.

- Provide repeated opportunities for students to subtract. During those practices, encourage students to discover a formal rule for subtraction of rational numbers during a large class discussion so that students can justify their rules to one another.

- Engage students with real-world contexts to demonstrate the distance between two rational numbers on the number line as the absolute value of their difference such as, *"How far did the temperature rise on Monday if the low temperature was –1 and the high was 3?"*

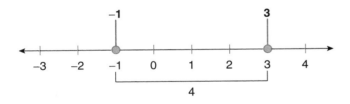

What the STUDENTS do:

- Discover that subtraction and adding with an additive inverse provide the same results. For example, $(-\frac{1}{2}) - 5$ is the same as $(-\frac{1}{2}) + (-5)$.

- Clarify their reasoning about subtraction and additive inverse through oral and/or written communication.

- Model real-world contexts that involve subtraction of rational numbers using a number line.

- Discover that the solutions to real-world subtraction problems using the absolute value of the distance between two rational numbers on the number line give the same result as subtracting through examples given in class.

Addressing Student Misconceptions and Common Errors

For students having difficulty understanding subtraction as adding the inverse using a number line, use the mats and two-color chips. Demonstrate the equation $5 - 6 = (-1)$ on the mat. First, place 5 positive chips on the mat.

Then, try to remove 6. Since this is not possible, add a zero as a pair of chips.

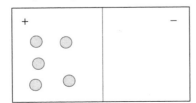

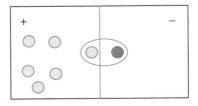

Now it is possible to remove 6 chips (subtract 6). You are left with one chip on the negative side of the map. This mat exercise can be used to model any subtraction.

Students have previously used the commutative, associative, and additive identity properties with whole numbers. These properties apply to rational numbers. For example:

Commutative Property of Addition: $4.5 + (-6) = (-6) + 4.5$

Associative Property of Addition: $6.9 + (-5) + 3.1 = 6.1 + 3.9 + (-5)$

Additive Identity Property of Addition (also called the Zero Property): $(-4.8) + 0 = (-4.8)$

What the TEACHER does:

- Provide students with examples and non-examples of commutativity, associativity, and additive identity of addition with rational numbers for students to use to clarify their understanding of the properties.

- Use an advanced organizer such as the Frayer vocabulary model (see Reproducible 2) to help students clarify their understanding of the properties as they apply to rational number operations.

- Provide students with numerical equations to solve using the properties of the operations, such as: $-\frac{1}{2} + 2.4 + \frac{1}{2} = (-\frac{1}{2} + \frac{1}{2}) + 2.4 = 0 + 2.4 = 2.4$.

What the STUDENTS do:

- Discover that the properties of operations apply to addition and subtraction of rational numbers by identifying examples and non-examples.

- Clarify their understanding of the properties of operations as they apply to addition and subtraction of rational numbers by completing an advanced organizer.

- Solve numerical addition and subtraction equations using the properties of the operations.

Addressing Student Misconceptions and Common Errors

In previous grades students learned that subtraction is not commutative. This holds true with rational numbers even though students now understand that $6 - 8 = (-2)$. It is still the case that $6 - 8 \neq 8 - 6$.

Notes

GRADE 7

Apply and extend previous understandings of multiplication and division of fractions to multiply and divide rational numbers.

    a. *Understand that multiplication is extended from fractions to rational numbers by requiring that operations continue to satisfy the properties of operations, particularly the distributive property, leading to products such as (–1)(–1) = 1 and the rules for multiplying signed numbers. Interpret products of rational numbers by describing real-world contexts.*

Standards 7.NS.A.2 a–d break down the understandings needed to multiply and divide rational numbers.

Real-world contexts help students make sense of multiplication of rational numbers. For example, it makes sense that $4 \times (–6.50) = –26$ when the context for this equation is Janene owes $6.50 to each of 4 people. How much does Janene owe altogether?

It is common to read and understand (–6) as "the opposite of six" as well as "negative six." Use "the opposite of" wording to make sense of equations such as $(–2) \times (–5)$ so that we read "the opposite of 2 times negative 5" or $((–1) \times 2) \times (–5) = –(2 \times –5) = –(–10) = 10$.

Students should discover the rules for multiplying signed numbers, and the rules make more sense when given context. For example, the chart below shows equations with context.

Selling 2 packs of pens at $4 per pack	$2 \times 4 = 8$	
Owing $4 each to 2 friends	$2 \times –4 = –8$	
Spending $2 on 4 packs of pens that cost $2 each	$–2 \times 4 = –8$	
Forgiving 2 debts of $4 each	$–2 \times –4 = 8$	

What the TEACHER does:

- Give several examples of multiplication with rational numbers to students in real-world contexts where the signs of the answers make sense. Examples can include, *"I owe $6.50 to each of 4 people. How much money do I owe altogether?"* $4 \times (–6.50) = (–26)$. After several stories for each combination of signs (+ +, + –, – –), ask students to suggest rules for multiplying rational numbers.

- It is common to read and understand (–6) as "the opposite of six" as well as "negative six." Use "the opposite of" wording to make sense of equations such as $(–2) \times (–5)$ so that we read "the opposite of 2 times negative 5."

- Help students generalize rules for multiplying signed numbers from tables of related facts.

- Provide students with an opportunity to determine which properties of multiplication hold true for rational numbers. This can be accomplished by giving students a list of properties and asking them to write multiplication equations with rational numbers that make use of the properties or giving students examples of multiplication equations with rational numbers and asking students which properties are shown in the equations.

- Provide opportunities for students to write the rules for multiplication of signed numbers or answer questions about properties in journals, letters, and exit and/or entrance slips.

What the STUDENTS do:

- Discover the rules for multiplying rational numbers by reasoning from real-world examples.

- Use different interpretations for the (–) sign such as "negative" or "the opposite of" to make sense of real-world contexts using rational numbers.

- Conclude that the properties of the operations for multiplication hold for rational number multiplication.

Addressing Student Misconceptions and Common Errors

Students who have difficulty generalizing rules for multiplication from real-world contexts can be given a mathematical context. Provide a number of equations with like signs and have students find the answers with a calculator. From there students can formulate a rule for multiplying rational numbers with like signs from a pattern they see in the equations they solve. Repeat with equations having unlike signs.

> b. *Understand that integers can be divided, provided that the divisor is not zero, and every quotient of integers (with non-zero divisor) is a rational number. If p and q are integers, then $-\frac{p}{q} = \frac{-p}{q} = \frac{p}{-q}$. Interpret quotients of rational numbers by describing real-world contexts.*

Division of rational numbers can be thought of as the inverse of multiplication relying on previous understandings of the relationship between multiplication and division. For example, $(-25) \div 5 = -5$ because $5 \times (-5) = 25$. This preserves the relationship between multiplication and division found with whole numbers, including the fact that division by 0 is undefined. One explanation is: $x \times 0 = 5$, so $5 \div 0 = x$. There is no possible number for x. The equation $-\frac{p}{q} = \frac{-p}{q} = \frac{p}{-q}$ is for the teacher, not the students. Use both $p \div (-q)$ and $\frac{p}{-q}$ notations for division.

What the TEACHER does:

- Relate the meaning of division with signed numbers to the meaning of division with whole numbers by using the inverse relationship of multiplication and division such as, "*Since $7 \times 3 = 21$, we know that $21 \div 3 = 7$. Following the same reasoning, $7 \times (-3) = (-21)$ so $(-21) \div (-3) = 7$.*"

- Expose students to many examples of division with integers so they can discover/establish formal rules.

- Use multiplication and division as inverse operations. Ask students to work in groups to explain why it is not possible to divide by 0. Encourage them to divide by 0 and see what happens. One explanation is $x \times 0 = 5$, so $5 \div 0 = x$. There is no possible number for x.

- Relate the meaning of division with signed numbers to the meaning of division with whole numbers by using the inverse relationship of multiplication and division such as "*Since $7 \times 3 = 21$ we know that $21 \div 3 = 7$. Following the same reasoning $7 \times (-3) = (-21)$ so $(-21) \div (-3) = 7$.*"

- Use both $p \div (-q)$ and $\frac{p}{-q}$ notations for division.

- Challenge students with questions such as, "*–5 is the quotient. What is the equation?*"

- Provide real-world contexts where quotients of rational numbers can be interpreted. For example, if the temperature on Sunday was 0 °F and 7 days later it was –21 °F, what does –3 represent? How was –3 calculated?

- Provide opportunities for students to create real-world problems using division of rational numbers.

- Use writing as a formative assessment to learn about students' understanding of multiplication and division of rational numbers.

- Provide on-going practice with multiplication and division of rational numbers in real-world and mathematical contexts so that students may develop fluency.

What the STUDENTS do:

- Use reasoning to determine that division by zero is not defined.

- Discover that division as the inverse of multiplication holds true with integers.

- Generalize rules for division with signed numbers from examples.

- Use $p \div (-q)$ and $\frac{p}{-q}$ notations interchangeably.

- Interpret a rational quotient in a real-world context.

- Clarify their own understanding of the relationship between multiplication and division of rational numbers through writing.

- Develop fluency through practice with multiplication and division of rational numbers.

Addressing Student Misconceptions and Common Errors

Students who are not fluent with basic multiplication and division facts will have difficulty performing fluently with rational numbers. These students need additional practice. Many computer-based programs have success with basic fact mastery.

For students who do not understand why division by 0 is undefined, give specific examples of the relationship between multiplication and division that would not make sense. For example, $x \times 0 = 5$, so $5 \div 0 = x$. There is no possible number for x.

Present problems in real-world contexts that allow students to see the meaning of the properties of the operations. Properties include:

Commutative Property of Multiplication: $3.6 \times 2 = 2 \times 3.6$

Associative Property of Multiplication: $3 \times (6 \times (-7)) \times (-2) = (3 \times 6) \times ((-7) \times (-2))$

Distributive Property: $-4(4 + (-3)) = ((-4) \times 4) + ((-4) \times (-3))$

Multiplicative Identity: $1 \times (-9) = (-9)$

Zero Property of Multiplication: $(-4.6) \times 0 = 0$

What the TEACHER does:

- Use real-world contexts as examples for students to reason using properties of the operations. Let students solve in pairs and explain the operations they used such as:

  o Maria needed to borrow 1 cup of sugar to finish the icing on her cake. Her mother had 2 containers with a $\frac{1}{2}$ cup of sugar in each. Her father had $\frac{1}{2}$ of a 2-cup bag. Explain why it does not matter whose sugar Maria borrows.

  o Ms. Core bought stock in Harley Davidson Motorcycles. For the first 3 days she owned the stock, the shares changed price by $-2\frac{1}{4}$ a day. For the next 5 days, it changed $+\frac{3}{4}$ per day. Did Ms. Core show a profit during the first 8 days that she owned the stock? Would there be a difference if the stock changed $+\frac{3}{4}$ for the first 5 days and changed $-2\frac{1}{4}$ the next 3 days? Explain your reasoning mathematically.

- Encourage the use of precise mathematical vocabulary as students explain their reasoning.

What the STUDENTS do:

- Use properties of the operations to explain the solutions to real-world problems.

- Clarify their understanding of properties of operations by discussing with their partners and explaining their reasoning to the class.

- Practice use of appropriate mathematical vocabulary in discussions. Vocabulary includes the names of the properties.

Addressing Student Misconceptions and Common Errors

Students often confuse the associate property with the distributive because both properties use parentheses. This is a common error for students who do not understand what is happening in the equation. Try modeling the properties with simple examples such as this one for the distributive property: I have 3 tetras and 4 goldfish in each of my 5 fish tanks. How many fish do I have?

$$5(3 + 4) = (5 \times 3) + (5 \times 4)$$

Notes

d. *Convert a rational number to a decimal using long division; know that the decimal form of a rational number terminates in 0s or eventually repeats.*

To convert rational numbers in fraction form to decimal form, use the meaning of fractions as division. For example, $\frac{4}{5} = 4 \div 5$. Using long division, $4 \div 5 = 0.80$. From repeated examples, students learn that the decimal form either ends in 0s (as in the example) or repeats digits/sets of digits. Students learn to use the bar above a digit/set of digits to designate digits that repeat. For example, $\frac{2}{3} = 2 \div 3 = 0.\overline{6}$ and $\frac{39}{99} = 0.\overline{39}$. This prepares students to learn about irrational numbers in Grade 8.

What the TEACHER does:

- Define $\frac{a}{b}$ as $a \div b$. This may be a new understanding of fraction notation for many students.

- Use rational numbers that will end in 0s when converted to decimals such as $\frac{3}{4} = 0.750$ and $\frac{33}{2} = 22.50$.

- Provide students with fraction sets to convert such as the thirds, sevenths, ninths, and so on. Using long division, students will find patterns of repeating digits. Use the bar over the first digit or set of digits that repeat such as $\frac{1}{7} = 0.\overline{142857}$.

- Provide students opportunities to reflect on why they think the patterns are occurring in the thirds, sevenths, and so on. Opportunities may be in writing or conversations with classmates.

- Pose the following question to the class: Can you group the decimal forms of rational numbers into types? What do you notice?

What the STUDENTS do:

- Use long division to convert rational numbers in fraction form to decimal form.

- Explain why and how they know a long division quotient will repeat such as in the case of $\frac{1}{7}$.

- Sort the decimal form of rational numbers into two types, ending in 0/terminating or repeating. Students conclude that rational numbers can be written as repeating or terminating decimals.

Addressing Student Misconceptions and Common Errors

Some students may have difficulty with long division. Look for patterns in repeated errors made by these students and target these specific errors. Common division errors are forgetting to add zeroes in the dividend and placing the decimal point in the wrong place in the quotient. Try some alternate algorithms that focus on place value. Some students may have tracking difficulties. Doing long division on graph paper is a solution for many students.

Perseverance is important in converting to decimal form if there are many digits that repeat. Students should be encouraged to continue until they find a repeating pattern or 0 because it is a common error that they stop the division algorithm too soon. Calculators are a useful tool for decimals that have over four digits that repeat.

Sometimes students want to use the repeat bar over two or three repeating digits when only one digit repeats such as $\frac{3}{9} = 0.\overline{3}$, not $0.\overline{333}$. This error can be corrected through the use of error analysis exercises where students are presented with incorrect work done by a fictitious student. The problems should re-create a common error or misconception and the students try to identify it, thereby clarifying their own thinking. In this case, an example is as follows: Mario wrote the answer to a problem as $\frac{1}{3} = 0.\overline{333}$. He made an error. Correct his mistake and explain to Mario how to avoid making the same mistake in the future.

Notes

STANDARD 3 (7.NS.A.3)

Solve real-world and mathematical problems involving the four operations with rational numbers.[1]

[1]Computations with rational numbers extend the rules for manipulating fractions to complex fractions.

Extend the work with order of operations to all rational numbers. An example of a mathematical problem is $-3 \times 2\left(\frac{5}{6} + -\frac{1}{2}\right) = -2$.

Complex fractions are fractions with a fraction in the numerator and/or a fraction in the denominator such as $\frac{\frac{3}{4}}{\frac{1}{2}}$. Interpret the

division bar to turn a complex fraction into division: $\frac{\frac{3}{4}}{\frac{1}{2}} = \frac{3}{4} \div \frac{1}{2}$.

What the TEACHER does:

- Extend the work with order of operations to all rational numbers.

- Provide real-world problems that build on previously studied skills. For example: *"You want to buy a new tablet. The service agreement will deduct $22.50 from your savings every month to pay for it. How much will the deductions be at the end of the year?"* $12(-22.50) = -270$. Include problems that apply all four operations with rational numbers and complex fractions.

What the STUDENTS do:

- Apply operations with rational numbers to problems that involve the order of operations.

- Solve mathematical problems that use the four operations with rational numbers.

- Solve real-world problems that involve the four operations with rational numbers.

- Compute with complex fractions.

Addressing Student Misconceptions and Common Errors

As equations become longer with more terms and more complex using rational numbers, some students are overwhelmed and do not know where to begin. Help these students by reviewing the order of operations and demonstrating how to solve equations one step at a time. Flip books created by the students that do a step-by-step breakdown of a computation aid some students. For such a book, students can begin with a problem and perform one step on the first page, then repeat that step and add a second step to the next page, continuing in this manner.

Notes

The Number System

Cluster A: Apply and extend previous understandings of operations with fractions to add, subtract, multiply, and divide rational numbers.

Standard: 7.NS.A.1.b. *Understand* p + q *as the number located a distance* |q| *from* p, *in the positive or negative direction depending on whether* q *is positive or negative. Show that a number and its opposite have a sum of 0 (are additive inverses). Interpret sums of rational numbers by describing real-world contexts.*

Standards for Mathematical Practice:

SFMP 4. Model with mathematics.

Students explain what they know about addition of rational numbers by justifying their conclusions with models.

SFMP 6. Attend to precision.

Students find rational numbers that make true equations.

Goal:

Students use their understanding of addition of rational numbers to justify with models the possible values to create true equations.

Planning:

Materials: chart paper, markers

Sample Activity:

- Assign students to partner pairs. Distribute the following task: Your teacher needs a break and has assigned you the task of creating the questions for next week's quiz. His instructions are as follows:
  - Write two addition equations with a sum of −10.
  - Write two subtraction equations with a difference of −8.
  - Write a real-world problem that models the equation −15 + 5 = 10.
  - Using models, convince your teacher that your equations are true.

- Students prepare a short class presentation to convince their teacher that their equations are correct. Teacher should encourage classmates to ask questions and challenge group answers where appropriate.

Notes

Questions/Prompts:

- Are students using guess and check to find their answers? Ask, *"Do you know any models that might help you?"*

- If no one is challenging group presentations, offer a challenge of your own as a model to start the critique. Ask, *"Did anyone do this differently?"*

- Are students having difficulty finding real-world contexts? Brainstorm topics with them such as finance, sports, weather, and so on.

Differentiating Instruction:

Struggling Students:

- Some students may have difficulty since there is no one correct answer on several steps of the task. Encourage them to use a number line so they can see the options.

Extension:

- Alter the assignment to finding and explaining how to find all the possible values of x that make the following equations true:

$$-5 + x = \text{a positive number}$$

$$x - 3 = \text{a negative number}$$

Notes

The Number System

Cluster A: Apply and extend previous understandings of operations with fractions to add, subtract, multiply, and divide rational numbers.

Standard:

Standards for Mathematical Practice:

Goal:

Planning:

Materials:

Sample Activity:

Questions/Prompts:

Differentiating Instruction:

Struggling Students:

Extension:

The Number System
8.NS.A*

Know that there are numbers that are not rational, and approximate them by rational numbers.

STANDARD 1	**8.NS.A.1:** Know that numbers that are not rational are called irrational. Understand informally that every number has a decimal expansion; for rational numbers show that the decimal expansion repeats eventually, and convert a decimal expansion which repeats eventually into a rational number.
STANDARD 2	**8.NS.A.2:** Use rational approximations of irrational numbers to compare the size of irrational numbers, locate them approximately on a number line diagram, and estimate the value of expressions (e.g., π^2). *For example, by truncating the decimal expansion of $\sqrt{2}$, show that $\sqrt{2}$ is between 1 and 2, then between 1.4 and 1.5, and explain how to continue on to get better approximations.*

*Supporting cluster

The Number System   8.NS.A

Cluster A: Know that there are numbers that are not rational, and approximate them by rational numbers.

Grade 8 Overview

In this cluster students expand their knowledge of the real numbers to include irrationals. Students reason with approximations of irrational numbers and explain how to get more precise approximations. Students compare and locate irrational numbers on a number line. In grade 7 students converted fractions into their decimal expansions. Eighth graders convert the decimal expansions into fraction form.

Standards for Mathematical Practice

SFMP 2. Reason abstractly and quantitatively.

Students are reasoning as they explain how to get more precise approximations of irrational numbers.

SFMP 6. Attend to precision.

Students are using rational approximations of irrational numbers to compare and locate irrational numbers on a number line.

SFMP 8. Look for and express regularity in repeated reasoning.

Students explain how to get more precise rational approximations of irrational numbers.

Related Content Standards

6.NS.C.6   7.NS.A.2.d   8.EE.A.2

Notes

Know that numbers that are not rational are called irrational. Understand informally that every number has a decimal expansion; for rational numbers show that the decimal expansion repeats eventually, and convert a decimal expansion which repeats eventually into a rational number.

Students expand their knowledge of the Real Number System to include irrational numbers. A diagram shows the relationship of the subsets:

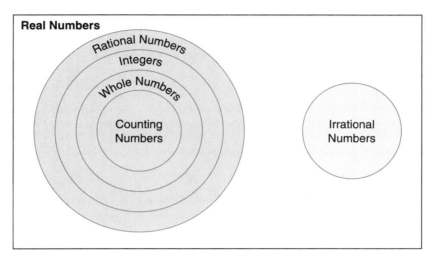

An irrational number is a decimal whose expansion does not terminate or repeat. Irrational numbers cannot be written in fraction form. Using decimal expressions, students compare rational numbers and irrational numbers to show that rational number expansions repeat and irrational numbers expansions do not. The notation " . . ." means "continues indefinitely without repeating." For example, $0.\bar{3}$ is a rational number that repeats but $\pi = 3.1415 \ldots$ does not repeat.

To convert a decimal expansion into a fraction:

Change $0.\bar{5}$ to a fraction

1. Let $x = 0.555 \ldots$

2. Multiply both sides so that the repeating digits will be in front of the decimal. In this case, one digit repeats so both sides are multiplied by 10, giving $10x = 5.555 \ldots$

3. Subtract the original equation from the new equation.

    $10x = 5.555 \ldots$
    $\underline{-x = 0.555 \ldots}$
    $9x = 5$

4. Solve the equation by dividing both sides of the equation by 9.

5. $x = \frac{5}{9}$

What the TEACHER does:

-   Pose questions such as the following: *"Will all rational numbers eventually repeat? Can you find a rational number that does not repeat?"* Use this discussion as an introduction for students to discover irrational numbers.

-   Have students reason about the inclusive nature of the subsets of the Real Number System and complete a Venn diagram of the Real Number System.

-   Access prior knowledge about converting fractions to decimals. Relate the concept to changing the decimal

expansion of a repeating decimal into a fraction and a fraction into a repeating decimal. Provide examples.

What the STUDENTS do:

-   Clarify understanding of rational numbers as repeating or terminating through discussion about irrational numbers.

-   Recognize and use the notation for decimal expansions of irrational numbers.

(continued)

GRADE 8

What the STUDENTS do (continued):

- Complete a Venn diagram to clarify their understanding of the Real Number System as the set of numbers made up of the rational and the irrational numbers.

- Convert decimal expansions into equivalent fractions using an algorithm.

- Use strategies other than conversions for some decimal expansions; for example, after exploring the ninths, students may remember the repeating pattern ($\frac{1}{9} = 0.\bar{1}$, $\frac{2}{9} = 0.\bar{2}$).

- Recall common fractions such as $\frac{3}{4} = 0.75$.

Addressing Student Misconceptions and Common Errors

Some students have difficulty understanding the relationship of the subsets of the Real Number System with a Venn diagram. Try a hands-on approach using boxes or bags that fit inside one another to represent the subsets.

Some students need more practice than others converting repeating decimals to equivalent fractions. This can be done over time with mini-practice sessions weekly.

Notes

STANDARD 2 (8.NS.A.2)

Use rational approximations of irrational numbers to compare the size of irrational numbers, locate them approximately on a number line diagram, and estimate the value of expressions (e.g., π^2). For example, by truncating the decimal expansion of $\sqrt{2}$, show that $\sqrt{2}$ is between 1 and 2, then between 1.4 and 1.5, and explain how to continue on to get better approximations.

Students compare irrational numbers and locate them on a number line by finding their rational approximations. Find rational approximations by creating lists of numbers by answering the following question: Between which two numbers will you find $\sqrt{2}$? Since $1^2 = 1$ and $2^2 = 4$, it is between 1 and 2. To be more precise, is it closer to 1 or 2? Systematically square 1.1, 1.2, 1.3, 1.4 . . . 1.9. Between which two numbers do you find 2? Repeat the process until you have the degree of precision you are seeking.

What the TEACHER does:

- Pose the following question: Where should you place 3.14159 . . . on the number line? Provide a number line to fill in with rational numbers. Provide several integers and fractions along with 3.14159 . . . and allow them to reason where they will place 3.1459. . . . Discuss how precise they were in their placement. Did they place it between 3 and 4 or between 3.141 and 3.142? Is between 3 and 4 precise enough? Through this questioning, lead students to conclude that approximations of irrational numbers are used to compare and locate them on a number line.

- Allow students to compare the size of irrational numbers based on their location on the number line. Highlight the reasoning students already use to compare the size of integers, fractions, and so on based on distance and direction on a number line.

- Provide opportunities for students to practice approximating irrational numbers. Be sure to provide instructions on how precise the approximation should be, such as, *"to 3 decimal places."*

- Provide students opportunities to explain in writing how to get more precise approximations for irrational numbers. For example, they could write a letter to next year's seventh-grade class explaining how to approximate the $\sqrt{5}$ to three decimal places.

What the STUDENTS do:

- Reason abstractly to determine where to place an irrational number on the number line. Students begin to focus on the precision required of the task. It is not unreasonable to expect them to ask how precise they should be for the given exercises. Tenths? Hundredths?

- Look for and express regularity in the repeated reasoning used in finding approximations of irrational numbers.

- Reason abstractly as they become more familiar with the process to find approximations of irrational numbers to streamline the algorithm.

- Express thinking in writing to clarify understanding about how to find precise approximations of irrational numbers.

Addressing Student Misconceptions and Common Errors

When rational numbers written in decimal form have more than three digits that repeat, some students stop the division process and call it an irrational number. These students need to be encouraged to persevere with the division until they are convinced there is no repeat. These students may not have a clear understanding of rational numbers as numbers that can be written in fraction form. This fact should be made explicit during instruction.

To help students who become overwhelmed with the process to approximate irrational numbers, suggest an organized format. For example, set up three columns with questions that need to be answered for each. Some students may need the template at first.

____ falls between which two whole numbers?	Is ____ closer to ____ or ____?	Is ____ closer to ____ or ____?

The Number System

Cluster A: Know that there are numbers that are not rational, and approximate them by rational numbers.

Standard: 8.NS.A.2. *Use rational approximations of irrational numbers to compare the size of irrational numbers, locate them approximately on a number line diagram, and estimate the value of expressions (e.g., π^2). For example, by truncating the decimal expansion of $\sqrt{2}$, show that $\sqrt{2}$ is between 1 and 2, then between 1.4 and 1.5, and explain how to continue on to get better approximations.*

Standards for Mathematical Practice:

SFMP 2. Reason abstractly and quantitatively.
Students are reasoning abstractly as they determine where to place rational and irrational numbers on the number line.

SFMP 6. Attend to precision.
Students are using rational approximations of irrational numbers to compare size and locate on a number line.

Goal:
Students demonstrate abstract reasoning in their explanations of how they compare the size of irrational numbers, locate irrational numbers on the number line, and estimate the value of expressions that contain irrational numbers.

Planning:

Materials: paper and pencil, prepared blank number lines (or students can draw their own)

Sample Activity:

- Provide groups of students with a set of rational numbers containing integers and fractions. Include 3.14159 . . . and ask students to place the numbers on a display number line.
- Have a class discussion on where students placed the irrational number and the justification.
- Discuss how to compare the size of irrational numbers based on their location on the number line.
- Demonstrate how to find a rational approximation for an irrational number.
- Give students the level of precision and ask them to find the rational approximations for irrational numbers such as $\sqrt{5}$.
- Close the lesson with a number line and a set of rational and irrational numbers (including expressions such as π^2) for students to locate on the number line. Students should give a written justification for the placement of the numbers.

Questions/Prompts:

- Are students having trouble with the irrational number placement? Ask, *"What do you know for sure about the size of the number?"*

- Are students not sure how to begin to find the rational approximation of $\sqrt{5}$? Ask, *"Between which two whole numbers is $\sqrt{5}$?"*

- Are some students confused about where to stop the approximation? Ask questions to be sure they understand place value of decimals.

Differentiating Instruction:

Struggling Students: Spend time guiding students having difficulty by asking them questions to scaffold the activity such as, *"Which numbers do you know the location of on the number line?"* Continue with questions such as, *"What do you know about the size of $3.14159\ldots$?"*

Extension: Ask, *"How many irrational numbers do you think are between 1.4 and 1.5? Explain your reasoning."*

Notes

The Number System

Cluster A: Know that there are numbers that are not rational, and approximate them by rational numbers.

Standard:

Standards for Mathematical Practice:

Goal:

Planning:

Materials:

Sample Activity:

Questions/Prompts:

Differentiating Instruction:

Struggling Students:

Extension:

Reflection Questions: The Number System

The order of these materials is not meant to be linear—in other words you do not teach one standard and then move to the next. Rather, they connect within a cluster, across clusters, and across domains.

1. Look at the standards in Grade 8, Cluster B. How do they relate to one another? Support or build on one another?

2. The domain The Number System calls for much computation. How do the Standards for Mathematical Practice inform this domain? Focus on one grade level.

Expressions and Equations

Expressions and Equations

Domain Overview

GRADE 6

At this level, the study of expressions and equations centers on the use of variables in mathematical expressions. Students write and evaluate numerical expressions and use expressions and formulas to solve problems. Students also solve simple one-step equations and use equations such as $3x = y$ to describe relationships between quantities. The sixth-grade study of expressions and equations is foundational in the transition to algebraic representation and problem solving, which is extended and formalized in Grade 7.

GRADE 7

Seventh graders use properties of operations to generate equivalent expressions. They use the arithmetic of rational numbers to formulate expressions and equations in one variable and use these equations to solve problems.

The seventh-grade focus of solving real-world and mathematical problems using numerical and algebraic expressions and equations provides the foundation for equation work in Grade 8 and assists in building the foundation work for writing equivalent nonlinear expressions in later grades.

GRADE 8

Eighth graders focus on more complex equations by learning about and applying the properties of integer exponents, square and cube roots, and scientific notation. They also connect previous understandings about proportional relationships to linear equations. Systems of two linear equations in two variables are introduced, and three methods for finding solutions are learned.

6	7	8	
		✓	Books: *My Full Moon is Square* by Elinor Pinczes and *Sea Squares* by Joy Hulme
✓		✓	Cubes such as linking cubes, Unifix cubes™, wooden cubes
✓			Number line
✓	✓	✓	Square tiles (paper or commercially produced)

KEY VOCABULARY

6	7	8	
✓	✓		**base** in 4^2, 4 is the base; the number multiplied by itself
	✓	✓	**bivariate data** data in two variables, one to be graphed on the x-axis and the other on the y-axis
✓	✓		**coefficient** a number or variable used to multiply a variable; in $3x + 7$, 3 is the numerical coefficient; in $y = mx + b$, x is the variable and m is the variable coefficient
✓	✓		**constant** a fixed value; in $3c + 5 = 11$, 5 and 11 are constants
✓	✓		**dependent variable** the output variable in a function; the variable whose value depends on the input
✓	✓	✓	**distributive property** property that states that multiplying a sum by a number is the same as multiplying each addend by the number and then adding the products. The distributive property states that if a, b, and c are real numbers, then $a \times (b + c) = (a \times b) + (a \times c)$.
✓	✓	✓	**equation** statement using an equal sign (=) showing that two expressions have the same value
✓		✓	**equivalent** the same as; equal to
✓		✓	**evaluate** solve
✓		✓	**exponents** in 4^2, 2 is the exponent; the number that dictates how many times the base multiplies by itself; $4^2 = 4 \times 4$
✓			**exponential notation** written in the form of B^x
✓	✓	✓	**expression** a value expressed as numbers and/or variables, and operation symbols (such as +, −, ×) grouped together; $9y + 7$ is an expression; one side of an equation
✓	✓		**factor** as a verb, to break down into the terms that multiply to make the quantity to be factored

(Continued)

KEY VOCABULARY

6	7	8	
✓			**independent variable** the input value in a function; the variable whose value determines the value of the dependent variable
✓	✓		**inequality** statement that two values are not equal; the inequality symbol is ≠; inequalities can also use the symbols > and <
		✓	**irrational number** any real number that cannot be expressed as a ratio $\frac{a}{b}$, where a and b are integers, with b non-zero, and is therefore not a rational number
		✓	**linear equation** an equation whose graph is a straight line
✓		✓	**numerical expressions** expressions using all numbers such as 34×82
✓		✓	**rational numbers** any number that can be expressed as the quotient $\frac{a}{b}$ of two integers, with the denominator b not equal to zero
		✓	**scientific notation** a number written in the form of a number between 1 and 10 (including 1) times a power of 10; 4.2×10^6 is 4,200,000 written in scientific notation
✓			**simplify** to change an expression or equation into its lowest terms; combining like terms is one method to simplify an equation or expression
		✓	**simultaneous equations** a set of equations whose solution(s) are all the points that make all the equations in the set true; when graphed, the solutions are shown as the point(s) of intersection; also known as a system of equations
✓			**substitution** use of a numerical value to replace a variable
✓	✓	✓	**variable** a symbol that stands for an unknown number or any number in a specified set

Notes

Expressions and Equations
6.EE.A*

Cluster A

Apply and extend previous understandings of arithmetic to algebraic expressions.

STANDARD 1	**6.EE.A.1:** Write and evaluate numerical expressions involving whole-number exponents.
STANDARD 2	**6.EE.A.2:** Write, read, and evaluate expressions in which letters stand for numbers.

    a. Write expressions that record operations with numbers and with letters standing for numbers. *For example, express the calculation "Subtract y from 5" as 5 − y.*

    b. Identify parts of an expression using mathematical terms (sum, term, product, factor, quotient, coefficient); view one or more parts of an expression as a single entity. *For example, describe the expression 2(8 + 7) as a product of two factors; view (8 + 7) as both a single entity and a sum of two terms.*

    c. Evaluate expressions at specific values of their variables. Include expressions that arise from formulas used in real-world problems. Perform arithmetic operations, including those involving whole-number exponents, in the conventional order when there are no parentheses to specify a particular order (Order of Operations). *For example, use the formulas $V = s^3$ and $A = 6s^2$ to find the volume and surface area of a cube with sides of length s = $\frac{1}{2}$.*

STANDARD 3	**6.EE.A.3:** Apply the properties of operations to generate equivalent expressions. *For example, apply the distributive property to the expression 3(2 + x) to produce the equivalent expression 6 + 3x; apply the distributive property to the expression 24x + 18y to produce the equivalent expression 6(4x + 3y); apply properties of operations to y + y + y to produce the equivalent expression 3y.*
STANDARD 4	**6.EE.A.4:** Identify when two expressions are equivalent (i.e., when the two expressions name the same number regardless of which value is substituted into them). *For example, the expressions y + y + y and 3y are equivalent because they name the same number regardless of which number y stands for.*

*Major cluster

Expressions and Equations   6.EE.A

Cluster A: Apply and extend previous understandings of arithmetic to algebraic expressions.
Grade 6 Overview

The focus for this cluster is writing and evaluating numerical expressions involving whole number exponents, finding the value of an expression using exponential notation such as $3^3 = 27$, and using the appropriate terminology to explain how to evaluate an expression. Students are applying the properties of operations to generate equivalent expressions including the distributive property to produce equivalent representation.

Standards for Mathematical Practice
SFMP 2. Reason abstractly and quantitatively.

Sixth graders decontextualize to manipulate symbolic representations by applying properties of operations.

SFMP 4. Model with mathematics.

Students model real-world scenarios with equations and expressions.

STANDARD 3 (6.EE.A.3)

Apply the properties of operations to generate equivalent expressions. For example, apply the distributive property to the expression $3(2 + x)$ to produce the equivalent expression $6 + 3x$; apply the distributive property to the expression $24x + 18y$ to produce the equivalent expression $6(4x + 3y)$; apply properties of operations to $y + y + y$ to produce the equivalent expression $3y$.

Standard 3 spotlights applying the properties (distributive property, the multiplicative identity property of 1, and the commutative property for multiplication of operations) with expressions involving variables to generate equivalent expressions.

What the TEACHER does:

- Provide learning opportunities for students to use multiplication to interpret $3(2 + x)$ as three groups of $(2 + x)$. Have students create an array with three columns and $x + 2$ in each column to show the meaning of $3(2 + x)$. Ask students to discuss and explain why $3(2 + x)$ is equal to $6 + 3x$. (Note that the bars below represent x and the small boxes represent units.)

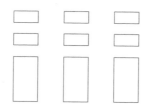

- Use manipulatives to interpret y as referring to one y, and y plus y plus y is $3y$. Discuss the distributive property, the multiplicative identity property of 1, and the commutative property for multiplication to prove that $y + y + y = 3y$.

- Encourage students to generate equivalent expressions for $5(x - 2)$ and $4x + 3y$.

- Ensure students have opportunities to talk with the teacher and each other to make sense of equivalent expressions.

- Focus on the following vocabulary terms: *equivalent expressions, properties, multiplicative identity, distributive,* and the *commutative property for multiplication.*

- Provide cyclical, distributed practice over time to review applying the properties of operations to generate equivalent expressions.

What the STUDENTS do:

- Understand that the properties used with numbers also apply to expressions with variables.

- Apply the properties of operations with expressions involving variables to generate equivalent expressions.

Addressing Student Misconceptions and Common Errors

When using the distributive property, some students may multiply the first term in the parentheses but forget to do the same to the second term. To address this error, give students a plastic ziplock bag of approximately 25 counters in two different colors mixed in each bag. Direct students to empty the bag and count the number of each color counter such as there are 14 yellows and 11 reds. Ask students to use the distributive property to write an expression to show how many of each color would be in 4 bags. Students write the expression $4(14y + 11r)$. Using the distributive property, the expression is $56y + 44r$. Interpret this as 56 yellows and 44 reds in 4 bags. Provide other examples.

Give students error analysis problems such as the following: *"Fred said $3(2 + x)$ and $6 + x$ are equivalent expressions. He was incorrect. Tell Fred what he did incorrectly."* One solution is to remind Fred that 3 must be distributed through both terms in the parentheses.

Using manipulatives such as Algeblocks™ or Algebra Tiles™ is also helpful in modeling the distributive property.

Notes

Identify when two expressions are equivalent (i.e., when the two expressions name the same number regardless of which value is substituted into them). For example, the expressions $y + y + y$ and $3y$ are equivalent because they name the same number regardless of which number y stands for.

This standard focuses on combining like terms in expressions. Students substitute values into expressions to prove equivalence. For example, *Are $3(x + 4)$ and $3x + 12$ equivalent expressions?* Substitute a numerical value for x such as 2. Then, $3(2 + 4) = 18$ and $(3 \times 2) + 12 = 18$ so the expressions are equivalent.

What the TEACHER does:

- Have students explore adding or subtracting like terms as quantities that contain the same variables and exponents. For example, $5x + 4x$ are like terms and can be combined as $9x$; however, $5x + 4x^2$ are not like terms since x and x^2 are not the same. Manipulatives such as Algeblocks™ or Algebra Tiles™ can be used to explore this concept.

- Provide practice for students to prove equivalence with substitution. They will use substitution to verify that both expressions are equivalent such as $3(2 + x) = 6 + x$. They should substitute any number for x. If the expressions have different values, they are not equivalent.

- Ensure students have adequate practice with equivalent expressions using the associative, commutative, and distributive properties.

- Focus on the following vocabulary terms: *equation, equivalent, expression, variable,* and *substitution.*

- Provide cyclical, distributed practice over time to review how to identify when two expressions are equivalent.

What the STUDENTS do:

- Explore the concept of like terms and apply combining like terms in expressions accurately.

- Reason that two expressions are equivalent through the use of substitution.

- Explain reasoning to other classmates and the teacher using precise mathematical vocabulary.

Addressing Student Misconceptions and Common Errors

Some sixth graders do not recognize when letters are used to represent variables and when letters are used to represent units of measure such as, $4m$ and 4 m as in meters or $3h$ and 3 h as in hours. Use contextual examples to distinguish between the two.

Some students may continue to combine $4x$ and $4x^2$. Use a manipulative such as square tiles to demonstrate the difference between the two terms.

Notes

Expressions and Equations
6.EE.B*

GRADE 6

Cluster B

Reason about and solve one-variable equations and inequalities.

STANDARD 5 **6.EE.B.5:** Understand solving an equation or inequality as a process of answering a question: which values from a specified set, if any, make the equation or inequality true? Use substitution to determine whether a given number in a specified set makes an equation or inequality true.

STANDARD 6 **6.EE.B.6:** Use variables to represent numbers and write expressions when solving a real-world or mathematical problem; understand that a variable can represent an unknown number, or, depending on the purpose at hand, any number in a specified set.

STANDARD 7 **6.EE.B.7:** Solve real-world and mathematical problems by writing and solving equations of the form $x + p = q$ and $px = q$ for cases in which p, q and x are all nonnegative rational numbers.

STANDARD 8 **6.EE.B.8:** Write an inequality of the form $x > c$ or $x < c$ to represent a constraint or condition in a real-world or mathematical problem. Recognize that inequalities of the form $x > c$ or $x < c$ have infinitely many solutions; represent solutions of such inequalities on number line diagrams.

*Major cluster

Expressions and Equations   6.EE.B

Cluster B: Reason about and solve one-variable equations and inequalities.
Grade 6 Overview

Students focus on the meaning of an equation and use reasoning and prior knowledge to solve it. They use variables to represent numbers and write expressions when solving problems. Students learn to write inequalities of the form $x > c$ or $x < c$ and use number line representation to show the solutions of the inequalities.

Standards for Mathematical Practice
SFMP 1. Make sense of problems and persevere in solving them.

Sixth graders solve real-world and mathematical problems through the application of algebraic concepts. They look for meaning of a problem and find efficient ways to represent and solve it.

SFMP 2. Reason abstractly and quantitatively.

Grade 6 students use properties of operations to generate equivalent expressions and use the number line to understand multiplication and division of rational numbers.

SFMP 4. Model with mathematics.

Students write expressions, equations, or inequalities from real-world contexts and connect symbolic and graphical representations. They use number lines to compare numbers and represent inequalities.

SFMP 6. Attend to precision.

Students communicate precisely with others and use clear mathematical language when describing equations and inequalities.

SFMP 7. Look for and make use of structure.

Sixth graders apply properties to generate equivalent expressions and solve equations by the subtraction property of equality.

Related Content Standards

5.OA.A.1   7.EE.A.2   7.EE.B.3   7.EE.B.4   7.EE.B.4.a   7.EE.B.4.b

Part 3   Expressions and Equations   **91**

Understand solving an equation or inequality as a process of answering a question: which values from a specified set, if any, make the equation or inequality true? Use substitution to determine whether a given number in a specified set makes an equation or inequality true.

The center of attention for this standard is solving an equation or inequality as a process of answering the following question: *Which values from a specified set make the equation or inequality true?* Students simplify numerical expressions by substituting values for given variables and use substitution to determine whether a given number in a specified set makes an equation true or which set of numbers makes an inequality true. Limit solving inequalities to selecting values from a given set that would make the inequality true. For example, find the value(s) of y that will make $7.2 + y \geq 9$. Select your value(s) from the set $= \{1, 1.3, 1.8, 2, 3\}$.

What the TEACHER does:

- Provide experiences for students to focus on understanding the meaning of solving an equation before developing the procedural knowledge. Start with a balance scale model to represent and solve equations. Say, *"There are 42 centimeter cubes on the left side of the scale and 200 cubes on the right side of the scale. All the blocks are the same size. How many cubes must be added to the left side of the scale to make the scale balance?"*

- Pose questions for variable equations such as the following: *What numbers could possibly be the solution for* $x + 17 = 27$? Note that equations should not require using the rules for operations with negative numbers.

- Supply scenarios where the solution is a single answer or multiple answers for the students to explore. This helps students establish the difference between equations and inequalities.

- Ask questions for variable inequalities such as the following: *What numbers could possibly be the solution for* $x + 17 > 27$? Present a set of possible solutions for students to select from. Include rational numbers in the set.

- Emphasize simple equations for students to solve using reasoning and prior knowledge such as *"Maria has 42 dollars in her bank. For her birthday she received some more dollars and now has $200. How many dollars did she receive for her birthday?"* Provide a set of possible solutions so that students may use substitution to find the solution. One possible set is $\{78, 58, 158, 258\}$.

- Focus on the following vocabulary terms: *inequalities* and *equations*.

- Provide cyclical, distributed reviews over time to practice solving an equation or inequality as a process of answering a question.

What the STUDENTS do:

- Use precise mathematical vocabulary to explain the differences between equations and inequalities.

- Discover that solutions to inequalities represent a range of possible values rather than a single solution.

- Reason the value(s) that make an equation or inequality true and select from a given set of values.

- Simplify numerical expressions by substituting values for given variables.

Addressing Student Misconceptions and Common Errors

Many students have difficulty understanding that an inequality can have more than one solution. The best way to work on this concept is to use real-world examples that are familiar to students. For example, I have $25 and want to buy some bracelets. The bracelets cost $8 each. How many could I buy? This results in the inequality $8b \leq 25$ where b is the number of bracelets I can buy. Since students are not solving inequalities in this standard, if you include a negative number in the set of possible solutions, have a discussion about how the negative value only works for the equation and not the real-world scenario.

STANDARD 6 (6.EE.B.6)

Use variables to represent numbers and write expressions when solving a real-world or mathematical problem; understand that a variable can represent an unknown number, or, depending on the purpose at hand, any number in a specified set.

This standard concentrates on writing expressions using variables that represent real-world or mathematical problems. Students learn that a variable represents an unknown number or any number in a specified set.

What the TEACHER does:

- Provide a variety of experiences for students to write expressions for solving real-world word problems. Focus on reading algebraic expressions to make the connection that a variable represents a number, such as the following: *"Sean has five more than twice as many pencils as John. Write an algebraic expression to represent the number of pencils Sean has."* $2j + 5$ where j represents the number of pencils John has.

- Encourage students to identify what the variable represents in each real-world scenario when they write an expression.

- Help students describe problem situations solved using an equation such as $4c + 5 = 25$, where c represents the cost of an item. Provide other problems where a variable represents any number in a specified set.

- Emphasize the following vocabulary terms: *expressions*, *equations*, and *variables*.

- Provide cyclical, distributed reviews over time to practice using variables to represent numbers and to read/write expressions when solving real-world or mathematical problems.

What the STUDENTS do:

- Understand that a variable represents a number or a specified set of numbers.

- Represent real-world scenarios with variable expressions, identifying what the variable represents.

- Use precise mathematical vocabulary when discussing expressions and variables.

Addressing Student Misconceptions and Common Errors

Some students continually misrepresent real-world scenarios with expressions. They each make different errors. Do an error analysis on the work of the students who repeatedly make errors. Are they mistaking what the variable is? Do they have trouble translating verbal expressions to variable expressions? Are they seeking to write equations instead of expressions? Write error analysis questions for the students to solve that use each of the common student errors being made in class that you have identified. An example of such a problem is as follows: Fred wrote $x + 6$ when asked to find an expression for *Sam has 6 times as many fish as Paul.* Fred was incorrect. Write Fred a note explaining his error. Note: Do not use real student names. This is meant to clarify misconceptions generally, not embarrass students who made the errors initially.

Notes

Solve real-world and mathematical problems by writing and solving equations of the form x + p = q and px = q for cases in which p, q and x are all nonnegative rational numbers.

Attention for Standard 7 is placed with solving equations for real-world and mathematical problems that involve positive rational numbers and zero. To solve the equation, students can draw pictures such as this example: *"Juan spent $48.99 on three T-shirts. If each shirt is the same amount, write an algebraic equation that represents this situation and solve to determine how much one T-shirt costs. The picture created is a bar model chart."* Each bar is labeled S for T-shirt, so each pair of jeans costs the same amount of money. The bar model represents the equation 3S = $48.99. To solve the problem, students divide the total cost of $48.99 by 3.

$48.99		
S	S	S

What the TEACHER does:

- Pose problems for students to explore solving equations based on real-world scenarios such as *"Corry bought 6 CDs that each cost the same amount. Without tax, he spent $89.94. How much did he spend on each CD? Write and solve an equation to solve the problem."* Note that problems should only use positive rational numbers (including 0), fractions, and decimals. Encourage students to illustrate the equation in problem situations by drawing a picture or using reasoning and prior knowledge. Solving equations using reasoning, pictures, diagrams, and prior knowledge allows students to develop effective strategies on their own.

- Ask students to generate equations based on situations from their daily lives such as texting friends. Have students explain the meaning of the variables used.

- Ensure students have opportunities to talk with the teacher and each other to make sense of equations in the form of *x + p = q* and *px = q*.

- Focus on the following vocabulary terms: *equations* and *nonnegative rational numbers*.

- Provide cyclical, distributed review over time to continually practice solving real-world and mathematical problems by writing and solving equations.

What the STUDENTS do:

- Solve equations that represent real-world mathematical problems that involve positive rational numbers and zero.

- Model real-world situations with equations and use a variety of strategies to solve them.

- Use precise mathematical vocabulary to communicate with the teacher and classmates.

Addressing Student Misconceptions and Common Errors

Some students may need additional, on-going practice with writing and solving equations. Use advertisements in newspapers to generate real-world scenarios that may be used to write and solve the equations.

Notes

STANDARD 8 (6.EE.B.8)

Write an inequality of the form x > c or x < c to represent a constraint or condition in a real-world or mathematical problem. Recognize that inequalities of the form x > c or x < c have infinitely many solutions; represent solutions of such inequalities on number line diagrams.

The essence of Standard 8 is graphing inequalities on a number line and writing inequalities to solve real-world mathematical problems. Students check by substitution to determine if the graph of an inequality is correct.

What the TEACHER does:

- Provide opportunities for students to represent inequalities on a number line. Present problems such as *"Less than $200.00 was spent by the Mrs. Smith for the class party. Write an inequality to represent this amount and graph this inequality on a number line."* Explain that the open circle above the 200 means that 200 is not included in the solution boundary set. The ray represents all numbers in the solution set. Check the solution by having students each select a number represented on the number line as part of the solution set and determine if it makes the inequality $x < 200$ true. Ask students if -200, which makes the statement $x < 200$ true, is a realistic answer to the word problem. Then, facilitate a class discussion.

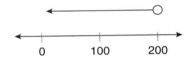

- Focus on the vocabulary term *inequality*.
- Provide cyclical, distributed reviews over time to practice writing an inequality of the form $x > c$ or $x < c$.

What the STUDENTS do:

- Discover that a variable can stand for an infinite number of solutions when used in inequalities.
- Graph inequalities on a number line.
- Write inequalities to solve real-world mathematical problems.
- Check by substitution to determine if the graph of an inequality is correct.

Addressing Student Misconceptions and Common Errors

Some students may need additional on-going practice with writing inequalities to represent a real-world mathematics situation. Use advertisements in newspapers to generate ideas of real-world scenarios that can be used to write an inequality to represent an amount. Ask students to talk about the problems and the number lines they created to show the inequalities.

Notes

Expressions and Equations
6.EE.C

Represent and analyze quantitative relationships between dependent and independent variables.

STANDARD 9	**6.EE.C.9:** Use variables to represent two quantities in a real-world problem that change in relationship to one another; write an equation to express one quantity, thought of as the dependent variable, in terms of the other quantity, thought of as the independent variable. Analyze the relationship between the dependent and independent variables using graphs and tables, and relate these to the equation. *For example, in a problem involving motion at constant speed, list and graph ordered pairs of distances and times, and write the equation* $d = 65t$ *to represent the relationship between distance and time.*

Expressions and Equations 6.EE.C

Cluster C: Represent and analyze quantitative relationships between dependent and independent variables.
Grade 6 Overview

The focus for this cluster is using variables to represent two quantities in a real-world problem that change in relationship to one another. Students write an equation and analyze the relationship between the dependent and independent variables using graphs and tables.

Standards for Mathematical Practice
SFMP 1. Make sense of problems and persevere in solving them.

Sixth graders solve real-world problems through the application of algebraic concepts.

SFMP 4. Model with mathematics.

Students model real-life situations with mathematics and use variables to represent two quantities in real-world problems. Problem situations are modeled symbolically, graphically, tabularly, and contextually.

SFMP 6. Attend to precision.

Students communicate precisely with others and use clear mathematical language when describing dependent and independent variables.

SFMP 7. Look for and make use of structure.

Sixth graders represent mathematics to describe a situation with either an equation or a diagram and interpret the results.

Related Content Standards

5.OA.A.1   7.EE.B.3   7.EE.B.4

Notes

STANDARD 9 (6.EE.C.9)

Use variables to represent two quantities in a real-world problem that change in relationship to one another; write an equation to express one quantity, thought of as the dependent variable, in terms of the other quantity, thought of as the independent variable. Analyze the relationship between the dependent and independent variables using graphs and tables, and relate these to the equation. For example, in a problem involving motion at constant speed, list and graph ordered pairs of distances and times, and write the equation $d = 65t$ to represent the relationship between distance and time.

This standard accents using variables to represent two quantities in real-world scenarios. Students recognize that a change in the independent variable creates a change in the dependent variable, such as the following: As x changes, y also changes. Emphasis is placed on writing an equation to express the quantity in terms of the dependent and independent variables. Students also identify relationships between tables, graphs, and equations and relate these back to the equation.

What the TEACHER does:

- Provide experiences for students to understand multiple representations such as tables, equations, and graphs that can be used to analyze relationships between quantities. Students should describe the relationships using language. Ensure students understand that each representation shows the same relationship.

- Include numerous situations for students to analyze and determine the unknown that is dependent on the other components such as how far someone travels is dependent on the time and rate.

- Focus on the following vocabulary terms: *dependent variable* and *independent variable*.

- Provide cyclical, distributed practice over time to continually review using variables to represent two quantities in a real-world problem that change in relationship to one another.

What the STUDENTS do:

- Use variables to represent two quantities.

- Identify relationships between tables, graphs, and equations.

- Recognize that a change in the independent variable creates a change in the dependent variable such as the following: As x changes, y also changes.

- Write an equation to express the quantity in terms of the dependent and independent variables.

Addressing Student Misconceptions and Common Errors

Some students may confuse what a graph represents. To help, have students explain in their own words what the graph means.

Notes

Expressions and Equations

Cluster C: Represent and analyze quantitative relationships between dependent and independent variables.

Standard: 6.EE.C.9. *Use variables to represent two quantities in a real-world problem that change in relationship to one another; write an equation to express one quantity, thought of as the dependent variable, in terms of the other quantity, thought of as the independent variable. Analyze the relationship between the dependent and independent variables using graphs and tables, and relate these to the equation.* For example, in a problem involving motion at constant speed, list and graph ordered pairs of distances and times, and write the equation $d = 65t$ to represent the relationship between distance and time.

Standards for Mathematical Practice:

SFMP 1. Make sense of problems and persevere in solving them.

Sixth graders solve real-world problems through the application of algebraic concepts.

SFMP 4. Model with mathematics.

Students model real-life situations with mathematics and use variables to represent two quantities in real-world problems. Problem situations are modeled symbolically, graphically, tabularly, and contextually.

SFMP 6. Attend to precision.

Students communicate precisely with others and use clear mathematical language when describing dependent and independent variables.

SFMP 7. Look for and make use of structure.

Sixth graders represent mathematics to describe a situation with either an equation or a diagram and interpret the results.

Goal:

To focus on independent and dependent variables using real-world problems, sixth graders make connections between different representations of the problem using a table, an equation, and a graph.

Planning:

Materials: pencil and paper for each partner pair of students

Sample Activity:

• Provide the following real-world problem and allow students to work as partners.

Our sixth-grade class is selling wrapping paper to fund our class party. Each roll of wrapping paper sells for $2.50 and is packaged 12 rolls to a box. Our class sold a total of 15 boxes of wrapping paper.

• Give students the following directions:

  o Complete the table to show the money collected for 15 boxes.
  o Write an equation to show the amount of money collected and the boxes of wrapping paper sold.
  o Graph the equation using ordered pairs from the table.

# of Boxes Sold	Money Collected
1	$30.00
2	$60.00
3	
4	$120.00
5	
6	
7	
8	
9	$270.00
10	
11	
12	
13	
14	
15	

○ Look at the equation you wrote to show the amount of m money collected if b boxes of wrapping paper were sold. Explain which is the independent variable and which is the dependent variable.

Questions/Prompts:

- Ask, *"What is the relationship between the variables? Write an expression that illustrates the relationship."*

- Ask, *"How many boxes of wrapping paper do the students in the class need to sell if they want to make approximately $2,000?"*

Differentiating Instruction:

Struggling Students: Some students may need more experience with completing tables, writing equations, and constructing graphs with ordered pairs. With these students, try the problem again, making it a simpler problem and an easier table for students to complete.

Extension: Extend this work by having students generate their own scenarios to create a table, write an equation, and construct the graph with ordered pairs.

Expressions and Equations

Cluster A: Apply and extend previous understandings of arithmetic to algebraic expressions.

Standard:

Standards for Mathematical Practice:

Goal:

Planning:

Materials:

Sample Activity:

Questions/Prompts:

Differentiating Instruction:

Struggling Students:

Extension:

Expressions and Equations

Cluster B: Reason about and solve one-variable equations and inequalities.

Standard:

Standards for Mathematical Practice:

Goal:

Planning:

Materials:

Sample Activity:

Questions/Prompts:

Differentiating Instruction:

Struggling Students:

Extension:

Expressions and Equations

Cluster C: Represent and analyze quantitative relationships between dependent and independent variables.

Standard:

Standards for Mathematical Practice:

Goal:

Planning:

Materials:

Sample Activity:

Questions/Prompts:

Differentiating Instruction:

Struggling Students:

Extension:

Expressions and Equations
7.EE.A*

Cluster A

Use properties of operations to generate equivalent expressions.

STANDARD 1   **7.EE.A.1:** Apply properties of operations as strategies to add, subtract, factor, and expand linear expressions with rational coefficients.

STANDARD 2   **7.EE.A.2:** Understand that rewriting an expression in different forms in a problem context can shed light on the problem and how the quantities in it are related. *For example, a + 0.05a = 1.05a means that "increase by 5%" is the same as "multiply by 1.05."*

*Major cluster

Expressions and Equations   7.EE.A

Cluster A: Use properties of operations to generate equivalent expressions.
Grade 7 Overview

In this cluster students apply properties of operations previously learned as strategies to add, subtract, factor, and expand linear equations that have rational coefficients. This skill leads to students being able to rewrite expressions in different forms so they can solve contextual problems and understand how the quantities in the problem are related.

Standards for Mathematical Practice
SFMP 2. Reason abstractly and quantitatively.

Students use expressions in different forms to understand how quantities in an equation are related.

SFMP 4. Model with mathematics.

Students write expressions and equations to model contextual problems.

SFMP 6. Attend to precision.

Students communicate their reasoning using precise mathematical vocabulary.

Related Content Standards

6.EE.A.3   6.EE.A.4   7.NS.A.1.d   7.NS.A.2.c   8.EE.C.7.b

Notes

Apply properties of operations as strategies to add, subtract, factor, and expand linear expressions with rational coefficients.

Apply previously learned properties of operations (distributive, commutative, associative, identity, and inverse properties of addition and multiplication, as well as the zero property of multiplication) as strategies for adding, subtracting, factoring, and expanding linear expressions. Coefficients are limited to rational numbers that include integers, positive/negative fractions, and decimals. Use the properties to write equivalent expressions; for example, $3(4a + 2) = 12a + 6$ uses the distributive property.

Substituting a numerical value for the variable and then evaluating the expressions to find the same solution is a tool to determine whether two expressions are equivalent. For example, $3(4a + 2)$ is equal to $12a + 6$. Let $a = 5$ and substitute 5 for a in both expressions.

$3(4a + 2)$	$12a + 6$
$3((4 \cdot 5) + 2)$	$(12 \cdot 5) + 6$
$3(20 + 2)$	$60 + 6$
$3(22)$	66
66	

What the TEACHER does:

- Present sets of expressions and ask which are equivalent. Allow time for students to reason using properties. For example, *"Maria thinks the two expressions $2(3a - 2) + 4a$ and $10a - 2$ are equivalent. Is she correct?"* Explain your reasoning.

- Provide students with opportunities to explain their reasoning in writing about how they are creating an equivalent expression using precise mathematical vocabulary. For example, vocabulary includes the terms *distributive property, identity*, and so on.

- Use substitution as a method to determine if two expressions are equivalent.

- Use equivalent expressions for real-world problems. For example: *"A rectangle is twice as wide as long. One expression to find the area is $l \cdot 2l$. Write the expression another way."*

Solution: $2l^2$

l

$2l$

What the STUDENTS do:

- Reason to identify sets of equivalent expressions.

- Discover that there can be more than one expression equivalent to a given expression.

- Change an expression into an equivalent expression using properties of operations and combining like terms.

- Represent real-world problems with equivalent expressions using properties of operations, combining like terms and substitution, and solve them.

- Communicate orally and/or in writing using precise mathematical vocabulary how an equivalent expression is created.

- Defend why two expressions are or are not equivalent.

Addressing Student Misconceptions and Common Errors

When students work with several steps in an expression, sometimes they forget about the order of operations such as in the following example: $7 + 2(3x - 5) + 2x$. Students may want to add the $7 + 2$ first or only multiply the 2 by the $3x$ and not the -5. A review of the order of operations can help. For students who need more assistance, have them create their own order of operations card with steps outlined to reference when needed to check their work. Students can also create their own pneumonic device to help them recall the steps.

STANDARD 2 (7.EE.A.2)

Understand that rewriting an expression in different forms in a problem context can shed light on the problem and how the quantities in it are related. For example, $a + 0.05a = 1.05a$ means that "increase by 5%" is the same as "multiply by 1.05."

Using equivalent expressions from the previous standard, focus on how writing an equivalent statement can better show the relationship among the terms in the expressions. For example, $6x + 15 = 3(2x + 5)$ means that three groups of $2x + 5$ is the same as one group of $6x$ and 15.

What the TEACHER does:

- Present students with real-world problems that can be modeled with more than one expression. For example: *"An item that is on sale for 20% off costs 80% of the original price. Write an expression using x as the original price."* Allow students to explain their expressions, decide if one another's expressions are equivalent, and explain how a particular expression relates the quantities in the problem. This can be done individually, in groups or as projects.

What the STUDENTS do:

- Model contextual problems with multiple variable expressions.

- Explain orally and/or in writing, using precise mathematical vocabulary, how two equivalent expressions relate the quantities.

Addressing Student Misconceptions and Common Errors

Many students have difficulty seeing that expressions are equivalent when the expressions are out of context. Use simple contexts so that students can reason with a context to explain why two expressions are equivalent. For example: *"Write two equivalent expressions for the following situation—All music downloads are 99 cents today. Maria wants to download 2 R&B hits, 1 rap hit, and 3 hits by her favorite artist. Two equivalent expressions are 6×0.99 and $(2 \times 0.99) + (1 \times 0.99) + (3 \times 0.99)$."* Focus student attention on how 6 hits for 0.99 each is the same as 2 hits and 1 hit and 3 hits for 0.99 each.

Notes

Expressions and Equations
7.EE.B*

Solve real-life and mathematical problems using numerical and algebraic expressions and equations.

STANDARD 3   **7.EE.B.3:** Solve multi-step real-life and mathematical problems posed with positive and negative rational numbers in any form (whole numbers, fractions, and decimals), using tools strategically. Apply properties of operations to calculate with numbers in any form; convert between forms as appropriate; and assess the reasonableness of answers using mental computation and estimation strategies. *For example: If a woman making $25 an hour gets a 10% raise, she will make an additional $\frac{1}{10}$ of her salary an hour, or $2.50, for a new salary of $27.50. If you want to place a towel bar $9\frac{3}{4}$ inches long in the center of a door that is $27\frac{1}{2}$ inches wide, you will need to place the bar about 9 inches from each edge; this estimate can be used as a check on the exact computation.*

STANDARD 4   **7.EE.B.4:** Use variables to represent quantities in a real-world or mathematical problem, and construct simple equations and inequalities to solve problems by reasoning about the quantities.

   a. Solve word problems leading to equations of the form $px + q = r$ and $p(x + q) = r$, where p, q, and r are specific rational numbers. Solve equations of these forms fluently. Compare an algebraic solution to an arithmetic solution, identifying the sequence of the operations used in each approach. *For example, the perimeter of a rectangle is 54 cm. Its length is 6 cm. What is its width?*

   b. Solve word problems leading to inequalities of the form $px + q > r$ or $px + q < r$, where p, q, and r are specific rational numbers. Graph the solution set of the inequality and interpret it in the context of the problem. *For example: As a salesperson, you are paid $50 per week plus $3 per sale. This week you want your pay to be at least $100. Write an inequality for the number of sales you need to make, and describe the solutions.*

*Major cluster

Expressions and Equations   7.EE.B

Cluster B: Solve real-life and mathematical problems using numerical and algebraic expressions and equations.
Grade 7 Overview

Students focus on solving real-world problems and learn to use equations and inequalities to solve the problems by reasoning about the quantities. Students learn to solve equations in the forms $px + q = r$ and $p(x + q) = r$ fluently through practice. They compare algebraic solutions to arithmetic ones to demonstrate that they understand the sequence of operations in each approach and how they are the same and different. For inequalities, students graph solutions and then describe the solutions in terms of the context of the problem.

Standards for Mathematical Practice
SFMP 1. Make sense of problems and persevere in solving them.

Students solve multi-step real-world mathematical problems. Students use equations and inequalities to solve problems.

SFMP 2. Reason abstractly and quantitatively.

Students solve problems by reasoning about quantities.

SFMP 4. Model with mathematics.

Students write equations to model contextual problems.

SFMP 6. Attend to precision.

Students estimate answers to problems as a check to accurate solutions.

Related Content Standards

7.NS.A.3   6.EE.B.6   6.EE.B.7   8.EE.C.7   8.F.A.3

Notes

STANDARD 3 (7.EE.B.3)

Solve multi-step real-life and mathematical problems posed with positive and negative rational numbers in any form (whole numbers, fractions, and decimals), using tools strategically. Apply properties of operations to calculate with numbers in any form; convert between forms as appropriate; and assess the reasonableness of answers using mental computation and estimation strategies. For example: If a woman making $25 an hour gets a 10% raise, she will make an additional $\frac{1}{10}$ of her salary an hour, or $2.50, for a new salary of $27.50. If you want to place a towel bar $9\frac{3}{4}$ inches long in the center of a door that is $27\frac{1}{2}$ inches wide, you will need to place the bar about 9 inches from each edge; this estimate can be used as a check on the exact computation.

Students solve multi-step real-world and mathematical problems. The problems should contain a combination of whole numbers, positive and negative integers, fractions, and decimals. Students will apply what they learned in previous standards about converting fractions, decimals, and percents and use properties of operations to find equivalent forms of expressions as needed. Students will be expected to check their work for reasonableness using estimation strategies, which may include but are not limited to the following:

- rounding the values in the problem up or down and then adjusting the estimate to make up for the closeness of the rounded values to the originals,

- using friendly or compatible numbers for the values in the problem that allow for common factors for multiplication or easy addition such as grouping hundreds or thousands, and

- using benchmark numbers that are easy to work with such as using 2 for $1\frac{7}{8}$ to make an estimate.

What the TEACHER does:

- Pose a variety of multistep real-world and mathematical problems to solve, including integers, fractions, decimals, and percents. Students should convert fractions, decimals, and percents as in the example in the Standard where a 10% raise was interpreted as $\frac{1}{10}$ of the base salary.

- Encourage the use of rounding, compatible numbers, and benchmark numbers to check for reasonableness of results.

- Expect students to use a check for reasonableness on every problem. Have them explain orally and/or in writing their estimation strategies for some of the problems using journals or on exit slips.

What the STUDENTS do:

- Solve multi-step real-world and mathematical problems with precision.

- Select an appropriate estimation strategy and apply it to a problem. Values in problems lend themselves to different strategies.

- Justify the estimation process used by explaining, orally and/or in writing, how it proved their answer to be reasonable. If the estimate did not show an answer to be reasonable, explain how it helped lead to an accurate answer.

Addressing Student Misconceptions and Common Errors

It is common for students to have difficulty with multi-step problems. Scaffold the problems by adding a question mid-way. Display the first step of the problem, allow students to find the answer, and then present the next part that relies on the first step. Gradually remove the middle question as students get used to finding a middle question and identifying it themselves. For example: *"Fred goes out to eat and buys a pizza that costs $12.75, including $.50 tax. He wants to leave a tip based on the cost of the food. What must Fred do?"*

First, present the following: *"Fred goes out to eat and buys a pizza that costs $12.75, including $.50 tax. How much did the pizza cost?"* Solve this part of the problem. Then, using the answer from Part 1, introduce the second part of the problem: *"He wants to leave a tip based on the cost of the food. What must Fred do?"*

Some students' work may indicate a weakness representing numbers in different forms such as 10% as $\frac{1}{10}$. These students need additional practice. Use number lines, visuals such as bars, and hands-on materials instead of memorizing rules.

STANDARD 4 (7.EE.B.4)

Use variables to represent quantities in a real-world or mathematical problem, and construct simple equations and inequalities to solve problems by reasoning about the quantities.

   a. *Solve word problems leading to equations of the form* $px + q = r$ *and* $p(x + q) = r$, *where p, q, and r are specific rational numbers. Solve equations of these forms fluently. Compare an algebraic solution to an arithmetic solution, identifying the sequence of the operations used in each approach.* For example, the perimeter of a rectangle is 54 cm. Its length is 6 cm. What is its width?

Students will become fluent in solving equations. Students use the arithmetic from the problem to generalize an algebraic solution.

Use word problems that lend themselves to equations in the forms of $px + q = r$ and $p(x + q) = r$. Two examples are as follows:

1. Three consecutive even numbers add up to 48. What is the lowest number of the three? $x + x + 2 + x + 4 = 3x + 6 = 48$ ($px + q = r$)

2. Ms. Thomas had $25 to spend on party favors. She had $10.40 left after buying 10 balloons. How much did she spend on each balloon? $0.1(25 - 10.40) = r$ ($p(x + q) = r$)

Students should develop fluency solving word problems that can be modeled by linear equations in the form $px + q = r$. Integers, fractions, and decimals should be included as values in the word problems.

What the TEACHER does:

- Select word problems for students that lend themselves to algebraic equations in the forms $px + q = r$ and $p(x + q) = r$, such as:

  o Diane had $30 to spend on party favors. She had $17.50 left after buying 10 balloons. How much did she spend on each balloon? $0.1(30 - 17.50) = r$.

  o Three consecutive even numbers add up to 48. What is the lowest number of the three?

  $$x + (x + 2) + (x + 4) = 48$$

  $$x + x + 2 + x + 4 = 48$$

  $$3x + 6 = 48$$

- Facilitate a classroom discussion about the importance of using the order of the operations. Demonstrate with an incorrect sequence of operations to emphasize the point.

- Provide students with problems that can be solved arithmetically but also have an algebraic solution such as problems that apply formulas for area or perimeter as in the example in the Standard. Ensure students can relate an arithmetic solution to an algebraic one using the example from the Standard.

What the STUDENTS do:

- Model word problems with equations in the forms $px + q = r$ and $p(x + q) = r$.

- Fluently solve equations of the forms $px + q = r$ and $p(x + q) = r$.

- Compare algebraic equations with arithmetic solutions for the same problem using precise mathematical vocabulary.

Addressing Student Misconceptions and Common Errors

Students who have difficulty becoming fluent in solving equations may need a hands-on approach. Manipulatives such as Algeblocks™, Hands-On Equations,™ and Algebra Tiles™ can be useful.

b. *Solve word problems leading to inequalities of the form* px + q > r *or* px + q < r, *where p, q, and r are specific rational numbers. Graph the solution set of the inequality and interpret it in the context of the problem. For example: As a salesperson, you are paid $50 per week plus $3 per sale. This week you want your pay to be at least $100. Write an inequality for the number of sales you need to make, and describe the solutions.*

In this standard, students move from solving word problems with equations to word problems with inequalities. Inequalities follow a similar form to those of the equations, $px + q > r$ and $px + q < r$. Students graph the solution set of the inequality on a number line and describe what it means in terms of the context of the word problem. Be aware that sometimes the solution set to the inequality contains values that do not make sense as solutions for the word problem. For example, in the word problem, *"Donna has at most $60 to spend on a shopping spree. She wants to buy a dress for $22 dollars and spend the rest on bracelets. Each bracelet costs $8. How many bracelets can she purchase?"* we see a solution of

$$\$60 - \$22 = \$38$$

$$8x \le 38$$

$$\frac{8x}{8} \le \frac{38}{8}$$

$$x \le 4.75$$

The number of bracelets is less than or equal to 4.75. However, Donna cannot buy .75 of a bracelet, so when we graph the inequality as below:

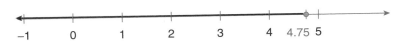

we see that the only viable solutions to the word problem are 4, 3, 2, 1, or no bracelets.

What the TEACHER does:

- Compare word problems that can be modeled with equations to those where an inequality is needed to find a solution set. Inequalities may have negative coefficients. Ask the students to compare how they are the same and how they are different.

- Model solving an inequality while facilitating a classroom discussion about how the procedure for solving inequalities is similar to that of equations.

- Present students with many examples of word problems that can be modeled by and solved with inequalities such as the following:

  o Erin has at most $73 to spend on jewelry. She wants to buy a watch for $25 and spend the rest on necklaces. Each necklace costs $8. Write an inequality for the number of necklaces she can purchase and solve it.

- Provide examples of inequalities with negatives so that students learn to reverse the direction of the inequality sign when multiplying or dividing by a negative.

- Encourage students to substitute the answer in the inequality to see if it makes the inequality true.

- Have students graph the solution sets of the inequalities on a number line and make sense of the solution set in context as opposed to whether it is a correct solution set to the mathematical inequality. Ask students to identify the maximum and minimum numbers that make sense within the context of the problem.

What the STUDENTS do:

- Recognize whether a word problem can be represented with an equation or an inequality.

- Create inequalities of the forms $px + q > r$ and $px + q < r$.

- Solve inequalities that contain the symbols <, >, ≤, ≥.

- Check answers with substitution.

- Graph solutions to inequalities on number lines and discuss whether all of the answers in the solution set make sense in the context of the problem.

Students may forget to switch the inequality sign when multiplying or dividing by a negative. Help students by asking them to check answers in their solution sets in the original inequality to see if they satisfy the inequality. For other students who consistently make errors, check their number line graphs. Some seventh graders may have difficulty drawing the graphs accurately. For example, some students will reverse the location of negative and positive integers. For these students, supply them with graph paper or simply a sheet of pre-drawn number lines for them to fill out.

Notes

GRADE 7

Expressions and Equations

Cluster A: Use properties of operations to generate equivalent expressions.

Standard: 7.EE.A.2. *Understand that rewriting an expression in different forms in a problem context can shed light on the problem and how the quantities in it are related.* For example, $a + 0.05a = 1.05a$ means that "increase by 5%" is the same as "multiply by 1.05."

Standards for Mathematical Practice:

SFMP 2. Reason abstractly and quantitatively.

Students use expressions in different forms to understand how quantities in an equation are related.

SFMP 4. Model with mathematics.

Students write expressions and equations to model contextual problems.

SFMP 6. Attend to precision.

Students communicate their reasoning to one another using precise mathematical vocabulary.

Goal:

Students understand that equivalent expressions can help show the relationship between the quantities in the problem more clearly and, thus, make it easier to explain the relationship.

Planning:

Materials: copies of the problem, paper and pencil, 1 sheet of chart paper per group

Sample Activity:

• Students work in groups to solve the following problem:

> Pablo is making a square picture frame of square tiles as shown:
>
>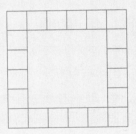
>
> On a sheet of poster paper, write three different expressions Pablo can use to find the total number of tiles in the frame.
>
> 1. Explain how each expression relates to the diagram.
>
> 2. Demonstrate that the expressions are equivalent.
>
> 3. Which expression does your group think is the most useful? Explain your thinking to the class.

- Have groups make class presentations. Ask questions during the presentations to facilitate class discussion such as, *"That is an interesting expression. Did any other group come up with that one? What did you need to understand to create that expression?"*

Questions/Prompts:

- For groups having trouble getting started, ask them to describe the problem in their own words.

- When students need to look at the problem from a different perspective, ask, *"How is this side related to this side?"* (as you point).

- If a group needs more practice, say, *"Talk to me about the thinking you have used so far."*

Differentiating Instruction:

Struggling Students: Struggling students may better understand the problem if they model it with square tiles and manipulate them to make sense of the problem.

Extension: Ask students to find a fourth equivalent expression for this problem.

Notes

Expressions and Equations

Cluster A: Use properties of operations to generate equivalent expressions.

Standard:

Standards for Mathematical Practice:

Goal:

Planning:

Materials:

Sample Activity:

Questions/Prompts:

Differentiating Instruction:

Struggling Students:

Extension:

Expressions and Equations

Cluster B: Solve real-life mathematical problems using numerical and algebraic expressions and equations.

Standard:

Standards for Mathematical Practice:

Goal:

Planning:

Materials:

Sample Activity:

Questions/Prompts:

Differentiating Instruction:

Struggling Students:

Extension:

Expressions and Equations
8.EE.A*

Work with radicals and integer exponents.

STANDARD 1	**8.EE.A.1:** Know and apply the properties of integer exponents to generate equivalent numerical expressions. *For example, $3^2 \times 3^{-5} = 3^{-3} = \frac{1}{3^3} = \frac{1}{27}$.*
STANDARD 2	**8.EE.A.2:** Use square root and cube root symbols to represent solutions to equations of the form $x^2 = p$ and $x^3 = p$, where p is a positive rational number. Evaluate square roots of small perfect squares and cube roots of small perfect cubes. Know that $\sqrt{2}$ is irrational.
STANDARD 3	**8.EE.A.3:** Use numbers expressed in the form of a single digit times an integer power of 10 to estimate very large or very small quantities, and to express how many times as much one is than the other. *For example, estimate the population of the United States as 3 times 10^8 and the population of the world as 7 times 10^9, and determine that the world population is more than 20 times larger.*
STANDARD 4	**8.EE.A.4:** Perform operations with numbers expressed in scientific notation, including problems where both decimal and scientific notation are used. Use scientific notation and choose units of appropriate size for measurements of very large or very small quantities (e.g., use millimeters per year for seafloor spreading). Interpret scientific notation that has been generated by technology.

*Major cluster

Expressions and Equations   8.EE.A

Cluster A: Work with radicals and integer exponents.
Grade 8 Overview

In this cluster students learn how to compute with integer exponents. Students build on what they have learned about square roots to solve equations in the form of $x^2 = p$ and $x^3 = p$, where p is a positive rational number, evaluating perfect square and perfect cube roots. Students learn how to express very large and very small numbers in scientific notation and express how many times larger or smaller one number written in scientific notation is than another. Students use the properties of integer exponents to perform operations with numbers written in scientific notation. Students interpret numbers written in scientific notation using technology.

Standards for Mathematical Practice
SFMP 2. Reason abstractly and quantitatively.

Students use reasoning to express how many times larger (or smaller) one number is than another when both are expressed in scientific notation.

SFMP 5. Use appropriate tools strategically.

Students learn to read scientific notation as expressed by technology.

SFMP 6. Attend to precision.

Students compute with integer exponents and numbers in scientific notation accurately.

SFMP 7. Look for and make use of structure.

Students will see and make use of patterns in scientific notation and in square and cube numbers.

Related Content Standards

7.NS.A.D.1   8.NS.A.1   8.NS.A.2

Notes

Know and apply the properties of integer exponents to generate equivalent numerical expressions. For example,
$3^2 \times 3^{-5} = 3^{-3} = \frac{1}{3^3} = \frac{1}{27}$.

Students learn how to compute using integer exponents building on their earlier experiences with adding and subtracting integers. For any non-zero real numbers a and b and integers n and m, the properties of integer exponents are as follows:

1. $a^n a^m = a^{n+m}$

2. $(a^n)^m = a^{nm}$

3. $a^n b^n = (ab)^n$

4. $a^0 = 1$

5. $a^{-n} = \frac{1}{a^n}$

6. $\frac{a^n}{a^m} = a^{n-m}$

What the TEACHER does:

- Introduce the laws of integer exponents one at time. Use a conceptual approach as opposed to asking students to memorize the rules.

- Provide examples of the processes that lead to the rules for each law, such as $4^2 \times 4^3 = (4 \times 4) \times (4 \times 4 \times 4) = 4 \times 4 \times 4 \times 4 \times 4 = 4^5$. Allow students to try a few similar expressions to see if they can find the solution and posit a rule or property they may discover.

- Provide examples: $6^2 7^2 = (6 \times 6)(7 \times 7) = (6 \times 7)(6 \times 7) = (6 \times 7)^2$. Ask students to try several of their own to see if they can discover a rule or property.

- Provide examples: $(5^3)^4 = (5 \cdot 5 \cdot 5) \times (5 \cdot 5 \cdot 5) \times (5 \cdot 5 \cdot 5) \times (5 \cdot 5 \cdot 5) = 5^{3\times4} = 5^{12}$ and $(3 \times 7)^4 = (3 \cdot 7) \times (3 \cdot 7) \times (3 \cdot 7) \times (3 \cdot 7) = (3 \cdot 3 \cdot 3 \cdot 3) \times (7 \cdot 7 \cdot 7 \cdot 7) = 3^4 \times 7^4$. Ask students to try several of their own to see if they can discover a rule or property.

- Have students practice the properties by generating equivalent expressions and writing them in simplest form such as $3^2 \times 3^{-5} = 3^{-3} = \frac{1}{3^3} = \frac{1}{27}$.

- Provide examples to lead students to discover how a negative exponent translates to a positive exponent in the denominator of a fraction, such as how $3^{-3} = \frac{1}{3^3}$.

- Assign a project for students to design and create posters summarizing the rules they discovered to hang in the classroom of the properties of exponents with integers.

What the STUDENTS do:

- Discover the properties of integer exponents by making sense of the examples presented. For example, $(3 \times 7)^4 = (3 \cdot 7) \times (3 \cdot 7) \times (3 \cdot 7) \times (3 \cdot 7) = (3 \cdot 3 \cdot 3 \cdot 3) \times (7 \cdot 7 \cdot 7 \cdot 7) = 3^4 \times 7^4$ with the rule discovered as $(ab)^n = a^n b^n$.

- Generate equivalent expressions in simplest form for products and quotients of numbers with integer exponents having the same bases.

Addressing Student Misconceptions and Common Errors

Students often confuse the rules. This occurs primarily when students are taught to memorize the rules rather than understand what is happening in the properties by working with numerical expressions as in the suggestions above. It is important to present examples and let students discover what the rules are. Then students should be encouraged to write their reasoning so they can clarify the explanations for themselves.

STANDARD 2 (8.EE.A.2)

Use square root and cube root symbols to represent solutions to equations of the form $x^2 = p$ and $x^3 = p$, where p is a positive rational number. Evaluate square roots of small perfect squares and cube roots of small perfect cubes. Know that $\sqrt{2}$ is irrational.

Students learn that squaring and cubing numbers are the inverse operations to finding square and cube roots. This standard works with perfect squares and perfect cubes, and students will begin to recognize those numbers. Equations should include rational numbers such as $x^2 = \frac{1}{4}$ and $x^3 = \frac{1}{64}$ and fractions where both the numerator and denominator are perfect squares or cubes:

$$x^2 = \frac{1}{4}$$

$$\sqrt{x^2} = \pm \frac{\sqrt{1}}{\sqrt{4}}$$

$$x = \pm \frac{1}{2}$$

Square roots can be positive or negative because $2 \times 2 = 4$ and $-2 \times -2 = 4$.

What the TEACHER does:

- Introduce squaring a number and taking the square root as inverse operations, providing students opportunities to practice squaring and taking roots.

- Repeat the previous instruction for cubes and cube roots, also including fractions where the numerator and denominator are both perfect cubes.

- Relate perfect square numbers and perfect cubes to geometric squares and cubes using square tiles and square cubes to build the numbers. A square root is the length of the side of a square, and a cube root is the length of the side of a cube.

- Encourage students to find patterns within the list of square numbers and then with cube numbers.

- Facilitate a class discussion around the question, *"In the equation $x^2 = p$, when can p be a negative number?"* Students should come to the conclusion that it is not possible.

- Discuss non-perfect squares and non-perfect cubes as irrational numbers such as $\sqrt{2}$.

What the STUDENTS do:

- Recognize perfect squares and perfect cubes.

- Solve equations containing cube and square roots.

- Discover and explain the relationship between square and cube roots and the sides of a square and the edges of a cube, respectively, by using hands-on materials.

- Reason that non-perfect squares and non-perfect cubes are irrational, including the square root of 2.

Addressing Student Misconceptions and Common Errors

It is important for students to have multiple opportunities and exposures with perfect cubes. This is a new concept in the curriculum and many students struggle with finding cube roots. A common misconception for cube roots is that any number times 3 is a perfect cube. Building larger cubes from smaller ones gives students a visual that they can rely on.

Notes

Use numbers expressed in the form of a single digit times an integer power of 10 to estimate very large or very small quantities, and to express how many times as much one is than the other. For example, estimate the population of the United States as 3 times 10^8 and the population of the world as 7 times 10^9, and determine that the world population is more than 20 times larger.

This standard emphasizes scientific notation. Students write very large and very small numbers in scientific notation using positive and negative exponents. For example, 123,000 written in scientific notation is 1.23×10^5, and 0.0008 written in scientific notation is 8×10^{-4}. When mastered, students use the skill to determine how many times larger (or smaller) one number written in scientific notation is than another. To compare, if the exponent increases by 1, the value increases 10 times. In the example of the U.S. and world populations, the exponent increased by 1, and the 7 is a little more than 2 times 3. So 2×10 makes for 20 times larger.

What the TEACHER does:

- Introduce examples of very large and very small numbers in contexts. Contexts can be found in sources such as government statistics websites, population sizes, land mass in area, and science. Ask students why writing very large and very small numbers in scientific notation would be beneficial. Who would use it?

- Provide students with the opportunity to research very large and very small numbers and present them written in scientific notation, along with the contexts, to the class. Discuss why these numbers are considered estimates. Keep a bank of these numbers and their contexts for students to use at a later time to create real-world problems.

- Provide contextual problems for students to compare numbers written in scientific notation.

- Use the bank of numbers created by the students to ask about how some of the numbers are related to one another by comparing similar contexts.

What the STUDENTS do:

- Understand the benefits of using scientific notation.

- Research to find examples of very large and very small numbers.

- Write very large and very small numbers in scientific notation.

- Understand that some numbers written in scientific notation are estimates. Explain why that is true.

- Compare numbers written in scientific notation to determine how many times larger (or smaller) one number written in scientific notation is than another.

Addressing Student Misconceptions and Common Errors

Students often confuse a very large number for a small number when written in scientific notation such as 4,000,000 for 4×10^{-6}. This usually is a result of students trying to memorize a rule about moving a decimal point to the left or the right. Instead of teaching a rule, rely on students' background knowledge of negative exponents. Before rewriting a number in standard form, look to the exponent to determine whether it is a small or large number. This can also be used as a check.

Students who do not understand the properties of exponents also make errors in computation with scientific notation. Teachers may need to review these properties.

Notes

Perform operations with numbers expressed in scientific notation, including problems where both decimal and scientific notation are used. Use scientific notation and choose units of appropriate size for measurements of very large or very small quantities (e.g., use millimeters per year for seafloor spreading). Interpret scientific notation that has been generated by technology.

This standard builds on previous standards as now students use what they know about scientific notation and properties of integer exponents to solve problems. Quantities in the problems can be expressed in scientific notation and decimal form. Students focus on the size of the measurement to determine which units are appropriate for the context such as millimeters for very small quantities. This standard also calls for students to use technology and be able to interpret the scientific notation used. The teacher needs to check the class calculators to be familiar with the notation used by those particular calculators as the notation used by calculators to express scientific notation is not standard.

GRADE 8

What the TEACHER does:

- Pose problems that require students to perform operations with numbers written in scientific notation.

- Present problem-solving opportunities for students to choose correct units of measurement when working with very large and very small numbers including making conversions between units such as in the following problem: *"An average ant is 10^{-1} centimeters long. If you laid ants end to end, how many would it take to make a line from New York City to Disney World?"* The distance to Disney World from NYC is 1,513 kilometers.

- Provide students with calculators. Give them a calculation to perform that results in a number displayed in scientific notation. Facilitate a large group discussion about what the notation in the display means and how it is a form of scientific notation. Provide other opportunities for students to interpret scientific notation expressed with technology. Ask, *"Do all calculators use the same display for scientific notation?"*

What the STUDENTS do:

- Perform operations with numbers written in scientific notation. Solve both mathematical and real-world problems.

- Choose correct units for very large and very small numbers when solving problems.

- Discover and interpret the rules for scientific notation displayed on a given calculator.

Addressing Student Misconceptions and Common Errors

When performing operations with numbers in scientific notation, such as $(7 \times 10^5) \times (18 \times 10^9)$, some students will be overwhelmed with keeping track of what they should do. Encourage these students to color code the numbers such as highlighting the numbers in exponential form in the given example so students remember to work them together.

Notes

Expressions and Equations
8.EE.B*

Understand the connections between proportional relationships, lines, and linear equations.

STANDARD 5	**8.EE.B.5:** Graph proportional relationships, interpreting the unit rate as the slope of the graph. Compare two different proportional relationships represented in different ways. *For example, compare a distance-time graph to a distance-time equation to determine which of two moving objects has greater speed.*
STANDARD 6	**8.EE.B.6:** Use similar triangles to explain why the slope m is the same between any two distinct points on a non-vertical line in the coordinate plane; derive the equation $y = mx$ for a line through the origin and the equation $y = mx + b$ for a line intercepting the vertical axis at b.

*Major cluster

Expressions and Equations 8.EE.B

Cluster B: Understand the connections between proportional relationships, lines, and linear equations.
Grade 8 Overview

In this cluster students connect proportional relationships, lines, and linear equations. First, students compare proportional relationships represented in different ways such as graphs, tables, and linear equations. Unit rate is interpreted as the slope of a line, and students learn that the slope is the same between any two points on a line by using similar triangles. Then the general equations for a line ($y = mx + b$ and $y = mx$) are derived.

Standards for Mathematical Practice
SFMP 2. Reason abstractly and quantitatively.

Students compare two proportional relationships represented in different forms.

SFMP 6. Attend to precision.

Students give explanations that are precise and use appropriate vocabulary.

SFMP 7. Look for and make use of structure.

Students see a pattern that results in the general form of a linear equation.

Related Content Standards

6.RP.A.3.b   7.EE.B.4.a   8.G.A.4   8.F.A.2   8.F.A.3

Notes

Graph proportional relationships, interpreting the unit rate as the slope of the graph. Compare two different proportional relationships represented in different ways. For example, compare a distance-time graph to a distance-time equation to determine which of two moving objects has greater speed.

Students build on their work from Grade 6 with unit rates and their work with proportional relationships in Grade 7 to compare graphs, tables, and equations of linear (proportional) relationships. Students identify the unit rate as slope in graphs, tables, and equations to compare proportional relationships presented using different representations. For example, compare the unit rate in a problem about a phone bill presented in graphic form on a Cartesian plane to a phone bill from a different company where the unit rate can be found represented in an equation or table.

What the TEACHER does:

- Present a single, graphed, proportional relationship to the class. Facilitate a class discussion about the unit rate, using students' background knowledge, and interpret the unit rate as the slope of the line.

- Present a second, related, proportional relationship, written in a different form such as a table or equation. Facilitate a class discussion about how to compare the two situations. Use questions such as, *"What is happening in each situation? How are they the same? Different? How can we tell? What about the slopes? What do they tell us? What can we do to help us compare the slopes (graph the second relationship)?"*

- Provide opportunities for students to compare proportional relationships and write their conclusions using precise mathematical vocabulary.

What the STUDENTS do:

- Make use of the structure of a representation to compare different representations. For example, students will find that if a problem asks them to compare the unit rates for information presented in a table and information presented in equation form, graphing both of them will make the comparison easier.

- Compare proportional relationships presented in different forms (graphs, tables, equations, verbal descriptions) and explain comparisons in writing using clear and precise mathematical language. Comparisons will include slope interpreted in context of the relationships.

Addressing Student Misconceptions and Common Errors

Errors occur when students are overwhelmed by being presented with too much information at a time. Encourage students having difficulty making the comparisons to work with one relationship at a time. Graphing may be a difficult skill for some students. Use graph paper larger than 1 cm for these students so they can see the unit rate easier.

Students who are overwhelmed can also be helped by using graphs of experiences that are familiar to them. This makes the information more accessible so students can better understand and interpret proportional relationships.

Notes

Use similar triangles to explain why the slope m is the same between any two distinct points on a non-vertical line in the coordinate plane; derive the equation y = mx for a line through the origin and the equation y = mx + b for a line intercepting the vertical axis at b.

Students gain additional knowledge about slope in this standard as they use similar triangles to explain how the slope m of a line is the same between any two points on a given non-vertical line. Students understand positive/negative slopes, 0 slope, and undefined slopes. Through the use of similar triangles, teachers lead students to derive the general equation ($y = mx + b$) of a line and discover that m is the slope and b is the y-intercept.

What the TEACHER does:

- Facilitate a class discussion about two similar triangles as in the example below:

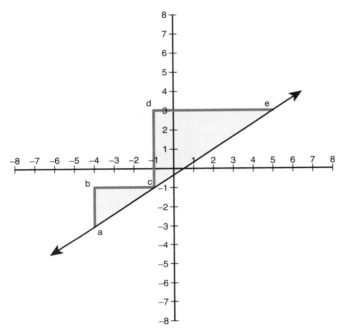

- Explain slope as rise over run (rise is the vertical distance and run is the horizontal distance) by having students see that $\overline{ab}$ (rise) is 2 units and $\overline{bc}$ (run) is 3 units for a ratio of 2 to 3 or written as $\frac{2}{3}$. On similar triangle CED, $\overline{cd}$ is 4 units and $\overline{de}$ is 6 units for a ratio of 4 to 6, which is the same as 2 to 3. Have students create other pairs of similar triangles to convince themselves that the slope of a line is the same between any two points on a non-vertical line.

- Challenge students to find the slope of a horizontal line (0) and a vertical line (undefined) and explain their reasoning.

- Demonstrate how to find a slope using the formula $\frac{y_1 - y_2}{x_1 - x_2}$.

- Lead students to discover the equation $y = mx$ for a line that goes through the origin and $y = mx + b$ for a line that goes through point b. Note that when $b = 0$, $y = mx$. The y-intercept is b.

What the STUDENTS do:

- Explain, orally and/or in writing, using similar triangles, why the slope of a line is the same between any two points on a non-vertical line. Use clear and precise language.

- Discover that b is the y-intercept and m is the slope in the general equation for a line, $y = mx + b$.

- Determine the slope of a line from a graph, table, or linear equation.

- Explain orally and/or in writing how proportional relationships, lines, and linear equations are related.

A common error students make is to misuse the formula for finding the slope of a line given two points. They use $x - y$ or use the difference of the x coordinates divided by the difference in the y coordinates. Look for these common errors. Focus students' attention on the errors by using error analysis tasks. For example, Jed used the following equation to find the slope of a line: $\frac{x_1}{y_1} - \frac{x_2}{y_2}$. Find Jed's mistake and correct it.

Notes

Expressions and Equations
8.EE.C*

Analyze and solve linear equations and pairs of simultaneous linear equations.

STANDARD 7   **8.EE.C.7:** Solve linear equations in one variable.

    a. Give examples of linear equations in one variable with one solution, infinitely many solutions, or no solutions. Show which of these possibilities is the case by successively transforming the given equation into simpler forms, until an equivalent equation of the form $x = a$, $a = a$, or $a = b$ results (where a and b are different numbers).

    b. Solve linear equations with rational number coefficients, including equations whose solutions require expanding expressions using the distributive property and collecting like terms.

STANDARD 8   **8.EE.C.8:** Analyze and solve pairs of simultaneous linear equations.

    a. Understand that solutions to a system of two linear equations in two variables correspond to points of intersection of their graphs, because points of intersection satisfy both equations simultaneously.

    b. Solve systems of two linear equations in two variables algebraically, and estimate solutions by graphing the equations. Solve simple cases by inspection. *For example, $3x + 2y = 5$ and $3x + 2y = 6$ have no solution because $3x + 2y$ cannot simultaneously be 5 and 6.*

    c. Solve real-world and mathematical problems leading to two linear equations in two variables. *For example, given coordinates for two pairs of points, determine whether the line through the first pair of points intersects the line through the second pair.*

*Major cluster

Expressions and Equations   8.EE.C

Cluster C: Analyze and solve linear equations and pairs of simultaneous linear equations.
Grade 8 Overview

Students analyze and solve one variable linear equations for one, zero, or infinitely many solutions, simplifying the equations until they reach $x = a$, $a = a$, or $a = b$ (where a and b are different numbers). Students then apply that knowledge to analyzing and solving pairs of simultaneous linear equations also known as systems of linear equations in two variables.

Standards for Mathematical Practice
SFMP 1. Make sense of problems and persevere in solving them.

Students solve problems with systems of linear equations.

SFMP 2. Reason abstractly and quantitatively.

Students analyze linear equations and systems of linear equations.

SFMP 4. Model with mathematics.

Students model real-world problems with systems of equations.

SFMP 6. Attend to precision.

Students give explanations that are precise and use appropriate vocabulary.

SFMP 7. Look for and make use of structure.

Students use the structure of an equation to know which steps to perform to solve it.

Related Content Standards

6.EE.B.7   7.EE.B.4.a

Notes

Solve linear equations in one variable.

   a. *Give examples of linear equations in one variable with one solution, infinitely many solutions, or no solutions. Show which of these possibilities is the case by successively transforming the given equation into simpler forms, until an equivalent equation of the form x = a, a = a, or a = b results (where a and b are different numbers).*

   b. *Solve linear equations with rational number coefficients, including equations whose solutions require expanding expressions using the distributive property and collecting like terms.*

This standard has students solving linear equations. It is explained by 8.EE.C.7.a and b. It is best to teach a and b together so that they are not considered isolated skills.

These standards provide the foundation for all future work with linear equations. Students solve equations that have one, zero, or infinitely many solutions and relate those solutions to the context. If the solution is in the form $x = a$, there is only one solution. If $a = a$, there are infinitely many solutions. If $a = b$ results (where a and b are different numbers), there are no solutions.

Linear equations can have fractions and decimals as coefficients and can be solved by expanding expressions with the distributive property and/or collecting like terms.

What the TEACHER does:

- Provide pairs of students with three one-variable linear equations: One equation has one solution, one has no solutions, and one has an infinite number of solutions. After students have a chance to solve, facilitate a discussion on the results students found. Demonstrate how when the result is $x = a$, there is only one solution that will make the equation true. Use substitution when student results are $a = b$ (a); ask the students to make sense of the results. Ask questions such as, *"Can a = b?"* Analyze the equation to see why there are no possible solutions. For results $a = a$, use substitution to demonstrate how there are an infinite number of solutions.

- Present students many opportunities to solve linear equations, including those with fraction, decimal, and positive/negative coefficients. Some equations should provide the opportunities to use the distributive property to expand terms and to combine like terms. Use Hands-On Equations™, Algeblocks™, Algebra Tiles™ or a similar set of manipulatives to demonstrate combining like terms and using the distributive property.

What the STUDENTS do:

- Solve and analyze one variable linear equations and explain whether the solution has one, zero, or infinitely many solutions.

- Solve linear equations with rational coefficients. Use the distributive property when appropriate and combine like terms when the equation calls for it.

Addressing Student Misconceptions and Common Errors

A common error students make involves applying the distributive property when negative integers are involved, such as $-2(-x - 4)$. The error occurs when they try to multiply the -2 and the -4. Students need repeated exposure to equations of this type. Prompting students to consider "minus 4" as "plus negative 4" helps correct the misconception. Providing and discussing tasks that involve students analyzing errors helps students self-correct many misconceptions.

Notes

STANDARD 8 (8.EE.C.8)

Analyze and solve pairs of simultaneous linear equations.

a. *Understand that solutions to a system of two linear equations in two variables correspond to points of intersection of their graphs, because points of intersection satisfy both equations simultaneously.*

b. *Solve systems of two linear equations in two variables algebraically, and estimate solutions by graphing the equations. Solve simple cases by inspection.* For example, $3x + 2y = 5$ and $3x + 2y = 6$ have no solution because $3x + 2y$ cannot simultaneously be 5 and 6.

c. *Solve real-world and mathematical problems leading to two linear equations in two variables.* For example, given coordinates for two pairs of points, determine whether the line through the first pair of points intersects the line through the second pair.

This standard has students solving simultaneous linear equations. It is explained by 8.EE.C.8.a–c. It is best to consider a, b, and c together as they are not isolated skills.

Students will understand that points of intersection are the solutions to pairs of simultaneous linear equations (also known as systems of linear equations). Students will solve systems graphically, algebraically, and by inspection. Examples in this standard are in real-world contexts and mathematical problems.

What the TEACHER does:

- Have students graph two linear equations that share a solution on the same coordinate plane. The lines should intersect. Facilitate a class discussion about what the point of intersection means. Ask students, *"What do you notice about the lines? What are the coordinates of the intersection? Which equation does the point of intersection satisfy?"* When students realize that the point of intersection satisfies both equations, introduce the terms system of equations/ simultaneous equations and graphing as a method to estimate solutions to systems of equations.

- Facilitate a discussion about what the graph would look like if there were no solutions to the system of equations and if there are an infinite number of solutions.

- Provide students with simple cases of simultaneous equations that have no solution and ask them to analyze the equations for a solution. A simple example is, *"3x + 2y = 5 and 3x + 2y = 6 have no solution because 3x + 2y cannot simultaneously be 5 and 6."*

- Introduce solving a system of linear equations algebraically and checking the results.

- Present opportunities to solve real-world and mathematical problems that are solved by systems of equations. Encourage students to use the most efficient method (graphing, inspection, or algebraic manipulation) to find the solution.

What the STUDENTS do:

- Reason that the intersection of two lines on a graph represents the solution to the system of linear equations. Explain, using clear and precise mathematical language, why this is true. Explain how to recognize if the solution set has one, zero, or an infinite number of points.

- Solve systems of equations graphically, algebraically, and by inspection depending on the problem presented.

- Solve real-world and mathematical problems that lead to pairs of simultaneous linear equations.

Addressing Student Misconceptions and Common Errors

Common errors for systems of equations include students who have trouble accurately graphing and, therefore, cannot correctly estimate the solution. Technology can be helpful as can graph paper with larger than 1-cm squares.

Expressions and Equations

Cluster A: Work with radicals and integer exponents.

Standard: 8.EE.A.2. *Use square root and cube root symbols to represent solutions to equations of the form* $x^2 = p$ *and* $x^3 = p$, *where p is a positive rational number. Evaluate square roots of small perfect squares and cube roots of small perfect cubes. Know that* $\sqrt{2}$ *is irrational.*

Standards for Mathematical Practice:

SFMP 7. Look for and make use of structure.

Students use square tiles to see the relationship to square numbers and cubes to cube numbers.

Goal:

Students work with manipulatives and discover that a square root is the side of a square and a cube root is the edge of a cube.

Planning:

Materials: square tiles, cubes (wooden cubes, Unifix cubes™, linking cubes), pencil and paper, 1 sheet poster paper per group

Sample Activity:

- Provide small groups with at least 49 tiles per group.
- Assign each group a square number: 49, 36, 25, 16, or 9.
- Each group makes a square with the number of tiles assigned and answers the following questions on their poster paper along with a drawing of their square: What is the area of your square? How did you calculate it? What is the formula for finding the area of a square? What do you notice about your number? What is the length of one side of your square? How does the length of one side of your square compare to the area of your square? Using your square, describe a square root.
- Repeat the procedure with cubes and adjust the questions to fit cube roots.
- Groups present their finding to the class. After presentations class discussion comes to a conclusion about square roots and cube roots.

Questions/Prompts:

- Are students able to see that they have made a square versus a rectangle? Ask, *"What do we know about a square that makes it a special rectangle?"*
- Are students recognizing that their numbers are perfect squares (or cubes)? Ask, *"What kinds of numbers have we learned about? List all the types and see which labels fit your number."*
- Have students noticed that the square root of the area of their square is the length of a side? Ask, *"How have you used the side of your square? Did you use it for any calculations in this activity? Which one? You may want to look back at the answers you wrote to your previous questions."*

Differentiating Instruction:

Struggling Students: Use heterogeneous groupings. Allow these students to manipulate the tiles and cubes if they seem to be confused. Some students may require their own set of manipulatives.

Extension: Assign students to read a children's book about square numbers such as *Sea Squares* by Joy Hulme or *My Full Moon Is Square* by Elinor Pinczes. After reading, have students outline their own children's book that teaches about cube numbers.

PLANNING PAGE

Expressions and Equations

Cluster A: Work with radicals and integer exponents.

Standard:

Standards for Mathematical Practice:

Goal:

Planning:

Materials:

Sample Activity:

Questions/Prompts:

Differentiating Instruction:

Struggling Students:

Extension:

Expressions and Equations

Cluster B: Understand the connections between proportional relationships, lines, and linear equations.

Standard:

Standards for Mathematical Practice:

Goal:

Planning:

Materials:

Sample Activity:

Questions/Prompts:

Differentiating Instruction:

Struggling Students:

Extension:

Expressions and Equations

Cluster C: Analyze and solve linear equations and pairs of simultaneous equations.

Standard:

Standards for Mathematical Practice:

Goal:

Planning:

Materials:

Sample Activity:

Questions/Prompts:

Differentiating Instruction:

Struggling Students:

Extension:

Reflection Questions: Expressions and Equations

1. Discuss how you respond to parents who feel that Grade 6 is too early to study algebraic expressions and equations.

2. Discuss the role manipulatives can play and the types of models that can be used in helping students understand expressions and equations in Grades 6–8.

3. Discuss how the Mathematical Practices "Reason abstractly" and "Critique the reasoning of others" are married to the mathematical standards in this domain.

## Part 4

Functions

Functions

Domain Overview

Eighth graders work with expressions and equations, including modeling an association in bivariate data with a linear equation, solving linear equations, and solving systems of linear equations with three different methods. Students learn about and use functions to describe quantitative relationships.

SUGGESTED MATERIALS FOR THIS DOMAIN

8

✓	Chart paper or poster-size Post-It Notes™
✓	Graph paper
✓	Graphing calculators and/or graphing software
✓	Markers

KEY VOCABULARY

8

✓	**function** a rule that assigns to each input exactly one output
✓	**initial value of a function** y-intercept; the y-value when $x = 0$
✓	**input** independent variable; the number put into an equation to get an output
✓	**linear function** a relationship whose graph is a straight line
✓	**nonlinear function** a relationship that does not graph into a straight line
✓	**output** dependent variable; the number that results when another number is put into the equation
✓	**rate of change** slope of a line

Functions
8.F.A*

Cluster A

Define, evaluate, and compare functions.

STANDARD 1 **8.F.A.1:** Understand that a function is a rule that assigns to each input exactly one output. The graph of a function is the set of ordered pairs consisting of an input and the corresponding output.[1]

[1]Function notation is not required for Grade 8.

STANDARD 2 **8.F.A.2:** Compare properties of two functions each represented in a different way (algebraically, graphically, numerically in tables, or by verbal descriptions). *For example, given a linear function represented by a table of values and a linear function represented by an algebraic expression, determine which function has the greater rate of change.*

STANDARD 3 **8.F.A.3:** Interpret the equation $y = mx + b$ as defining a linear function, whose graph is a straight line; give examples of functions that are not linear. *For example, the function $A = s^2$ giving the area of a square as a function of its side length is not linear because its graph contains the points $(1,1)$, $(2,4)$ and $(3,9)$, which are not on a straight line.*

*Major cluster

Functions   8.F.A

Cluster A: Define, evaluate, and compare functions.
Grade 8 Overview

Students are introduced to functions as rules that assign exactly one output to each input. Functions are represented graphically, algebraically, numerically in tables, and by verbal descriptions. Function notation $(f(x))$ is not required in Grade 8. Students compare the properties of two functions represented in different forms such as determining which function has a greater rate of change from two functions, one represented graphically and one numerically in tables. Students recognize equations in the form $y = mx + b$ as defining linear functions as opposed to those that are nonlinear (quadratic, exponential).

Standards for Mathematical Practice
SFMP 2. Reason abstractly and quantitatively.

Students determine if a relationship is a function.

SFMP 4. Model with mathematics.

Students represent linear functions in algebraic, graphical, numerical, and verbal forms.

SFMP 5. Use appropriate tools strategically.

Students use technological tools to explore and deepen their understanding of functions.

SFMP 7. Look for and make use of structure.

Students apply general mathematical rules such as $y = mx + b$ as the equation for a linear function.

Related Content Standards

7.RPA.2.a   7.RPA.2.b   8.EE.B.5   8.EE.C.7.b

STANDARD 1 (8.F.A.1)

Understand that a function is a rule that assigns to each input exactly one output. The graph of a function is the set of ordered pairs consisting of an input and the corresponding output.[1]

[1]Function notation is not required for Grade 8.

This standard is the students' introduction to functions and involves the definition of function as a rule that assigns to each input exactly one output. Students are not required to use or recognize function notation at this grade but will be able to identify functions using tables, graphs, and equations. A relationship is not a function when there is more than one y-value associated with any x-value. Using the definition, an example of a table that does not represent a function is as follows:

x	y
2	3
1	4
−1	3
2	5
Not a function	

x	y
0	1
1	3
−1	−1
0	1
Function	

What the TEACHER does:

- Provide graphs of relationships, some of which are functions and some not. Each graph should have a context so that students can reason whether or not the graph makes sense. For example, it does not make sense that a plane can be at different heights at the same point in time. Display this graphically and in a table to see that it is not a function.

  Allow students to make sense of other graphs where a rule assigns to each input exactly one output.

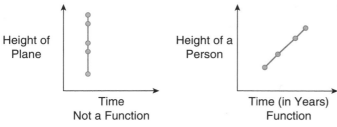

Height of Plane / Time — Not a Function

Height of a Person / Time (in Years) — Function

- Model use of the vocabulary terms *function*, *input*, and *output*.

- Present students with tables of relationships, some of which are functions and some are not. Encourage students to reason whether the example is a function or not and

justify their conclusion. Do not limit examples to linear relationships.

- Compare graphs of functions and non-functional relationships with their graphs. Discuss what students notice.

What the STUDENTS do:

- Reason whether a table or graph models a function or not and defend their reasoning.

- Use an advance organizer such as the Frayer model (see Reproducible 2) to clarify the definition of function.

Addressing Student Misconceptions and Common Errors

Students sometimes confuse the terms *input* and *output*, knowing that each input can have only one output. Function machines may help these students see that if you put in (input) a number in the machine, the rule only allows one number to be put out (output). Students can make or draw their own function machines.

GRADE 8

Compare properties of two functions each represented in a different way (algebraically, graphically, numerically in tables, or by verbal descriptions). For example, given a linear function represented by a table of values and a linear function represented by an algebraic expression, determine which function has the greater rate of change.

For this standard students will compare the properties of functions. One property of functions is slope. When students are given two different functions, each represented in a different form (algebraically, graphically, in a table, or by a verbal description), students should be able to determine which function has the greater slope. An example follows:

Ruth starts with a $50 gift card for Walmart. She spends $5.50 per week to buy cat food. Let y be the amount left on the card and x represents the number of weeks.

x	y
0	50
1	44.50
2	39.00
3	33.50
4	28.00

Boyce rents bikes for $5 an hour. He also collects a non-refundable fee of $10.00 for a rental to cover wear and tear. Write the rule for the total cost (c) of renting a bike as a function of the number of hours (h) rented.

Solution: Ruth's story is an example of a function with a negative slope. The amount of money left on the card decreases each week. The graph has a negative slope of -5.5, which is the amount the card balance decreases every time Ruth buys cat food.

Boyce's bike rental is an example of a function with a positive slope. This function has a positive slope of 5, which is the amount to rent a bike for an hour. An equation for Boyce's bikes could be $c = 5h + 10$.

What the TEACHER does:

- Present two different linear functions using the same representation (algebraically, graphically, in a table, or by a verbal description). Ask the students if they can explain which has the greater slope (rate of change).

- Present two functions each represented in a different form and ask the students to work in groups to determine which has the greater slope. They may need some time to work in groups to change the representation of the functions. Have groups present their answers to the class along with their reasoning. Facilitate the discussion with questions such as, *"How did you determine which slope is greater? Why did you select to represent the functions in a different form?"*

- Present two different functions in similar context so that the question about comparing the slopes has meaning.

What the STUDENTS do:

- Compare properties of functions presented in the same and different forms.

- Communicate the reasoning involved in comparing two functions using precise mathematical language.

Addressing Student Misconceptions and Common Errors

A common error students make when working with slopes in context is understanding what the slope represents. If students are having this problem, work with a single function in a context and then, after identifying the slope and its meaning, add a second function in the same context so that students can work with the second slope separately before comparing to the first slope.

Interpret the equation y = mx + b as defining a linear function, whose graph is a straight line; give examples of functions that are not linear. For example, the function A = s² giving the area of a square as a function of its side length is not linear because its graph contains the points (1,1), (2,4) and (3,9), which are not on a straight line.

In this standard students become familiar with the equation $y = mx + b$ as defining a linear function that will graph as a straight line. Students distinguish between linear (functions that graph into a straight line) and nonlinear functions (functions that do not graph into a straight line such as a curve). Note that standard form and point-slope form are not studied in this grade.

What the TEACHER does:

- Present students with examples of functions that are linear and nonlinear for them to graph. Facilitate a class discussion about the similarities and differences in the graphs. The graphs that are not linear are those with points not on a straight line. The area of a square as a function of its side length, $A = s^2$, is an example of a nonlinear function because points (1,1), (2,4), and (3,9) are not on a straight line.

- Present a series of linear equations such as the following:

$$y = \frac{1}{2}x + 7$$

$$y = -4x + 8$$

$$y = 6x - 2$$

$$y = 0.5x + 5$$

Ask students to find the similarities and differences among the equations and their graphs. Facilitate a discussion that results in students recognizing the structure and naming $y = mx + b$ as the general equation for a linear function. Point out that when using a graphing calculator, the general equation for a line is usually expressed as $y = ax + b$.

- Present some linear equations in the form $y = b + mx$ as many contextual problems will present information in this order. Ask students to write examples of linear functions. This may be a group challenge allowing groups to present their work to the class using correct terminology.

What the STUDENTS do:

- Discern the similarities and differences between linear and nonlinear graphs.

- Look for and make use of structure in identifying $y = mx + b$ as the general form of an equation for a straight line.

- Model functions that are nonlinear and explain, using precise mathematical language, how to tell the difference.

GRADE 8

Addressing Student Misconceptions and Common Errors

Some students have difficulty with the general equation $y = mx + b$ for equations presented as subtraction such as $y = 5x - 4$. Students can be asked to graph a series of such equations to convince themselves that they are linear. In addition, point out that "minus 4" is the same as "adding −4"

Notes

Functions
8.F.B*

Use functions to model relationships between quantities.

STANDARD 4
8.F.B.4: Construct a function to model a linear relationship between two quantities. Determine the rate of change and initial value of the function from a description of a relationship or from two (x, y) values, including reading these from a table or from a graph. Interpret the rate of change and initial value of a linear function in terms of the situation it models, and in terms of its graph or a table of values.

STANDARD 5
8.F.B.5: Describe qualitatively the functional relationship between two quantities by analyzing a graph (e.g., where the function is increasing or decreasing, linear or nonlinear). Sketch a graph that exhibits the qualitative features of a function that has been described verbally.

*Major cluster

Functions   8.F.B

Cluster B: Use functions to model relationships between quantities.
Grade 8 Overview

In this standard students use what they have learned previously and apply it in context to model functional relationships. Students construct functions and determine the slope and y-intercept (initial value) of a function from a verbal description of a relationship or from two (x, y) values, including finding those values in a graph or a table. Students give contextual meaning to the rate of change and y-intercept and interpret rate of change and the y-intercept in terms of the graph or table of the function. Given a graph, students analyze the functional relationship (does the function increase or decrease? Is it linear?). Given a verbal description of a function, students sketch the function showing the qualitative features.

Standards for Mathematical Practice
SFMP 4. Model with mathematics.

Students construct a function to model a linear relationship between two quantities.

SFMP 7. Look for and make use of structure.

Students make use of the qualitative features (structure) found in a verbal description of a function and sketch that function.

Related Content Standards

7.EE.B.4.a   8.SP.2   8.SP.3   8.EE.5

Notes

Construct a function to model a linear relationship between two quantities. Determine the rate of change and initial value of the function from a description of a relationship or from two (x, y) values, including reading these from a table or from a graph. Interpret the rate of change and initial value of a linear function in terms of the situation it models, and in terms of its graph or a table of values.

Students identify the rate of change (slope) and *y*-intercept (initial value) from tables, graphs, equations, and verbal descriptions of linear relationships. The *y*-intercept is the *y*-value when the *x*-value is 0. Interpretation of slope and the initial value of the function is accomplished using real-world situations.

What the TEACHER does:

- Present students with graphs of linear functions and focus a discussion on the *y*-intercept. From examples, lead students to discover that the *y*-intercept is the *y*-value when the *x*-value is 0. Provide students with opportunities to identify the *y*-intercept on several graphs.

- Pose the following challenge: Show a table for each of the graphs recently presented and identify the *y*-intercept in the table. For the table below, the *y*-intercept is at (0,4).

x	y
−2	−2
0	4
1	7

- Ask students to find the equations for the linear functions previously used and see if they can figure out how to find the *y*-intercept when the function is in equation form. (It is the constant in the equation $y = mx + b$.) Present some equations where the format is $y = b + mx$. Present some equations where the *y*-intercept is negative.

- Provide context as much as possible so that students learn to interpret the meaning of the initial value in a function.

- Explain slope of a line by presenting a graph of a linear equation and introducing the slope as the ratio of the change in the *y*-values of two points to the change in the *x*-value of the same two points. Relate this back to unit rate from Grade 6.

- Display tables for students to use to determine rate of change using the rise to run ratio, such as the following:

x	y
−2	−2
0	4
1	7

Select any points, for example (−2, −2) and (1, 7). The difference between −2 and 7 is −9.

The difference between −2 and 1 is −3. The ratio of $\frac{-9}{-3} = 3$.

- Provide students the opportunity to discover that the coefficient of *x* in the equation $y = mx + b$ is the slope by allowing them to look at the tables, calculate slope, and compare to the equations of the lines.

- Provide context as often as possible so that students can interpret the meaning of the slope in a given situation.

- Provide students verbal descriptions of situations where they can create the equation of the function. Identify the slope and initial value and relate them to the $y = mx + b$ general equation.

What the STUDENTS do:

- Discover the *y*-intercept (initial value of a function) from a function represented in table, graph, algebraic form, and by verbal description.

- Calculate slope of a line using the rise to run ratio.

- Discover slope of a line when the function is presented in table, graph, algebraic (equation) form, or by verbal descriptions.

- Communicate the meaning of the slope and *y*-intercept in a given situation using precise mathematical vocabulary.

Addressing Student Misconceptions and Common Errors

The most common error students make is confusing the rise and run in the ratio for slope. This mistake is easily observed as students calculate slope. Vocabulary foldables using the terms *rise* and *run* may help students remember the differences.

Describe qualitatively the functional relationship between two quantities by analyzing a graph (e.g., where the function is increasing or decreasing, linear or nonlinear). Sketch a graph that exhibits the qualitative features of a function that has been described verbally.

Given a graph, students will provide a verbal description of the function, including whether the graph is linear or nonlinear or where the function is increasing or decreasing. Given a function's verbal description, students will be able to sketch the graph displaying qualitative properties of that function. The quantitative features of the graph are not displayed (specific quantities on the axes).

What the TEACHER does:

- Challenge students with a graph and situation such as the following:

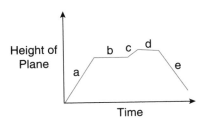

A plane travels from a West Coast airport to Denver. Take off is fine and the plane cruises. Then the pilot is warned of bad weather ahead, so he climbs above the clouds. Travel continues until it is time to land. Ask students to match the parts of the story to the parts of the graph. Use this example (or a similar one) to help students learn that graphs can tell stories. Even though time and height cannot be quantified in this graph, the situation can be described qualitatively.

- Model the use of mathematical vocabulary to describe the parts of the graph that are linear, increasing, decreasing, and so on.

- Present students with a graph and ask them to tell/write the story and label the axes. A classic example is to write a story about the height of the water in a bathtub over time to match a graph similar to the one used in the airplane story previously mentioned.

- Provide students with opportunities to sketch graphs given the stories.

- Allow students to create their own graphs and stories to share with the class.

- Select stories where the graph may appear counterintuitive such as the graph of a plane's distance from its destination city to its time in the air. This graph has a negative slope since as the time increases, the distance to the destination decreases.

What the STUDENTS do:

- Model stories with graphs and vice versa.

- Interpret parts of a story to coincide with parts of the function displayed on a graph.

- Sketch a graph that shows the qualitative features of a function described verbally.

- Create a story that matches the qualitative features of a given graph.

Addressing Student Misconceptions and Common Errors

A common error students make is that they do not read the labels on the axes carefully. Eighth graders who sketch graphs that appear counterintuitive from the story are making assumptions about the axes without analyzing them. These students should be asked to describe what the axes mean on a graph before they begin to analyze or write a story.

Functions

Cluster A: Define, evaluate, and compare functions.

Standard: 8.F.A.3. *Interpret the equation* y = mx + b *as defining a linear function, whose graph is a straight line; give examples of functions that are not linear.* For example, the function $A = s^2$ giving the area of a square as a function of its side length is not linear because its graph contains the points (1,1), (2,4) and (3,9), which are not on a straight line.

Standards for Mathematical Practice:

SFMP 2. Reason abstractly and quantitatively.

Students take linear equations and abstract them to the general form of $y = mx + b$.

SFMP 4. Model with mathematics.

Students take verbal descriptions and represent them as graphs.

SFMP 7. Look for and make use of structure.

Students look for patterns in the graphs of the verbal descriptions.

Goal:

Students learn that some functions are linear and others are nonlinear, and linear functions share a common equation form of $y = mx + b$.

Planning:

Materials: markers, chart paper, or large Post-It Notes™

Sample Activity:

- Prepare verbal descriptions of five or six functions. At least three should be linear relationships and the remainder nonlinear.
- Give each group one function to graph on chart paper or large Post-It Notes™.
- After groups graph the relationships (including appropriate labels), display them so the entire class can see all of the graphs.
- Ask the groups to look at the graphs of the functions and sort them any way they see fit.
- Lead a whole class discussion on how the students sorted the graphs and why. The obvious sort will be graphs that are straight lines and those that are not. After discussing the sorted graphs, introduce the vocabulary of linear and nonlinear functions.
- Follow-up by having groups represent the linear functions as equations.
- Discuss the similarities of the equations and introduce the general equation $y = mx + b$.

Questions/Prompts:

- Are students able to graph their verbal descriptions? Ask, *"What do you need to make a graph? What values are represented on the x-axis? y-axis?"*

- Are students having difficulty with the sort? Ask, *"What do you notice is the same about some graphs?"*

- Ask students to focus on the place where the line crosses the y-axis on the linear graphs. Ask, *"What do you notice about where the line crosses the axis?"* (Note that this question will help when the lesson gets to the point of introducing $y = mx + b$.)

Differentiating Instruction:

Struggling Students: Students may have difficulty with the general form since it is abstract. After the lesson, give students only linear equations and linear graphs and have them compare the m and the b from the graph to its respective equation. Do this as many times as the students need to make the connection using many different examples.

Extension: Students can examine their daily lives and find linear relationships. These relationships can then be graphed and written as equations.

Notes

Functions

Cluster A: Define, evaluate, and compare functions.

Standard:

Standards for Mathematical Practice:

Goal:

Planning:

Materials:

Sample Activity:

Questions/Prompts:

Differentiating Instruction:

Struggling Students:

Extension:

PLANNING PAGE

Functions

Cluster B: Use functions to model relationships between quantities.

Standard:

Standards for Mathematical Practice:

Goal:

Planning:

Materials:

Sample Activity:

Questions/Prompts:

Differentiating Instruction:

Struggling Students:

Extension:

Reflection Questions: Functions

1. Review the Grades 6 and 7 standards. Discuss how they prepare students for functions in Grade 8.

2. Linear relationships are a big idea for this domain. Talk about linear relationships that you and your students encounter daily. Discuss how these examples can be used to ground your instruction in the real world.

3. There are two clusters in this domain. You may teach them sequentially or weave them together. Discuss the advantages for your students with each method.

## Part 5

Geometry

Geometry

Domain Overview

GRADE 6

Students in Grade 6 build on their understanding of area and volume from Grade 5 to deepen understanding of volume and develop the concept of surface area. Students prepare for their work in Grade 8 with transformations by working with polygons in the coordinate plane in Grade 6. Reasoning about relationships in their work on surface area, composing and decomposing shapes, and finding distance on a coordinate plane using endpoint coordinates for horizontal and vertical lines prepare them for Grade 7 relationships.

GRADE 7

Seventh graders solve problems involving scale drawings and informal geometric constructions, and they work with two- and three-dimensional shapes to solve problems involving area, surface area, and volume. Students take their study of area from Grade 6 to circles. Students work

with three-dimensional figures, relating them to two-dimensional figures by examining cross sections. They solve real-world and mathematical problems involving area, surface area, and volume of objects composed of triangles, quadrilaterals, polygons, cubes, and right prisms.

GRADE 8

The geometry focus in Grade 8 is on transformations. At this level, students describe their effects on figures in the coordinate plane to use the ideas they have developed about distance and angles. Students investigate angles created when a transversal crosses parallel lines and investigate the angle-angle criterion for similarity of triangles. Students understand the Pythagorean Theorem and its converse and use it to find distances on the coordinate plane. The study of volume culminates with problem solving for volume for cones, spheres, and cylinders.

6	7	8	
✓	✓	✓	Attribute shapes, Power Polygons™
✓			Empty cardboard boxes
		✓	Geometric software
	✓		Geometric solids
✓	✓	✓	Graph paper
✓	✓		Inch or centimeter cubes
✓			Nets for cubes, prisms, and pyramids
	✓		Protractors
	✓		Round objects to measure circumference such as CDs, can lids, etc.
✓	✓	✓	Rulers
	✓		Styrofoam three-dimensional figures such as cones and prisms
✓			Tangrams

KEY VOCABULARY

6	7	8	
	✓		**adjacent angles** two angles that share a common vertex and a common side
✓	✓	✓	**area** number of square units needed to cover a surface
	✓		**circumference** distance around the outside of a circle
	✓		**complementary angles** two angles whose sum is 90°
✓	✓	✓	**congruent figures** figures having the same size and shape
		✓	**dilation** a transformation where all distances are changed by a common factor
		✓	**exterior angle** an angle formed by one side of a polygon and the extension of an adjacent side
		✓	**hypotenuse** the side of a right triangle opposite the right angle
		✓	**legs** sides of a right triangle that form the right angle
		✓	**line of symmetry** line dividing a figure into two congruent halves

(Continued)

(Continued)

KEY VOCABULARY

6	7	8	
✓			**net** two-dimensional representation of a three-dimensional figure that can be folded up into the three-dimensional figure
✓	✓	✓	**parallel lines** lines in a plane that will never intersect
✓			**polygon** a many-sided, closed, simple figure whose sides are line segments
✓	✓		**prism** a solid with parallel congruent polygons for bases and parallelograms for faces
	✓		**pyramid** a polyhedron with a polygon for the base and triangular faces that meet at the apex
		✓	**Pythagorean Theorem** for every right triangle, the sum of the squares of the length of the legs is equal to the square of the length of the hypotenuse
✓			**quadrilateral** a polygon with four sides
		✓	**reflection** a transformation that flips the plane over a fixed line
✓	✓		**right rectangular prism** a prism where all of the lateral faces are rectangles
		✓	**rotation** transformation where a figure turns around a fixed point
	✓	✓	**scale drawing** a drawing that shows the original drawing or object with its accurate dimensions enlarged or reduced by a scale factor
✓	✓	✓	**similar figures** figures having the same shape but not necessarily the same size
		✓	**sphere** the set of all points in three-dimensional space that is equidistant from a fixed point called the center
	✓		**supplementary angles** two angles whose sum is 180°
✓	✓	✓	**surface area** total area of the exterior faces of a three-dimensional figure
		✓	**transformation** a one-to-one correspondence of points in the plane such that each point P is associated with a unique point P', known as the image of P. Transformations can be dilations, translations, reflections, or rotations
		✓	**translation** a transformation where the original figure is moved to a new location without changing size or orientation. Also known as a slide
		✓	**transversal** a line that intersects two or more lines
	✓		**vertical angles** nonadjacent angles with equal measure located across a common vertex
✓	✓	✓	**volume** the amount of space contained in a solid; measured in cubic units

Geometry
6.G.A*

Solve real-world and mathematical problems involving area, surface area, and volume.

STANDARD 1 **6.G.A.1:** Find the area of right triangles, other triangles, special quadrilaterals, and polygons by composing into rectangles or decomposing into triangles or other shapes; apply these techniques in the context of solving real-world and mathematical problems.

STANDARD 2 **6.G.A.2:** Find the volume of a right rectangular prism with fractional edge lengths by packing it with unit cubes of the appropriate unit fraction edge lengths, and show that the volume is the same as would be found by multiplying the edge lengths of the prism. Apply the formulas $V = lwh$ and $V = bh$ to find volumes of right rectangular prisms with fractional edge lengths in the context of solving real-world and mathematical problems.

STANDARD 3 **6.G.A.3:** Draw polygons in the coordinate plane given coordinates for the vertices; use coordinates to find the length of a side joining points with the same first coordinate of the same second coordinate. Apply these techniques in the context of solving real-world and mathematical problems.

STANDARD 4 **6.G.A.4:** Represent three-dimensional figures using nets made up of rectangles and triangles, and use the nets to find the surface area of these figures. Apply these techniques in the context of real-world and mathematical problems.

*Supporting cluster

Geometry 6.G.A

Cluster A: Solve real-world and mathematical problems involving area, surface area, and volume.
Grade 6 Overview

This cluster focuses on area, volume, and surface area. Students use knowledge and skills to solve real-world and mathematical problems and apply the concepts by manipulating nets, cubes, and other real-world materials.

Standards for Mathematical Practice
SFMP 4. Model with mathematics.

Students apply what they learn about area, surface area, and volume to real-world and mathematical problems.

Related Content Standards

5.MD.C.3   6 NS.C.6   7.G.B.4   8.G.C.9

Notes

STANDARD 1 (6.G.A.1)

Find the area of right triangles, other triangles, special quadrilaterals, and polygons by composing into rectangles or decomposing into triangles and other shapes; apply these techniques in the context of solving real-world and mathematical problems.

Students take triangles and quadrilaterals and form rectangles, or take rectangles and/or other quadrilaterals and decompose them (take apart) into familiar shapes to find the area of the composite shape. A composite shape is a shape formed from other shapes. Students study composite shapes that are unfamiliar and decompose them into familiar shapes such as triangles and rectangles (which they know how to calculate the areas of) to find the area. This practice with familiar and irregular composite shapes and decomposition is applied to real-world situations.

What the TEACHER does:

- Make tangram puzzles available for practice in recognizing that several familiar shapes can be put together to compose a rectangle.

- Provide students with a variety of triangles, special quadrilaterals, and polygons and allow them to find the areas of the given shapes. Encourage students to put these shapes together to create new shapes. Challenge them to find the area of the newly composed shapes.

- Allow students the opportunity to work backward by giving them shapes that may be decomposed into familiar shapes. Begin this as a hands-on experience where students cut apart a polygon into familiar shapes and use what they know about area of the familiar shapes to find the area of the given shape.

What the STUDENTS do:

- Reason that familiar shapes can be put together to create composite shapes whose area is equal to that of the sum of the areas of the joining shapes.

- Model composite shapes and their decomposition with hands-on materials such as attribute shapes, Power Polygons™, and tangrams.

- Compare decompositions among classmates to see that a shape can be decomposed more than one way.

- Gain confidence in decomposing composite shapes into familiar shapes and use the areas of the familiar shapes to find the area of the composite shapes.

- Generalize how the area of a shape is the sum of the areas of the shapes that make up the composite shape. Write the generalizations to clarify understandings.

- Use mathematical vocabulary appropriately.

- Solve problems from the real-world using composite figures to model real-world examples such as the size of a lake or a crater on the moon.

Composite shape

Shape decomposed into a center square and 4 rectangles

- Ensure students have experiences to write about what they are learning. Use exit slips, entrance slips, daily journal entries, and so forth. This allows students to explain how decomposing a polygon into familiar shapes such as triangles and rectangles can help find the area of the polygon.

- Model using appropriate mathematical vocabulary.

- Use a variety of mathematical and real-world examples of composite figures for students to apply what they are learning about decomposing figures and area of composite figures.

Addressing Student Misconceptions and Common Errors

Students who have difficulty performing more than two steps in solving a problem may have difficulty finding the area of the composite figures even after decomposing them. These students benefit from writing the areas of the joined shapes directly in the composite figure to help keep track of the parts. Students can also color code the decomposition.

STANDARD 2 (6.G.A.2)

Find the volume of a right rectangular prism with fractional edge lengths by packing it with unit cubes of the appropriate unit fraction edge lengths, and show that the volume is the same as would be found by multiplying the edge lengths of the prism. Apply the formulas V = lwh and V = bh to find volumes of right rectangular prisms with fractional edge lengths in the context of solving real-world and mathematical problems.

With this standard students build on their background knowledge of volume of right rectangular prisms with whole number dimensions by using manipulatives to determine the volume of a right rectangular prism with fractional side lengths.

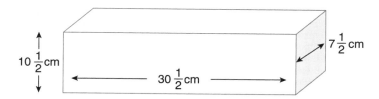

Students relate this experience to the formulas for volume ($V = lwh$ and $V = bh$) and find that their experience of counting the unit cubes yields the same result as using the formulas. Students then solve real-world and mathematical problems by applying volume formulas appropriately.

What the TEACHER does:

- Provide students with the opportunity to fill a right rectangular prism (a box, a folded net, etc.) with cubes. The edges of the cubes should represent a fractional length such as $\frac{1}{2}$ of a unit. If cubes with fractional length edges are not available, use centimeter cubes (or other unit cubes) naming the length of the edges as $\frac{1}{2}$ units. At least one of the edges of the box needs to be a fractional length such as $3\frac{1}{2}$ units.

- Pose questions that relate this volume activity to one in which the cubes are whole units. Pose questions about how the number of cubes that filled the box relates to the volume of the box arrived at by using the formula(s).

- Have students write about how this activity compares to one in which whole unit edges are used.

- Prepare real-world problems for students to solve that create a need to calculate volume with fractional units.

What the STUDENTS do:

- Model volume by filling a rectangular prism with unit cubes of a fractional length and use the model to determine volume of the prism.

- Discover that filling a solid with cubes and counting them gives the same result as using the volume formula.

- Reason that finding volume is the same process and uses the same formulas whether the edge lengths are whole units or fractional units.

- Solve real-world volume problems where one of the edge lengths is a fractional unit.

Addressing Student Misconceptions and Common Errors

Students may understand the relationship between volume as the filling of a space with cubes and the volume formula but, due to weak fractional computation skills, may still produce incorrect responses. Provide additional opportunities for these students to improve their computational fluency. Technology offers many solutions for improving computational fluency.

Notes

Draw polygons in the coordinate plane given coordinates for the vertices; use coordinates to find the length of a side joining points with the same first coordinate or the same second coordinate. Apply these techniques in the context of solving real-world and mathematical problems.

Students plot points in all four quadrants of the coordinate plane. Coordinates are the vertices of polygons. Students connect the points and name the polygons. By giving students coordinates of vertices of the polygon that have the same first or same second coordinate (examples: (3,4) and (3,9) or (7,6) and (15,6)), students are challenged to find a technique to determine the length of a side of the polygon (subtract same coordinates). Students then apply this knowledge to solve real-world and mathematical problems.

What the TEACHER does:

- Provide students with opportunities to draw polygons in the coordinate plane by giving coordinates of triangles, rectangles, and parallelograms.

- Allow students to draw their own polygons and name the vertices with coordinate points. Students can then trade the coordinates they created with partners and uncover each other's polygons.

- Relate this lesson to the lessons on negative integers (6.NS.C.6) and include drawing polygons in all four quadrants.

- Pose a mathematical problem for students to find the length of a side of a polygon with the same first coordinate (or second coordinate) at the vertices.

- Prepare examples of polygons in Quadrants II, III, and IV so that students can apply their knowledge of absolute value.

- Model appropriate use of mathematical vocabulary.

- Promote writing opportunities, including exit and entrance slips and daily journals for students to explain what they are learning. Encourage students to use precise mathematical language in their writing.

- Use real-world and mathematical problems for students to apply this knowledge, such as, *"What is the area of a rectangle whose vertices are (7,4), (7,9), (4,4), (4,9)?"*

What the STUDENTS do:

- Draw polygons in the coordinate plane with attention to naming the vertices with coordinate points.

- Discover how to find the length of sides of polygons using the coordinates of the vertices having the same first coordinate (or second coordinate) and generalize a technique.

- Reflect in writing on the generalization, explaining what they learned about how to determine length of a line segment. This can be writing about how they solved a real-world problem where this generalization was applied.

Addressing Student Misconceptions and Common Errors

Students who confuse knowing which coordinates to subtract may have memorized an algorithm for finding the distance (length of side) without understanding how to use the coordinates on the plane. To address this, provide additional experiences drawing polygons and explaining (orally and in writing) how to find the length of a side with same first (and then same second) coordinates. Communication helps students clarify their understanding.

To prevent the misconception that coordinates only appear in the first quadrant, it is important to use coordinate points in all four quadrants. This means that students will need to have previous experience with negative integers so they can find points such as (−3,−2).

Notes

STANDARD 4 (6.G.A.4)

Represent three-dimensional figures using nets made up of rectangles and triangles, and use the nets to find the surface area of these figures. Apply these techniques in the context of solving real-world and mathematical problems.

Students begin learning about nets by cutting and folding nets of prisms. Nets are two-dimensional diagrams of three-dimensional shapes that can be folded into the three-dimensional shape. Building on students' previous knowledge of area, students can find the area of the rectangles and triangles that make up given nets. This leads to defining surface area as the sum of the area of the faces of the three-dimensional figure. Once students understand this concept, they solve real-world and mathematical problems involving surface area.

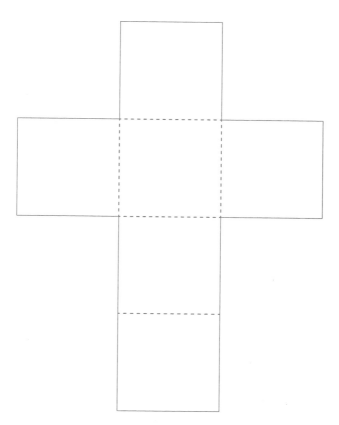

Net of a cube. Fold along the dotted lines.

What the TEACHER does:

- Plan opportunities to familiarize students with nets of prisms (see Reproducible 3). Examples include cutting out nets and folding them into three-dimensional figures, drawing nets for three-dimensional figures, finding the different nets that can fold to make a cube, drawing three-dimensional figures on isometric paper and labeling the faces, and so on.

- Promote problem-solving experiences using nets such as, *"How many different nets can be made to fold up to a cube?"*

- Lead students to find the area of the faces of a net. Model folding the net back to its three-dimensional figure and use this to define surface area. Shade the faces of the net different colors to help students see the relationship of the individual areas to the total surface area.

- Encourage students to find examples where the dimensions of faces repeat in a net. For example, in a rectangular prism, the opposite faces have the same dimensions.

- Pose prompts so students can write about surface area. An example of a prompt is the following: Peter has no idea what surface area is. Explain to him in words and pictures. One possible student solution is:

> Peter,
>
> Surface area is easy! All I do is add up the areas on all of the flat sides. We call these faces. Area is easy. I just multiply the length of the two sides like in this picture and then add up all the areas.

(continued)

What the TEACHER does (continued):

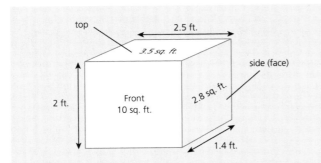

So the front and back faces are 2 × 2.5 = 10 sq. ft. The top and bottom are 2.5 × 1.4 = 3.5 sq. ft, and the left and right sides are 1.4 × 2 = 2.8 sq. ft. So now I add up all the square feet two times each, so I get 10 + 10 + 3.5 + 3.5 + 2.8 + 2.8 = 32.6 sq. ft.

- Encourage students to use correct mathematical vocabulary when speaking and writing about surface area, including the terms *face, vertex, edge, net, surface area, area, two-dimensional, three-dimensional, cube,* and *prism.*

- Facilitate a class discussion for students to share what they discovered about surface area and challenge one another's ideas.

- Provide real-world and mathematical problems for students to apply what they have learned about surface area. Include diagrams of the shapes that go along with the problems.

What the STUDENTS do:

- Visualize how nets relate to three-dimensional figures.

- Use a model to determine surface area.

- Understand how area of two-dimensional figures relates to surface area of three-dimensional figures.

- Compare and contrast area and surface area in writing using mathematical vocabulary.

- Find repetition of dimensions in some of the nets and explain them in terms of the structure of the three-dimensional figure; for example, a student may say or write, "*In this rectangular prism, the top and bottom polygons are the same and so are the front and back. That makes sense because the box has to stand up straight.*"

- Gain confidence as students share ideas in a supportive forum.

- Solve real-world and mathematical problems involving surface area.

Addressing Student Misconceptions and Common Errors

Some students who have difficulty with multi-step problem solving may also have difficulty with surface area because there are six areas to calculate and add together for a prism. To help, shade the faces different colors and write the areas of the faces directly on the net or on the diagram of the three-dimensional figure. Encouraging students to count the number of faces on the three-dimensional shape before they calculate the surface area may also help them account for all of the faces.

Another common error students make is confusing volume and surface area in problems where students must determine which concept should be applied. After students have been introduced to both terms, have students make paper foldables to compare the two terms.

Notes

Geometry

Cluster A: Solve real-world and mathematical problems involving area, surface area, and volume.

Standard: 6.G.A.4. *Represent three-dimensional figures using nets made up of rectangles and triangles, and use the nets to find the surface area of these figures. Apply these techniques in the context of solving real-world and mathematical problems.*

Standards for Mathematical Practice:

SFMP 4. Model with mathematics.

Students use real-world three-dimensional objects to create nets and find surface area.

SFMP 6. Attend to precision.

Students use correct vocabulary to talk about the parts of the nets and describe how to find surface area. Correct units should also be used.

SFMP 8. Look for and express regularity in repeated reasoning.

Students find repetition in the dimensions of the individual rectangles that make up the three-dimensional box.

Goal:

Students find surface area by using what they already know about area and composite figures using nets.

Planning:

Materials: 1 cardboard box per pair of students (cereal box, USPS mailing box, etc.), rulers, scissors

Sample Activity:

- Model cutting apart a box to find its net. Then, allow students to cut apart their own boxes to find the nets.
- Review the concept of area. As students measure and find the areas of the individual rectangles on their nets, direct them to write the areas on the respective faces on both sides of the net.
- Fold the nets back into the three-dimensional boxes and ask students to find the total outside area of their boxes. Then, introduce the term *surface area*.
- Discuss anything students noticed that helped them calculate the surface area. Some students may notice shapes that were repeated as well as the location of those repeated shapes.

Questions/Prompts:

- Are students able to see the composite shapes that make up the net? Ask, "*What shapes make up your net?*"
- Are students using the correct units? Ask, "*Which units represent area?*"
- Are students noticing that their nets have pairs of congruent rectangles? Ask, "*How do the areas of the rectangles compare? Where are the congruent shapes located? Why do you think that is so?*"

Differentiating Instruction:

Struggling Students: Some students may have difficulty physically cutting a box. In this case, the teacher may need to assist them. Other students may have weaknesses in measuring and may need to be shown how to round their measures. The many steps involved in calculating surface area may overwhelm some learners. Creating a list for the areas of the faces of the box will help.

Extension: Challenge students to formalize how they calculated the surface area of their boxes into a formula that will work for all rectangular prisms.

Geometry

Cluster A: Solve real-world and mathematical problems involving area, surface area, and volume.

Standard:

Standards for Mathematical Practice:

Goal:

Planning:

Materials:

Sample Activity:

Questions/Prompts:

Differentiating Instruction:

Struggling Students:

Extension:

Notes

Geometry
7.G.A

Draw, construct, and describe geometrical figures and describe the relationships between them.

STANDARD 1   **7.G.A.1:** Solve problems involving scale drawings of geometric figures, including computing actual lengths and areas from a scale drawing and reproducing a scale drawing at a different scale.

STANDARD 2   **7.G.A.2:** Draw (freehand, with ruler and protractor, and with technology) geometric shapes with given conditions. Focus on constructing triangles from three measures of angles or sides, noticing when the conditions determine a unique triangle, more than one triangle, or no triangle.

STANDARD 3   **7.G.A.3:** Describe the two-dimensional figures that result from slicing three-dimensional figures, as in plane sections of right rectangular prisms and right rectangular pyramids.

Geometry   7.G.A

Cluster A: Draw, construct, and describe geometrical figures and describe the relationships between them.
Grade 7 Overview

Students work with their hands drawing, constructing geometric shapes, and concentrating on triangles and building them given the three angle measures or the measures of side lengths. Students find relationships between figures such as the plane figures that result from slicing a three-dimensional figure. Using scale drawings, students solve problems including finding the actual lengths from scale drawings or redrawing a scale drawing to another scale.

Standards for Mathematical Practice
SFMP1. Make sense of problems and persevere in solving them.

Students solve problems using scale drawings.

SFMP 4. Model with mathematics.

Students use drawings and hands-on materials to model geometric shapes and relationships.

SFMP5. Use appropriate tools strategically.

Students draw free hand or use technology or other tools to draw geometric shapes.

Related Content Standards

6.RP.A.3.d   6.G.A.4   7.RP.A.2.a   7.G.B.4   7.G.B.5   7.G.B.6   8.G.A.4

Notes

STANDARD 1 (7.G.A.1)

Solve problems involving scale drawings of geometric figures, including computing actual lengths and areas from a scale drawing and reproducing a scale drawing at a different scale.

Students work with scale drawings. They learn how to read them, calculate the scale, compute the actual lengths from the scale in the drawing, and reproduce a scale drawing using another scale. Scale drawings are proportional to one another. Problems should center on experiences in the students' own lives. Examples include but are not limited to scale drawings of student rooms at home, the classroom, and comic book strips. The term *scale factor* should be used when students are asked to reproduce a scale drawing at a different scale. A scale factor is a number that multiplies some quantity. For example, doubling the length of a window that is 3 ft long corresponds to a scale factor of $2(2 \times 3 = 6)$.

What the TEACHER does:

- Pose a problem scenario that involves something familiar to students such as having to draw the classroom to scale for a set of blueprints. Allow students to do the measuring of the dimensions in the room and use this problem scenario to establish the basics about scale drawings and scale factors.

- Assign projects similar to the classroom scenario to work on, such as scaling their bedrooms, the school cafeteria, and so on. Let students present them to the class.

- Provide students with scale drawings and ask them to find the actual measures. Do one together as a class using a problem setting such as calculating the actual area of a space using a scale drawing. Pose questions such as the following: Does changing the scale factor affect the actual area?

- Prepare problems where students need to change the scale of a drawing. Relate to proportional reasoning and ratios.

What the STUDENTS do:

- Read and create scale drawings from familiar settings.

- Use precise mathematical language when presenting solutions to scale drawing problems to the class.

- Calculate actual measures such as area, perimeter, and volume from scale drawings using appropriate measurement units.

- Redraw a scale drawing using a different scale.

Addressing Student Misconceptions and Common Errors

Have students use graph paper to make their scale drawings as it will cut down on measurement errors. Students without a solid grasp of measurement units such as those for area will have difficulty with this standard, as will students who need more help with proportional reasoning. Take the opportunity while measuring the classroom or other hands-on measuring opportunity to reinforce measurement units for those students.

Notes

Draw (freehand, with ruler and protractor, and with technology) geometric shapes with given conditions. Focus on constructing triangles from three measures of angles or sides, noticing when the conditions determine a unique triangle, more than one triangle, or no triangle.

Students practice drawing geometric shapes using technology (computer programs both commercial and free on the Internet), rulers and protractors, and free hand. While giving practice with multiple shapes, focus on triangles and constructing them from three given angles or sides. Students should determine, by looking at the given measures, whether one, more than one, or no triangles can be created. Angles need to add up to 180° to make a triangle. The sum of two side lengths of a triangle is always greater than the third side. If this is true for all three combinations of added side lengths, then you will have a triangle.

What the TEACHER does:

- Provide students with multiple opportunities to draw geometric shapes free hand. Provide both regular graph paper and isometric graph paper.

- Model how to use rulers and protractors and allow students to use the tools to create geometric shapes with given measures.

- Introduce students to a variety of geometric software. Some products are free online and others will require school purchases. Provide ample time for students to explore how the software works and develop a degree of proficiency using the software to draw geometric shapes.

- Allow students to select the appropriate tool to solve problems where the teacher gives measures of three angles or sides and students draw the triangle(s).

- Provide different-sized lengths of spaghetti for students to discover how the lengths of sides relate to one another to make a triangle. Any stick-like hands-on manipulative will work.

- Provide many examples where the triangles students form are unique, many examples where it is impossible to construct a triangle, and some scenarios where more than one triangle can be drawn. Provide students time to figure out how they can tell from the givens, such as, *"If the three angles add up to more than 180°, can you make a triangle? How can you tell if three lines of given length will form a triangle?"*

What the STUDENTS do:

- Draw multiple geometric shapes using a variety of tools.

- Select the appropriate tools for drawing triangles in a given situation.

- Discover, through examples, whether the given information about triangles can create one, more than one, or no triangles.

Addressing Student Misconceptions and Common Errors

Some students may need graph or isometric paper to draw shapes.

Notes

STANDARD 3 (7.G.A.3)

Describe the two-dimensional figures that result from slicing three-dimensional figures, as in plane sections of right rectangular prisms and right rectangular pyramids.

Students relate the two-dimensional shape that results from slicing a three-dimensional figure. Three-dimensional shapes will include right rectangular prisms and right rectangular pyramids.

What the TEACHER does:

- Provide students with models of right rectangular prisms, cubes, and right rectangular pyramids that can be sliced such as those made of Styrofoam or florist forms.

- Ask students to create a table as below:

Name of 3-D Shape	2-D Shape	2-D Shape	2-D Shape	2-D Shape

As they consider the shapes, have students either imagine or slice through their shapes and determine the different planes that can be created with the slices.

- Challenge students with questions such as the following: *"How many different two-dimensional figures can be found by slicing a cube?"*

What the STUDENTS do:

- Discover the two-dimensional shapes that result from slicing a three-dimensional figure.

- Develop three-dimensional visualization skills as they see the resulting two-dimensional shapes.

Addressing Student Misconceptions and Common Errors

Some students who have difficulty developing three-dimensional visualization skills may need to use hands-on materials. In addition to Styrofoam, students can use clay shapes and slice through the shapes with a spatula.

Students sometimes confuse the entire remaining three-dimensional shape as the resulting two-dimensional shape created after the slicing. If you position a piece of paper over the slice and trace the outline of the slice, students can better see the resulting two-dimensional shape.

Notes

Geometry
7.G.B

Solve real-life and mathematical problems involving angle measure, area, surface area, and volume.

STANDARD 4   **7.G.B.4:** Know the formulas for the area and circumference of a circle and use them to solve problems; give an informal derivation of the relationship between the circumference and area of a circle.

STANDARD 5   **7.G.B.5:** Use facts about supplementary, complementary, vertical, and adjacent angles in a multi-step problem to write and solve simple equations for an unknown angle in a figure.

STANDARD 6   **7.G.B.6:** Solve real-world and mathematical problems involving area, volume and surface area of two- and three-dimensional objects composed of triangles, quadrilaterals, polygons, cubes, and right prisms.

Geometry   7.G.B

Cluster B: Solve real-life and mathematical problems involving angle measure, area, surface area, and volume.
Grade 7 Overview

This standard is about geometric problem solving. Students use basic information such as area, surface area, and volume formulas and facts about types of angles (supplementary, complementary, vertical, and adjacent) to solve real-world problems.

Standards for Mathematical Practice
SFMP1. Make sense of problems and persevere in solving them.

Students solve problems involving geometric principles.

SFMP 4. Model with mathematics.

Students use geometric models to solve problems.

Related Content Standards

6.G.A.1   6.G.A.2   6.G.A.4   8.G.C.9

Notes

STANDARD 4 (7.G.B.4)

Know the formulas for the area and circumference of a circle and use them to solve problems; give an informal derivation of the relationship between the circumference and area of a circle.

Students learn formulas for area ($A = \pi r^2$) and circumference ($C = 2\pi r$) of circles and then solve problems (mathematical and real-world) using these formulas. Students participate in discovering the relationship between the two formulas.

What the TEACHER does:

- Provide students an opportunity to discover the relationship between circumference and diameter. Have students work in groups to measure the circumference and diameter of several round objects in the classroom such as the clock face. Students combine their data and look for a relationship between the circumference and diameter.

- Facilitate a discussion about circumference to lead students to the formula for circumference of a circle. Do the same for area.

- Pose problems to solve that apply area and circumference formulas such as the following: *"The seventh grade is building a ring-toss game to raise money for a field trip. The bottles where we toss the rings will be placed on a green circle. If the circle is 10 feet in diameter, how many square feet of carpet will they need to buy to cover the circle? How might you communicate this information to the salesperson to make sure you receive a piece of carpet that is the correct size?"*

- Guide a derivation of the relationship between the circumference and area of a circle. Use a circle as a model. Cut the circle into as many equal-sized pie pieces as possible. Lay the pie pieces to form a shape similar to a parallelogram. Have students write an expression for the area of the parallelogram related to the radius (note: the length of the base of the parallelogram is half the circumference, or πr, and the height is r, resulting in an area of πr^2, which is the area of the circle). This derivation is the sample lesson at the end of this section.

What the STUDENTS do:

- Explain the relationship between circumference and diameter of a circle using correct mathematical vocabulary.

- Solve mathematical and real-world problems by applying the area of a circle and circumference formulas.

- Discover through hands-on experience, and explain the relationship between the circumference and area of a circle.

Addressing Student Misconceptions and Common Errors

The formulas for the area of a circle and the circumference of a circle are often confused by students. Teaching students to memorize these formulas without any understanding of how they relate to a circle increases the chance for confusion. Build the understanding before presenting the formulas.

Notes

Use facts about supplementary, complementary, vertical, and adjacent angles in a multi-step problem to write and solve simple equations for an unknown angle in a figure.

Explore supplementary, complementary, vertical, and adjacent angles and their relationships to one another. These facts are used in multi-step problems.

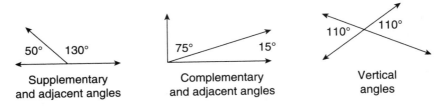

| Supplementary and adjacent angles | Complementary and adjacent angles | Vertical angles |

What the TEACHER does:

- Provide students the opportunities to explore supplementary, complementary, vertical, and adjacent angles first through measuring and then by finding the patterns. Apply these findings to look at the same angles in intersecting lines and many types of polygons.

- Assign multi-step problems where students apply what they know about supplementary, complementary, vertical, and adjacent angles to find solutions.

- Have students create dictionaries of new vocabulary words as there are many new ones in this standard such as *supplementary*, *complementary*, *vertical*, and *adjacent*.

What the STUDENTS do:

- Discover the definitions of supplementary, complementary, vertical, and adjacent angles.

- Solve multi-step problems by applying what they know about the types of angles.

- Clarify their understandings of the terms *supplementary, complementary, vertical,* and *adjacent angles* by writing in their own words.

Addressing Student Misconceptions and Common Errors

Students tend to confuse these vocabulary words. Making a foldable where they can look to distinguish between supplementary and complementary and then vertical and adjacent can be very helpful. A simple foldable would be a sheet of paper folded lengthwise as below:

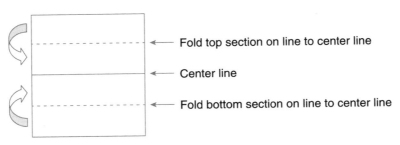

Students write *supplementary* on the outside of the top section folded down and *complementary* on the outside of the bottom section folded up. They write the definitions in their own words with pictures/diagrams inside the flaps and can use this as a visual to discriminate between the two words.

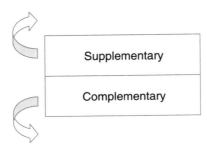

STANDARD 6 (7.G.B.6)

Solve real-world and mathematical problems involving area, volume and surface area of two- and three-dimensional objects composed of triangles, quadrilaterals, polygons, cubes, and right prisms.

This standard pulls together much of what the students know and can do in geometry through problem solving of both mathematical and real-world problems. Students will work with two- and three-dimensional objects and apply what they know about area, volume and surface area.

What the TEACHER does:

- Provide students with a variety of problems to solve from single to multi-step, from real-world to mathematical. Present opportunities to solve the problems as individuals, pairs, and small groups. Allow students to present their findings and justifications in writing such as journal entries and orally as in class presentations facilitated by the teacher.

- Model and highlight appropriate use of vocabulary whenever possible.

What the STUDENTS do:

- Solve a variety of real-world and mathematical problems involving geometry concepts such as area, volume, and surface area for two- and three-dimensional objects.

- Communicate orally and in writing solutions, including justifications for those solutions.

Addressing Student Misconceptions and Common Errors

A common error students make is to confuse when to use area, volume, or surface area. These students need to explore the concepts with concrete materials. They need to physically measure lengths and widths to find area, fill objects with cubes to develop their concept of volume, and use nets to determine surface area. Memorizing formulas makes it difficult for students to know when to use which concept.

Notes

Geometry

Cluster B: Solve real-life and mathematical problems involving angle measure, area, surface area, and volume.

Standard: 7.G.B.4. *Know the formulas for the area and circumference of a circle and use them to solve problems; give an informal derivation of the relationship between the circumference and area of a circle.*

Standards for Mathematical Practice:

SFMP 4. Model with mathematics.

Students use paper models of a circle to derive the relationship between the circumference and area of a circle.

Goal:

Students use a hands-on approach to derive the relationship between the circumference and area of a circle.

Planning:

Materials: paper circles with a diameter of 6–8 inches, scissors, tape, pencils, paper

Sample Activity:

- Facilitate a class discussion about the relationship between area and circle circumference to bring the ideas to the forefront.
- Have students, working in pairs, cut their circles into equal-sized pie pieces after determining the radius, circumference, and area of the circle.
- Have students rearrange the pie pieces to make a shape similar to a parallelogram as shown:

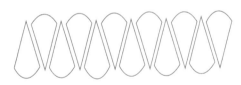

   Note that the more pieces the students use, the closer the rearranged pieces resemble a parallelogram.

- Lead students to note that the height of the parallelogram is *r*, the radius of the circle.
- Lead them to discover that the length of the parallelogram is equal to $\frac{1}{2}$ of the circumference of the circle. Therefore, the area of the parallelogram is $r\frac{1}{2}(2\pi r) = \pi r^2$.
- Ask students to write what they learned about the relationship of the area of a circle to the circumference.

Questions/Prompts:

- When students do not notice that *r* is the height of the parallelogram, ask, while pointing to the height, *"Where did this line on the pie wedge originally come from?"*

- When leading students to find that one side of the parallelogram is half the circumference of the circle ask, *"How did this line that makes the bottom of the parallelogram come about? Where was it in the original circle?"*

- For students who cannot see that the parallelogram and the circle have the same area, ask them to take the parallelogram apart and put the pieces back into a circle and redo the parallelogram.

Differentiating Instruction:

Struggling Students: This activity requires visualization skills. Students having difficulty may need to do this in steps. First, cut the circle into four wedges and make a parallelogram. Then cut those four into eight and redo the parallelogram. It may even take cutting the wedges one more time into 16 pieces. The more pieces, the smoother and straighter the edges of the parallelogram will be.

Extension: Provide little facilitation for these students. Write the instructions for them and allow them to draw the connections that lead to the derivation on their own.

Notes

Geometry

Cluster A: Draw, construct, and describe geometrical figures and describe the relationships between them.

Standard:

Standards for Mathematical Practice:

Goal:

Planning:

Materials:

Sample Activity:

Questions/Prompts:

Differentiating Instruction:

Struggling Students:

Extension:

Geometry

Cluster B: Solve real-life and mathematical problems involving angle measure, area, surface area, and volume.

Standard:

Standards for Mathematical Practice:

Goal:

Planning:

Materials:

Sample Activity:

Questions/Prompts:

Differentiating Instruction:

Struggling Students:

Extension:

Geometry
8.G.A*

Understand congruence and similarity using physical models, transparencies, or geometry software.

STANDARD 1

8.G.A.1: Verify experimentally the properties of rotations, reflections, and translations:

   a. Lines are taken to lines, and line segments to line segments of the same length.

   b. Angles are taken to angles of the same measure.

   c. Parallel lines are taken to parallel lines.

STANDARD 2

8.G.A.2: Understand that a two-dimensional figure is congruent to another if the second can be obtained from the first by a sequence of rotations, reflections, and translations; given two congruent figures, describe a sequence that exhibits the congruence between them.

STANDARD 3

8.G.A.3: Describe the effect of dilations, translations, rotations, and reflections on two-dimensional figures using coordinates.

STANDARD 4

8.G.A.4: Understand that a two-dimensional figure is similar to another if the second can be obtained from the first by a sequence of rotations, reflections, translations, and dilations; given two similar two-dimensional figures, describe a sequence that exhibits the similarity between them.

STANDARD 5

8.G.A.5: Use informal arguments to establish facts about the angle sum and exterior angle of triangles, about the angles created when parallel lines are cut by a transversal, and the angle-angle criterion for similarity of triangles. *For example, arrange three copies of the same triangle so that the sum of the three angles appears to form a line, and give an argument in terms of transversals why this is so.*

*Major cluster

Geometry 8.G.A

Cluster A: Understand congruence and similarity using physical models, transparencies, or geometry software.

Grade 8 Overview

This cluster focuses on the concepts of congruence and similarity. Students learn about transformations and use them to establish congruence and similarity of figures on a coordinate plane. Triangles and angles are studied by using informal arguments to establish facts about relationships between the angles of triangles and the different types of angles created when parallel lines are cut by a transversal.

Standards for Mathematical Practice
SFMP 3. Construct viable arguments and critique the reasoning of others.

Students use informal arguments to establish facts about the angle sum and exterior angle of triangles, the angles created when parallel lines are cut by a transversal, and the angle-angle criterion for similarity of triangles.

SFMP 4. Model with mathematics.

Students model on the coordinate plane to explore congruent and similar figures.

SFMP 6. Attend to precision.

Students are careful to bring lines to lines and angles to appropriate angles in transformations.

SFMP 7. Look for and make use of structure.

Students attend to the structure of the figures as they transform them.

Related Content Standards

6.RP.A.3   7.G.A.1   7.G.B.5

Notes

Verify experimentally the properties of rotations, reflections, and translations:

   a. *Lines are taken to lines, and line segments to line segments of the same length.*

   b. *Angles are taken to angles of the same measure.*

   c. *Parallel lines are taken to parallel lines.*

Eighth graders add rotations, reflections, and translations to their study of transformations from Grade 7 dilations. Students verify through experimentation with figures on a coordinate plane that lines are taken to lines and line segments to line segments of the same length; angles are taken to angles of the same measure, and parallel lines are taken to parallel lines. This standard is an introduction, and students should spend time exploring these transformations.

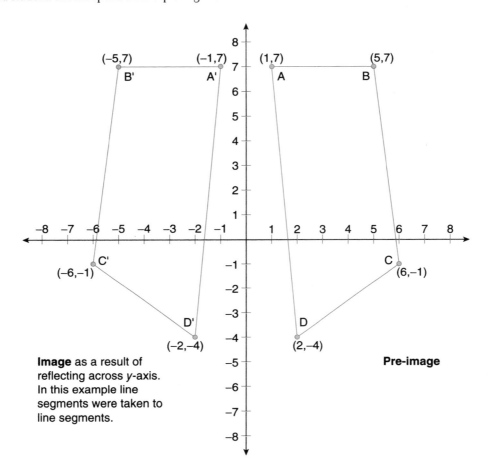

Image as a result of reflecting across *y*-axis. In this example line segments were taken to line segments.

Pre-image

What the TEACHER does:

- Provide basic exercises for the students to learn about rotations (turns), reflections (flips), and translations (slides) on the coordinate plane. Use hands-on materials such as shapes cut from paper to have students model the transformations before using the coordinate grid. Wallpaper patterns provide excellent models of rotations, translations, and reflections. Transparencies also illuminate the transformations. Students can go online to find examples of the transformations in art and architecture.

- Isolating each transformation, facilitate a class discussion about what they notice about the new figure compared

to the original. They should notice that lines are taken to lines, angles to angles of the same measure, and parallel lines to parallel lines. Use the correct mathematical notation of A and A′ (A′ read as "A *prime*") as the labels for the transformation and the original figure.

- Give students opportunities to identify the transformation(s) that occurred to take one figure to another. One activity is to let each student transform a figure on the coordinate plane using one, two, or three transformations. Then have the students trade papers to see if they can identify the transformations used by their classmates.

What the STUDENTS do:

- Accurately transform figures on the coordinate plane using rotations, reflections, and translations, and the correct notation.

- Identify the transformations used to transform one figure into another using hands-on materials and on the coordinate plane.

- Discover that for a transformation, lines are taken to lines, line segments to line segments, angles to angles of the same measure, and parallel lines to parallel lines.

Addressing Student Misconceptions and Common Errors

Students with spatial visualization problems will find this standard difficult. These students need much practice. The use of technology to show the transformations can help as the student can experience many transformations in a shorter period of time than if each had to be done by hand. There are numerous YouTube videos that deal with transformations.

Notes

GRADE 8

STANDARD 2 (8.G.A.2)

Understand that a two-dimensional figure is congruent to another if the second can be obtained from the first by a sequence of rotations, reflections, and translations; given two congruent figures, describe a sequence that exhibits the congruence between them.

Students use what they previously learned about transformations to determine congruency between figures. Congruent figures share the same size and shape. When given two congruent figures, students describe the sequence of transformations that occurred to create the congruent figure. Note that dilations cannot be used for congruent figures.

What the TEACHER does:

- Have students use one or two transformations to transform a figure. Display the student work to use as your example of congruent figures. Use the display to lead students to discover the definition of congruent.

- Provide students with examples of congruent figures and ask them to trace the sequence of transformations that created the congruent figure. Check that students are using the correct notation for the figure and the original of A and A′ (A′ read as "A *prime*").

- Present students with opportunities to write about congruent figures; for instance, trade examples of congruent figures created by students and the original figures. Have students justify in writing why the new shape is congruent to the original using appropriate vocabulary.

What the STUDENTS do:

- Discover that a series of transformations can create a figure that is congruent to the first. Communicate the understanding through writing.

- Create congruent figures by applying a series of transformations.

- Use correct notation in labeling congruent figures.

Addressing Student Misconceptions and Common Errors

Students with spatial visualization issues may have difficulty with this concept. Color coding the lines and angles in the congruent figure to match the original may help.

Notes

STANDARD 3 (8.G.A.3)

Describe the effect of dilations, translations, rotations, and reflections on two-dimensional figures using coordinates.

Students continue looking at two-dimensional figures on the coordinate plane, concentrating on the coordinates of the resulting figure after transformations, including dilations learned in Grade 7.

What the TEACHER does:

- Display several images (figures after transformation) and pre-images (original figures). Use different polygons. Focus student attention on the coordinates and pose questions so that students develop a sense of how the coordinates change during different transformations.

- Concentrate on moving one pre-image by adding, subtracting, and multiplying the coordinates such as add 2 to x, subtract 3 from y, combinations of changes to x and y, multiply coordinates by 3, and multiply coordinates by $\frac{1}{3}$.

  Then ask students questions such as the following: What happened to the figure? Did the change affect just one vertex or all? In what way?

- Facilitate students' generalizing about the changes that preserve size and/or shape. Note that dilations create distortions of the pre-image.

- Provide opportunities such as journals and exit slips for students to describe transformations with both words and coordinate points.

- Present examples to students for this standard not only on paper but using technology.

What the STUDENTS do:

- Discover that transformations change the coordinates of images from the pre-images in specific ways.

- Analyze images and pre-images to determine the transformations that took place and explain using words and coordinate points.

Addressing Student Misconceptions and Common Errors

Allowing students to use rulers to follow the lines from pre-image to image will help students with tracking difficulties.

Notes

Understand that a two-dimensional figure is similar to another if the second can be obtained from the first by a sequence of rotations, reflections, translations, and dilations; given two similar two-dimensional figures, describe a sequence that exhibits the similarity between them.

With this standard students move from congruence to similarity. Students develop the understanding that similar figures can be created by a series of transformations, including rotations, reflections, dilations, and translations, and can identify those transformations given an image and a pre-image.

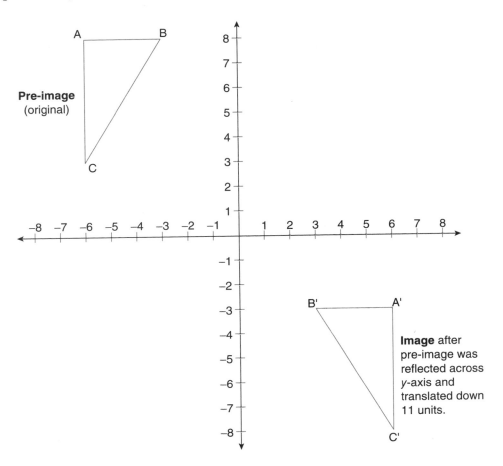

Pre-image (original)

Image after pre-image was reflected across *y*-axis and translated down 11 units.

What the TEACHER does:

- Display two images and pre-images. One should show congruent figures and the other should demonstrate similar figures. Use these to help students understand the difference between the two concepts.

- Present students with pre-images and images of similar polygons and trace, with students, the sequence of transformations that produced the image. Challenge students to find the most efficient combination of transformations. Give students practice doing the same using paper-and-pencil examples, but also those found in the real-world such as examples from art, architecture, and the natural world.

- Provide opportunities for students to communicate their reasoning through vehicles such as journals and exit slips.

What the STUDENTS do:

- Model similar figures from a pre-image using transformations.

- Trace the sequence of transformations that create a given image from a given pre-image.

- Communicate orally and/or in writing the transformation sequence found for creating a particular image from a pre-image.

Similarity and *congruence* are two words students frequently confuse. Help them by creating foldables such as those described for other standards and by using advance organizers such as the Frayer model (see Reproducible 2).

Notes

Use informal arguments to establish facts about the angle sum and exterior angle of triangles, about the angles created when parallel lines are cut by a transversal, and the angle-angle criterion for similarity of triangles. For example, arrange three copies of the same triangle so that the sum of the three angles appears to form a line, and give an argument in terms of transversals why this is so.

Students are expected to make informal arguments while exploring facts about the sum of the angles of a triangle, exterior angles of triangles, angles created when parallel lines are cut by a transversal, and the angle-angle criterion for similar triangles. The example demonstrates how these facts are interrelated. Note that formal two-column proofs are not expected at this grade.

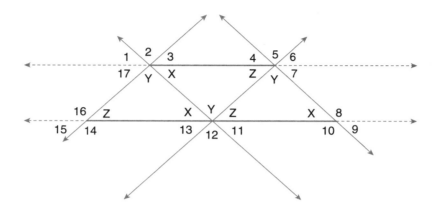

What the TEACHER does:

- Introduce students to the facts they need to learn in this standard through explorations such as the following: Have each student draw a triangle of his or her choice and tear off the angles. Rearrange the angles so they touch one another. Students should notice that each student was able to create a straight line, thus informally arguing that the three angles of a triangle add up to 180°. Note that formal two-column proofs are not expected at this grade.

- Introduce students to parallel lines cut by a transversal with projection equipment or other technology. Ask students to find pairs of equal angles using any tools they choose. Facilitate a class discussion in which adjacent, vertical, complementary, supplementary, alternate interior, and alternate exterior angles are found.

- Use the example from the standard to tie various facts together in an informal argument.

- Introduce the angle-angle criterion for similar triangles using an exploratory approach.

- Pose problems for students to solve using the facts and relationships they have learned in this standard.

- Model the use of geometric vocabulary from this standard. Encourage students to create their own dictionary of geometric terms complete with illustrations.

What the STUDENTS do:

- Explore angle sums and exterior angles of triangles, angles created when parallel lines are cut by a transversal, and the angle-angle criterion for similarity of triangles. Use correct mathematical vocabulary to describe these ideas.

- Create and defend informal arguments to justify the facts they have learned.

- Solve problems using the facts and relationships studied in this standard such as problems that can be solved by looking at angle relationships on parallel lines cut by a transversal as a model for the problem.

Addressing Student Misconceptions and Common Errors

Some students have difficulty reasoning with informal arguments. It is best to scaffold questions for those students to help them through an informal argument and supplement that with hands-on materials such as triangles that can be manipulated.

Geometry
8.G.B*

Understand and apply the Pythagorean Theorem.

| STANDARD 6 | **8.G.B.6:** Explain a proof of the Pythagorean Theorem and its converse. |

| STANDARD 7 | **8.G.B.7:** Apply the Pythagorean Theorem to determine unknown side lengths in right triangles in real-world and mathematical problems in two and three dimensions. |

| STANDARD 8 | **8.G.B.8:** Apply the Pythagorean Theorem to find the distance between two points in a coordinate system. |

*Major cluster

Geometry   8.G.B

Cluster B: Understand and apply the Pythagorean Theorem.
Grade 8 Overview

This cluster focuses on introducing the Pythagorean Theorem. Students explore the relationship between the sides of a right triangle to understand the formula $a^2 + b^2 = c^2$ and then solve problems by applying the theorem.

Standards for Mathematical Practice
SFMP 3. Construct viable arguments and critique the reasoning of others.

Students model an informal proof to understand the Pythagorean Theorem.

SFMP 4. Model with mathematics.

Students use modeling to understand the meaning of the Pythagorean Theorem.

SFMP 6. Attend to precision.

Students check their results to all computations.

SFMP 7. Look for and make use of structure.

Students look for patterns in right triangles to help solve problems.

Related Content Standards

6.G.A.1   8.NS.A.1   8.EE.A.2

Notes

Explain a proof of the Pythagorean Theorem and its converse.

There are many proofs of the Pythagorean Theorem. Students will work through one to understand the meaning of $a^2 + b^2 = c^2$ and its converse. The converse statement is as follows: If the square of one side of a triangle is equal to the sum of the squares of the other two sides, then the triangle is a right triangle.

What the TEACHER does:

- Explore right triangles to establish the vocabulary of hypotenuse and legs.

- Prepare graph chart paper so that each pair of students has one piece of chart paper with a right triangle drawn in the center. Triangles on different charts do not need to be the same size. Be sure that the side lengths of the triangles are whole numbers. Have students follow these steps:

  o Find the lengths of the hypotenuse and the legs and mark them beside the triangle.

  o Draw a square off of each side of the triangle.

  o Determine the area of each square. (Some students will count the boxes inside the square.)

  o Ask groups to write what they notice about the relationship of the areas of the squares.

What the STUDENTS do:

- Use the correct vocabulary when writing or talking about the Pythagorean Theorem.

- Model a proof of the Pythagorean Theorem.

- Reason that the converse of the Pythagorean Theorem is true as part of a class discussion.

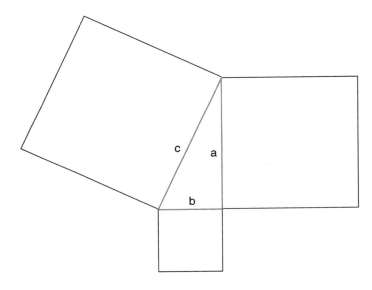

- Facilitate a whole-class discussion to arrive at the conclusion that $a^2 + b^2 = c^2$. Facilitate a whole-class discussion about the converse of the theorem and pose the following question: Do you think the converse is true? Defend your answer.

- Enrich discussion with stories about the history of Pythagoras and the roots of the theorem.

Addressing Student Misconceptions and Common Errors

Allow students to color code the triangle if necessary to see which square relates to which side of the right triangle they were provided. When stating the Theorem, many students miss the fact that the a^2 is the area of the square off of side a, not side a itself. Stress this fact clearly during the proof when students can see the square.

STANDARD 7 (8.G.B.7)

Apply the Pythagorean Theorem to determine unknown side lengths in right triangles in real-world and mathematical problems in two and three dimensions.

Students solve problems where they must apply the Pythagorean Theorem. Problems may be real-world or mathematical, and they may involve two- or three- dimensional situations.

What the TEACHER does:

- Model use of the Pythagorean Theorem to solve problems finding the unknown length of a side of a right triangle in two dimensions. "Walk through" problems with students. Use examples where the solutions are not all whole numbers. Encourage students to draw diagrams where they can see the right triangles being used. Students may need a review of solving equations with square roots.

- Model use of the Pythagorean Theorem with problems in three dimensions. Use real-world objects to help students see the right triangle in three dimensions such as using a box where the right triangle can be "drawn" in space using string. Use technology to illustrate the three dimensionalities in some problems.

- Assign students problems to solve individually, in pairs and in groups. Allow students to use any hands-on materials or technology they need to solve the problems. Justify solutions to the class.

What the STUDENTS do:

- Solve problems using many different modeling techniques such as hands-on materials or technology. Problems may involve two- or three-dimensional models.

- Use models with hands-on materials or technology to solve problems.

- Communicate with classmates using appropriate vocabulary.

- Check reasonableness of results to problems.

Addressing Student Misconceptions and Common Errors

Common errors can be the result of students having difficulty with the computation. A review of computation with square roots may be needed.

Students with spatial visualization issues will have difficulty with the three-dimensional problems. Teachers need to model those problems with objects for these students more so than with the rest of the class. Allowing technology to model for these problems is also helpful.

Notes

Apply the Pythagorean Theorem to find the distance between two points in a coordinate system.

Use the Pythagorean Theorem to find the distance between two points. Problems can best be modeled in a coordinate system.

What the TEACHER does:

- Present a real-world problem to the students where it is necessary to find the distance between two points. Allow students to struggle with it in pairs.

- Facilitate a class discussion about what the students tried and lead them to discover that using a coordinate plane and the Pythagorean Theorem can be a solution strategy.

- Provide opportunities for students to solve problems where they must use the Pythagorean Theorem to find the distance between two points working individually, in pairs, and in small groups. Students can present their work for critique by other students.

What the STUDENTS do:

- Adopt the use of the Pythagorean Theorem to find the distance between two points on the coordinate plane.

- Solve real-world problems using the Theorem as a strategy.

- Explain solution strategies using correct mathematical vocabulary.

Addressing Student Misconceptions and Common Errors

This standard requires the use of several steps as a solution strategy. Some students have trouble when more than one step is involved. Walk these students through the steps, asking them questions along the way so they can make sense of the solution and not just try to memorize the steps.

Some students use the Pythagorean Theorem to find missing sides for triangles that are not right triangles. To convince them that this will not work, have them reconstruct the proof with drawing squares on the sides of the triangle that is not right. They will see that the areas do not add up.

Notes

Geometry
8.G.C

Solve real-world and mathematical problems involving volume of cylinders, cones, and spheres.

STANDARD 9 **8.G.C.9:** Know the formulas for the volumes of cones, cylinders, and spheres and use them to solve real-world and mathematical problems.

Geometry 8.G.C

Cluster C: Solve real-world and mathematical problems involving volume of cylinders, cones, and spheres.
Grade 8 Overview

This cluster focuses on knowing and applying volume formulas for cylinders, cones, and spheres and then applying this knowledge to solving problems.

Standards for Mathematical Practice
SFMP 1. Make sense of problems and persevere in solving them.

Students solve problems involving volume of cones, cylinders, and spheres.

SFMP 4. Model with mathematics.

Students use modeling to understand the meaning of the Pythagorean Theorem.

SFMP 6. Attend to precision.

Students check their results to all computations.

SFMP 7. Look for and make use of structure.

Students look for patterns in right triangles to help solve problems.

Related Content Standards

6.G.A.2   7.G.B.6

Notes

Know the formulas for the volumes of cones, cylinders, and spheres and use them to solve real-world and mathematical problems.

This standard has two distinct parts. First, students learn the volume formulas for cones, cylinders, and spheres. Then they apply this knowledge to solve real-world and mathematical problems. The formulas should be taught through experiments where students figure out the formulas.

What the TEACHER does:

- Prepare students to discover the formulas through hands-on experiences. For the volume of a cylinder, compare it to what students already know about the volume for a right rectangular prism. Using the knowledge that the volume of a right rectangular prism is the area of the base times the height, compare a cylinder to a prism of the same height. Have physical models on hand. Note that the base of the prism is a rectangle, and the base of the cylinder is a circle. Lead students to reason that the formula for the volume is the same as the volume of a right rectangular prism in that both are the area of the base times the height. So for the cylinder, it is $V = h\pi r^2$, which is the base area (πr^2) times the height (h).

- Compare the volume of a cylinder to a cone to derive the formula for the volume for a cone. Use a cylinder and cone of equal heights. Let students fill the cone with rice or water and ask students to estimate how many times they need to fill the cone in order to fill the cylinder. Students will conclude that the cone holds $\frac{1}{3}$ the volume of the cylinder of the same height, thus the formula $V = \frac{1}{3} h\pi r^2$.

- Compare the volume of a sphere to the volume of a cylinder of the same height. Model half a sphere (hemisphere) placed inside the cylinder of same height and base. The area of the base of the cylinder and the area of the section created by cutting the sphere in half are both πr^2. In this model, the height of the cylinder is also r, so the volume of the cylinder is πr^3. Fill the hemisphere with rice or water and estimate how many will fill the cylinder. The volume of the hemisphere with radius r is $\frac{2}{3}$ that of the cylinder. Since the hemisphere is only half of the sphere, we double and find $V = \frac{4}{3}\pi r^3$.

- Provide opportunities for students to explain in writing how they understand the volume formulas for cones, cylinders, and spheres.

- Prepare a variety of problems and settings for students to solve real-world and mathematical problems by applying the volume formulas for cones, cylinders, and spheres.

What the STUDENTS do:

- Participate in experiments that help them derive the volume formulas for cones, cylinders, and spheres.

- Explain in writing their understanding of the volume formulas for cones, cylinders, and spheres.

- Solve mathematical and real-world problems that involve finding the volumes of cones, cylinders, and spheres.

Addressing Student Misconceptions and Common Errors

Students may confuse the three formulas if they are asked to memorize them without any understanding of why they make sense. It is important to spend time on the derivations and have students physically take part and make the discoveries for themselves.

Geometry

Cluster A: Understand congruence and similarity using physical models, transparencies, or geometry software.

Standard: 8.G.A.1. *Verify experimentally the properties of rotations, reflections, and translations:*

a. Lines are taken to lines, and line segments to line segments of the same length.

b. Angles are taken to angles of the same measure.

c. Parallel lines are taken to parallel lines.

Standards for Mathematical Practice:

SFMP 4. Model with mathematics.

Students find or create models of transformations: reflections, rotations, and translations.

Goal:

Students identify reflections, rotations, and translations for later use with congruency and similarity.

Planning:

Materials: job posting, art supplies, cameras, and computers

Sample Activity:

- Each student receives a copy of a job vacancy for a fictitious company. The announcement lists several requirements.

- Over the course of a week, students create a portfolio that matches the requirement in the job vacancy. They also create a cover letter demonstrating their knowledge of transformations. A sample job vacancy notice is as follows:

JOB VACANCY ANNOUNCEMENT

Design, Inc. is looking to hire an art designer who is familiar with translations.

Salary: $99,999/year

To apply, submit a cover letter along with a portfolio that contains the following items:

1. Three examples each of rotations, reflections, and translations. You may draw these or submit pictures, etc. as long as you show us you understand what they are. Be sure to label each with the name of the transformations.

2. Your cover letter should include why you want to work for us and explain how well you really understand transformations.

- Students have 1 week to complete the application and submit it.

Questions/Prompts:

- For students who do not know where to get the examples of the transformations, ask, *"Did we do anything in class where we explored transformations in the real-world? What did we find? Can you take pictures of them or print them?"*

- For students having trouble with the cover letter, ask them, *"Tell me what you know about reflections. Can you write that down?"*

Differentiating Instruction:

Struggling Students: Allow these students class time to consult with the teacher to keep them motivated. Have cameras, computers, and art supplies available for them. Throughout the unit, it is helpful to show examples of transformations found on the Internet, in wallpaper, on fabric, and so on.

Extension: Allow students to collect resources outside of school and bring them into the classroom for this project.

Notes

Geometry

Cluster A: Understand congruence and similarity using physical models, transparencies, or geometry software.

Standard:

Standards for Mathematical Practice:

Goal:

Planning:

Materials:

Sample Activity:

Questions/Prompts:

Differentiating Instruction:

Struggling Students:

Extension:

Geometry

Cluster B: Understand and apply the Pythagorean Theorem.

Standard:

Standards for Mathematical Practice:

Goal:

Planning:

Materials:

Sample Activity:

Questions/Prompts:

Differentiating Instruction:

Struggling Students:

Extension:

Geometry

Cluster C: Solve real-world and mathematical problems involving volume of cylinders, cones, and spheres.

Standard:

Standards for Mathematical Practice:

Goal:

Planning:

Materials:

Sample Activity:

Questions/Prompts:

Differentiating Instruction:

Struggling Students:

Extension:

Reflection Questions: Geometry

1. Discuss the big mathematical ideas in geometry at each grade level (6–8).

2. Discuss the Van Hiele Theory of Geometric Thought and how it informs the instruction for 6–8 geometry standards.

3. Discuss the difference in student learning when formulas are presented for memorization rather than derived with the students.

Statistics and Probability

Statistics and Probability

Domain Overview

GRADE 6
A major focus for sixth graders is to develop an understanding of statistical thinking. Students study measures of center and variability with newly learned knowledge of mean, median, mode, and range. Using dot plots, histograms, and box plots, students draw inferences and make comparisons between data sets. At this level, students recognize that a data distribution may not have a definite center and that different ways to measure center provide different values. Students discover that interpreting different measures of center for the same data develops the understanding of how each measure can change how data get interpreted.

GRADE 7
In seventh grade, students learn that statistics can be used to gain information about a population by examining a sample of the population. They draw inferences about a population and also draw informal comparative inferences about two populations. Seventh graders investigate and learn that the probability of a chance event is a number between 0 and 1. They develop a probability model and use it to find probabilities of events.

GRADE 8
The study of statistics in eighth grade focuses on constructing and interpreting scatter plots for bivariate measurement data to investigate patterns of association between two quantities. Students describe these patterns as clusters, outliers, positive or negative association, and linear or nonlinear association. Eighth graders learn that patterns of association can also be seen in bivariate categorical data by displaying frequencies and relative frequencies in a two-way table.

SUGGESTED MATERIALS FOR THIS DOMAIN

6	7	8	
	✓		Bags of colored marbles
	✓		Coins or two-sided counters
	✓		Dice or number cubes
	✓	✓	Graphing calculators
✓	✓	✓	Graph paper (large chart size and individual size)
	✓		Spinners

KEY VOCABULARY

6	7	8	
		✓	**bivariate data** data in two variables, one to be graphed on the *x*-axis and the other on the *y*-axis
✓			**box plot** a visual graphical display to show the median, quartiles, and extremes of a data set on a number line and the distribution of the data
✓		✓	**categorical data** data that can be sorted in groups or categories such as hair color, shoe size, and so on
	✓		**certain event** event with a probability of 1 on a scale from 0 to 1
	✓		**compound event** event in a sample space that has been constructed from two other sample spaces (sample space for tossing a coin and sample space for rolling a die)
✓	✓	✓	**data** descriptive facts or numbers
✓			**dot plot** a graphical number line display of data using dots
	✓		**event** a set of outcomes
	✓	✓	**frequency** the number of times a number or event occurs in a set of data
✓			**histogram** a visual graph that displays frequency of continuous data using bars. A histogram usually groups the data in ranges with no space between the bars.
✓	✓		**interquartile range** measure of variability; the difference between the first quartile and third quartile of a set of data. It is a way to describe the spread of a set of data or how the data are scattered.
	✓		**likelihood** how likely, unlikely, equally likely, certain, or impossible an event is to occur
	✓		**likely** an event that is likely has a probability approaching 1

(Continued)

(Continued)

6	7	8	
✓	✓	✓	**mean** the sum of the numbers in a set of data divided by the number of pieces of data; usually called "average"; arithmetic mean
✓	✓		**mean absolute deviation** the mean of the absolute deviations from the mean of each point in the data set
✓	✓		**measures of center** numerical values used to describe the overall clustering of data in a set; the overall "average" of a set of data. Three measures of central tendency are mean, median, and mode.
✓	✓		**measures of variation** range, interquartile range
✓	✓		**median** the number in the middle of a set of data when the data are arranged in order. When there are two middle numbers, the median is their mean.
	✓		**outcome** an element in the sample space
		✓	**outlier** a number in a data set that is significantly smaller or larger than the other number
	✓		**population** the entire set from which data can be selected
	✓		**probability** the measure of the likelihood of an event
	✓		**random sample** a sample chosen from a population in which each data in the population has an equal chance of being chosen
✓	✓		**sample** a selection from a population
✓	✓		**sample space** the set of all possible outcomes for a probability experiment. Sample spaces can be displayed as diagrams, lists, and tables.
	✓	✓	**scatter plot** the graph of a collection of ordered pairs
	✓		**simulation** an experiment that models a real-life situation; often done with technology
✓	✓	✓	**statistics** the collection, organization, and analysis of data
✓		✓	**statistical question** a question that anticipates variability in the data
	✓		**survey data** information (numerical or categorical) collected by asking questions of members of a population
	✓		**unlikely** an event that is unlikely has a probability approaching 0
✓	✓	✓	**variability** measure of spread. A measure of spread tells us how much a data sample is spread out or scattered.

Statistics and Probability
6.SP.A

Develop understanding of statistical variability.

STANDARD 1   **6.SP.A.1:** Recognize a statistical question as one that anticipates variability in the data related to the question and accounts for it in the answers. *For example, "How old am I?" is not a statistical question, but "How old are the students in my school?" is a statistical question because one anticipates variability in students' ages.*

STANDARD 2   **6.SP.A.2:** Understand that a set of data collected to answer a statistical question has a distribution which can be described by its center, spread, and overall shape.

STANDARD 3   **6.SP.A.3:** Recognize that a measure of center for a numerical data set summarizes all of its values with a single number, while a measure of variation describes how its values vary with a single number.

Statistics and Probability   6.SP.A

Cluster A: Develop understanding of statistical variability.

Grade 6 Overview

At the sixth-grade level, students learn how to write statistical questions used to survey and collect data. They study the key idea that data distribution may not have a definite center. Students discover that different ways to measure center produce different values and that interpreting measures of center for the same data develops the understanding of how each measure can change how the data get interpreted.

Standards for Mathematical Practice

SFMP 3. Construct viable arguments and critique the reasoning of others.

Students write and share their own statistical questions that can be used to survey and collect data from other classmates. They explain their thinking to others and respond to others' thinking.

SFMP 4. Model with mathematics.

Students use measures of center and variability and data displays to draw inferences about and make comparisons between data sets.

SFMP 6. Attend to precision.

Students communicate precisely with others and use clear mathematical language when describing and explaining the connections between different representations of data sets.

Related Content Standards

6.SP.B.4   6.SP.B.5   6.SP.B.5.a   6.SP.B.5.b   6.SP.B.5.c   6.SP.B.5.d   7.SP.A.1   7.SP.A.2
7.SP.B.3   7.SP.B.4

Recognize a statistical question as one that anticipates variability in the data related to the question and accounts for it in the answers. For example, "How old am I?" is not a statistical question, but "How old are the students in my school?" is a statistical question because one anticipates variability in students' ages.

The focus for this standard is identifying the difference between statistical and non-statistical questions and formulating/ writing simple questions to provide differences in responses. A statistical question must be stated so that responses will allow for differences. In the example, *"What color are the shoes I am wearing?"* only one response can be given. However, with the example, *"What colors of shoes are the students in our class wearing?"* a variety of responses can be collected. Students recognize responses to statistical questions have variations that may be used to draw conclusions about the data set.

What the TEACHER does:

- Allow students to discover that statistics is the study of numerical information, called data, through classroom discussion of examples. Statisticians collect, organize, and analyze data around a statistical question. A statistical question is used to collect statistical information. Discuss with students that a statistical question must be stated so that responses will allow for differences. In the example, *"What color are the shoes I am wearing?"* only one response can be given. However, with the example, *"What colors of shoes are the students in our class wearing?"* a variety of responses can be collected.

- Provide numerous examples for students to sort and categorize questions as statistical or non-statistical.

- Invite students to write and share their own statistical questions that can be used to survey and collect data from other classmates. Sixth graders need multiple experiences writing statistical questions.

- Focus on the following vocabulary terms: *statistics, data,* and *variability.*

- Allow students to talk with one another and the teacher to make sense of the definition of statistics, recognizing statistical questions and anticipating variability in the data related to the question.

What the STUDENTS do:

- Understand that data generated from statistical questions vary.

- Identify the difference between a statistical and non-statistical question.

- Recognize that responses to statistical questions have variations that can be used to draw conclusions about the data set.

- Formulate and write simple statistical questions that provide differences in responses.

Addressing Student Misconceptions and Common Errors

Since sixth grade introduces the first formal study of statistics, many students may write questions that do not allow for differences or a variety of responses. To help with this, provide repetitive practice and guidance to help the students write statistical questions having variations that may be used to draw conclusions about the data. Do many sorting activities with these students. Play the example/non-example game where the teacher displays two columns. In the first column, the teacher lists two or three examples, and in the second, the teacher lists two or three non-examples. From these lists, students try to guess what concept the teacher is making examples of. As students think they know the concept or want to test their hypothesis of what is the same about all the examples in the first column, the students add examples and non-examples to the lists, thereby providing more examples for the students who do not understand the concept. This aids students who need more time and more examples to help them focus on the concept.

STANDARD 2 (6.SP.A.2)

Understand that a set of data collected to answer a statistical question has a distribution which can be described by its center, spread, and overall shape.

Standard 2 focuses on the understanding that data collected to answer a statistical question can be analyzed by their distribution. A distribution is the arrangement of the values of a data set and is described as using its center (median or mean) and spread. The single value for each of the measures of center (mean, median, or mode) and measures of spread (range) is used to summarize the data. By finding the measures of center for a set of data, students use the value to describe the data in words. Students use histograms and box plots to describe a set of data using its center (mean, median, and mode), spread (range), and overall shape.

What the TEACHER does:

- Pose questions to the class to collect and analyze data, such as, *"How long does it take you to do your homework?"* Or, *"How many text messages do you estimate getting each day?"* Have the students create dot plots to examine the distribution of the data set and discuss the center, spread, and overall shape.

- Examine the data by finding the mean, median, mode, and range of the data. These concepts are new to the students, so let them discover and report back to the class what each term means and how they will find the mean, median, mode, and range for their dot plots. Divide the class into groups of four. Each group will study one of the concepts and report back to the class what they learned.

  ○ One group of students should report that the **mean** is a measure of center of that data summarized by a single number and that it represents the arithmetic average of the data. To find the mean of a data set, add all the values together and divide by the number of values in the set.

  ○ Another group should say that the **median** is a measure of center of that data summarized by a single number and represents the point at which 50% of the data is greater than or equal to that number and 50% is less than or equal to that number. To find the median, place the numbers in value order and then find the middle.

  ○ The third group of students should state that the **mode** of a set of numerical data represents the center of that data summarized by a single number. It represents the most frequent value of a set of data. To find the mode, put the numbers in order from least to greatest and count how many times each number occurs. The number that occurs the most is the mode. Note that some data sets are bimodal, meaning two numbers occur equally as much or more than the rest of the data points.

  ○ The last group of students should explain that the **range** of a set of numerical data is a measure of how the data vary, summarized by a single number. To find the range, subtract the highest and the lowest numbers in the set of data.

- Note that the suggested ideas will likely take 1 week to 10 days of instructional time. Keep in mind that students are *beginning* to develop their ability to think statistically with the key focus of describing and summarizing numerical data sets. After the graphs have been created by each student, focus on summarizing the data represented by the graphs. Describe the data using measures of center (mean, median, mode) and the spread and the overall shape of the data.

- Emphasize the following vocabulary terms: *distribution, center, spread, overall shape, histograms, line plots, box plots, outliers, quartiles, upper and lower extreme,* and *whiskers.*

- Provide cyclical, distributed reviews over time to practice collecting data to answer a statistical question with a distribution described by its center, spread, and overall shape.

What the STUDENTS do:

- Understand that data collected to answer a statistical question can be analyzed by their distribution.

- Calculate mean, median, mode, and range.

- Describe a set of data using its center (mean, median, and mode), spread (range), and overall shape.

- Create a line plot, histogram, and box plot.

Addressing Student Misconceptions and Common Errors

Some students may describe the spread of the data as low to high such as 6–21. Remind students that spread (range) is stated as a single number such as 15 and describes how the values vary across the data set. Stress that the purpose of the number is not the value itself but the interpretation it provides for the variation of the data.

Box plots seem complicated to some students because of the numerous steps involved in creating them. Keep in mind that students are *beginning* to develop their ability to think statistically, and this new learning must focus around students learning to *describe and summarize numerical data sets* and not just the procedure of creating the graphs. Technology can be used to create these graphs. Free programs are available on the Internet as are YouTube videos and commercially produced software packages.

The terms needed for describing data, including distribution, center, spread, overall shape, histograms, line plots, box plots, outliers, quartiles, upper and lower extreme, and whiskers, are all new to the students. Creating visual graphic vocabulary organizers such as the Frayer model (see Reproducible 2) will help students make sense of the terms they need to describe the data.

Notes

STANDARD 3 (6.SP.A.3)

Recognize that a measure of center for a numerical data set summarizes all of its values with a single number, while a measure of variation describes how its values vary with a single number.

This standard helps students understand that a data distribution may not have a definite center. Sixth graders discover that different ways to measure center produce different values. The median measures center as the middle value. The mean measures center as the value that each data point would take on if the total of the data values were redistributed equally. It is a balance point. Students recognize that a measure of variability can also summarize data because two very different sets of data can have the same median and mean but differ by their variability.

What the TEACHER does:

- Explain that interpreting different measures of center for the same data develops the understanding of how each measure can change how the data get interpreted.

- Plan activities that require students to match graphs to explanations or measures of center.

- Have students create a paper foldable such as a layered book with two sheets of layered paper to illustrate and compare the similarities and differences of mean, median, and mode. Include range, although it is not a measure of center. Stack and layer two sheets of 8½ × 11-inch paper. Be sure that the bottom sheet is about 1 inch higher than the top sheets in the stack. Create the layered book by folding the two sheets from the bottom up so that the layers leave flaps about the same distance apart. Write the terms as shown below and instruct students to flip up a tab to illustrate and write comparisons to show the similarities and differences. This may help students begin to understand the purposes among the measures of center (mean, median, and mode) and the distinction between center and spread.

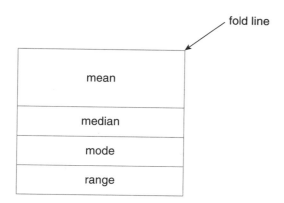

What the STUDENTS do:

- Understand how to find mean, median, mode, and range.

- Model with examples the difference between measures of center and measures of spread.

- Determine appropriate center and variation for various data sets.

- Focus on the following vocabulary terms: *measure of center, mean, median, mode,* and *range.*

- Allow students to talk with each other and the teacher to make sense of and recognize that a measure of center for a numerical data set summarizes all of its values with a single number, while a measure of variation describes how its values vary with a single number.

- Provide cyclical, distributed reviews over time to promote the understanding of measure of center and identify mean, median, and mode given different data sets.

Addressing Student Misconceptions and Common Errors

Some sixth graders may forget to divide when finding the mean. Additional practice may help. Students are often under the misconception that range is also a measure of center. This distinction between center and variation should be made.

Sometimes students use the word *average* when they want to discuss mean. Model use of the term *average* as an inclusive term for many different measures of center, not just the mean. The word *average* connotes many different concepts for students that are not mathematical because the word has many uses in everyday language. A short lesson where students offer mathematical terms that have different meanings in everyday life can be enlightening for these students. A few of those terms are: *table* (a kitchen table vs. a chart), *pie* (apple pie vs. π), and *ruler* (king vs. a measuring tool).

Notes

Statistics and Probability
6.SP.B

Cluster B

Summarize and describe distributions.

STANDARD 4 **6.SP.B.4:** Display numerical data in plots on a number line, including dot plots, histograms, and box plots.

STANDARD 5 **6.SP.B.5:** Summarize numerical data sets in relation to their context, such as by:

   a. Reporting the number of observations.
   b. Describing the nature of the attribute under investigation, including how it was measured and its units of measurement.
   c. Giving quantitative measures of center (median and/or mean) and variability (interquartile range and/or mean absolute deviation), as well as describing any overall pattern and any striking deviations from the overall pattern with reference to the context in which the data were gathered.
   d. Relating the choice of measures of center and variability to the shape of the data distribution and the context in which the data were gathered.

Statistics and Probability   6.SP.B

Cluster B: Summarize and describe distributions.
Grade 6 Overview

Students display data on line plots, histograms, and box plots with the focus of summarizing and describing distributions. Students summarize numerical data by providing background information about the attribute being measured, methods and unit of measurement, and the context of data collection activities, including random samples, the number of observations, and summary statistics.

Standards for Mathematical Practice
SFMP 4. Model with mathematics.

Students display data graphically in a format appropriate for a particular set of data.

SFMP 6. Attend to precision.

Students communicate precisely with others and use clear mathematical language when summarizing, describing, and reading data from graphs generated by other students.

Related Content Standards

6.SP.A.1   6.SP.A.2   6.SP.3   7.SP.A.1   7.SP.A.2   7.SP.B.3   7.SP.B.4

Notes
_____
_____
_____

Display numerical data in plots on a number line, including dot plots, histograms, and box plots.

Students learn how to display data on dot plots, histograms, and box plots (also known as box and whisker plots). A dot plot is appropriate for small- to moderate-size data sets of up to 25 numbers and is useful for highlighting the distribution and spread of the data, including clusters, gaps, and outliers. Histograms display the distribution of continuous data using intervals on a number line. Box plots display the distribution of values in a data set by dividing the set into quartiles. After creating the plots students interpret them, giving meaning to the context with statements such as, *"There is little variation in these data because the range on this box plot is 3."* Sixth graders learn to select the most appropriate display to represent the given data.

What the TEACHER does:

- Provide experiences for students to learn about displaying numerical data in plots on a number line, including dot plots, histograms, and box plots. Students must be able to choose an appropriate graph and display the data. They should be able to explain the data generated from the graphs.

- Pose a question or idea for students to create a dot plot. Dot plots are plots on a number line where each dot is representative of a piece of data in the set. To make a dot plot, first title the plot. Draw a horizontal line segment on grid paper. Make a scale of numbers below the line. The numbers should include the least value and the greatest value in the set of data. For each piece of data, draw an X *or* dot above the corresponding number.

- Ask students questions about the dot plots to ensure understanding, such as, *"What does each X on the graph represent?"* or *"What is the range of the data?"* Ask them to interpret the plot to give meaning to the context of the data with a summary.

- Pose a question or idea for students to create and explore histograms. The height of each bar represents the number of data values in that interval. Data are grouped into interval ranges. To make a histogram, it is helpful to make a frequency table first. Choose a range that contains all the data and divide it into equal intervals. After making the frequency table, it is easy to make the histogram because it is like making a bar graph, except each bar represents an interval and there are no spaces between the bars. Ask students questions about the histograms to ensure understanding, such as, *"How do the intervals on a histogram present different information than the bars on a bar graph?"* Ask them to interpret the histogram they create to give meaning to the context of the data with a summary. An example of a histogram follows.

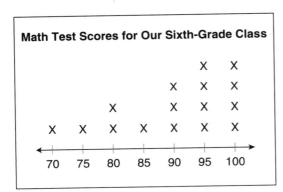

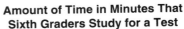
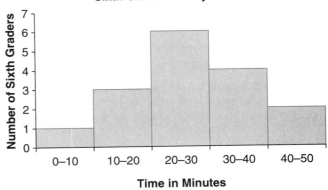

(continued)

What the TEACHER does (continued):

- Pose a question or an idea to help students experience a box plot. It can be graphed either vertically or horizontally and includes a lower quartile, a median, an upper quartile, and maximum. These values give a summary of the shape of a distribution. Students should understand that the size of the box or whiskers represents the middle 50% of the data. To make a box and whisker plot, first collect data. Organize them from least to greatest. Draw a number line that will show the data in equal intervals. Mark the median. Mark the median of the upper half (upper quartile). Mark the median of the lower half (lower quartile). Mark the upper extreme. Mark the lower extreme. Draw a box between the lower quartile and the upper quartile. Split the box by drawing a vertical line through the median. Draw 2 whiskers from the quartiles to the extremes. An example of a box plot for test grades from a mathematics class:

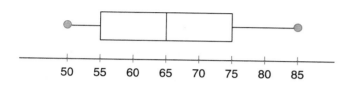

- After students create a box plot, ask questions to check for understanding about a box plot, such as, "*What does a whisker tell you about the data? What questions can you NOT answer from a box and whisker plot?*" Ask students to interpret the box and whisker plot to give meaning to the context of the data with a summary.

- Allow students to explore contextual sets of data and have them decide which statistical graph is best suited to the data.

- Model correct use of the following terms: *dot plots, histograms,* and *box plots.*

- Provide cyclical, distributed practice over time to review displaying numerical data in dot plots, histograms, and box plots and interpreting these graphs.

What the STUDENTS do:

- Understand that data are organized in graphs for the purpose of analyzing the data.

- Represent given data on the most appropriate graph (dot plot, histogram, or box plot).

- Interpret data represented on dot plots, box plots, and histograms for given situations.

Addressing Student Misconceptions and Common Errors

Confusing histograms and bar graphs is a common error students have that makes it difficult for them to interpret the intervals. Display histograms and bar graphs side by side with related data and ask students to compare and contrast what you can learn from each graph.

Notes

Summarize numerical data sets in relation to their context, such as by:

    a. *Reporting the number of observations.*

    b. *Describing the nature of the attribute under investigation, including how it was measured and its units of measurement.*

    c. *Giving quantitative measures of center (median and/or mean) and variability (interquartile range and/or mean absolute deviation), as well as describing any overall pattern and any striking deviations from the overall pattern with reference to the context in which the data were gathered.*

    d. *Relating the choice of measures of center and variability to the shape of the data distribution and the context in which the data were gathered.*

This standard emphasizes summarizing data. Students communicate a deep understanding of (1) observations (sample size, sometimes labeled as the n of the data), (2) appropriate measure of center and spread for a particular data set, (3) appropriate section of a graph to represent data collected, and (4) overall patterns in a distribution, including outliers, through statistical investigation.

What the TEACHER does:

- Begin by exploring plots (graphs) and asking students to find and report the number of observations. Ensure that students understand observation means sample size or n size and how it relates to numerical data sets. For example, a set of data with 10 data points has 10 observations, or we can say $n = 10$. Ensure that students understand and can explain why the number of observations is important to summarizing numerical data sets. Ensure students know the difference between intervals and observations.

- Provide a variety of samples of plots from newspapers and allow students to identify attributes under investigation, including how the attributes were measured and their units of measure.

- Invite students to ask a statistical question of interest, collect data to answer the question, and display the data on an appropriate graph. Ask students to summarize the data in a presentation given to the class that includes: (1) the number of observations; (2) a description of the attributes investigated, including how they were measured and the units used; (3) a measure of center and a measure of variability along with a defense for the various measures chosen; and (4) any overall pattern in the distribution or outliers noted.

- Teach mean absolute deviation (MAD) as a measure of variability. The mean absolute deviation of a set of data is the average distance between each data value and the mean. To find the mean absolute deviation, first find the mean. Next find the distance between each data value in the set and the mean. Then find the absolute value of the differences. Finally, find the mean of those differences. For an activity on mean absolution deviation, see the Sample Planning Page on page **212**.

- Design a class activity to interpret data with a box and whisker plot. Have each student estimate and record how many hours of TV they watch in a month and then graph the data as a class on a line plot. Interpret the data and create a box and whisker plot. Use the box and whisker plot to show variation of data.

- Focus on the following vocabulary terms: *box plots, dot plots, histograms, frequency tables, cluster, gap, mean, median, interquartile range, measures of center, measures of variability, data, mean absolute deviation, quartiles, lower quartile (first quartile or Q1), upper quartile (third quartile or Q3), symmetrical, skewed, summary statistics, outlier,* and *whiskers.*

- Provide cyclical, distributed practice over time to review and summarize numerical data sets in relation to their contexts.

- Allow students to talk with each other and their teacher to make sense of Standard 5.

What the STUDENTS do:

- Perform a statistical investigation, including the collection, organization, and analysis of the data. Analysis should include the appropriate statistics from mean, median, interquartile range, measures of center, measures of variability, data, mean absolute deviation, quartiles, lower quartile (first quartile or Q1), and upper quartile (third quartile or Q3).

- Calculate mean absolute deviation (MAD) for a data set and explain that MAD is the mean of the absolute values of the differences of each point in the data set from the mean of the data set.

- Communicate a deep understanding of (1) observations, (2) appropriate measure of center and spread for a particular data set, (3) appropriate section of a graph to represent data collected, and (4) overall patterns in a distribution, including outliers, through statistical investigation.

Addressing Student Misconceptions and Common Errors

Mean absolute deviation (MAD) is problematic for many students both procedurally and conceptually. Although the computation is clear, students forget steps, confuse the steps, and so on. To help with the procedure, it is useful to create a three-column table with the following headings: data, distance from the mean, and absolute value of distance from the mean. For example, if the mean of the following set of data is 60, a table to find the MAD would look like this:

Data Points	Distance From Mean	Absolute Value of Distances
65	+5	5
58	−2	2
60	0	0

From the table, students need to only calculate the mean of the values in column 3.

The concept is also very difficult at this age level. Be aware of this and allow adequate time to develop the concept of mean absolute deviation. This will make a difference with student understanding and application. Many of the challenges students often have will be avoided if students deeply understand the concept of MAD.

Notes

Statistics and Probability

Cluster B: Summarize and describe distributions.

Standard: 6.SP.B.5.c. *Giving quantitative measures of center (median and/or mean) and variability (interquartile range and/or mean absolute deviation), as well as describing any overall pattern and any striking deviations from the overall pattern with reference to the context in which the data were gathered.*

Standards for Mathematical Practice:

SFMP 4. Model with mathematics.

Students use measures of center and variability (range and mean absolute deviation) and data displays to draw inferences about a data set.

Goal:

Students collect data and interpret the mean absolute deviation for the data set.

Planning:

Materials: pencil and paper

Sample Activity:

- Begin by having students individually collect data from eight classmates with the task to find out approximately how many text messages the students send in 1 week.

- Students compile a list collected from their fellow students such as 40, 50, 58, 82, 66, 48, 72, and 88 texts.

- Direct students to find the mean absolute deviation of the set of data and describe the meaning of MAD and what it represents.

- First students need to find the arithmetic mean by adding together 40, 50, 58, 82, 66, 48, 72, and 88. The sum of the numbers is 504. Next divide by 8 to find the mean of 63. This is interpreted as 63 texts per person.

- Have students find the absolute value of the differences between each value in the data set and the mean. It is suggested that students create a dot plot (line plot) to visually observe the differences as shown:

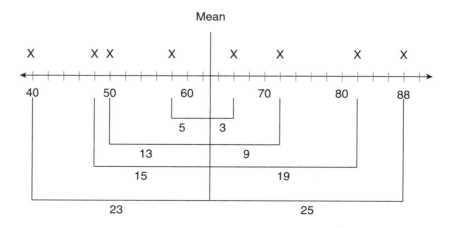

- Students should note that 82 is 19 units away from the mean of 63.
- Finally, ask students to find the average of the absolute value of the differences between each value in the data set and mean. Students add $5 + 3 + 13 + 9 + 15 + 19 + 23 + 25 = 112$ and then divide by $8 = 14$. This is the mean absolute deviation. Students interpret this as the average distance between each data value from the mean is 14 texts, meaning that this is how far apart the data is spread.

Questions/Prompts:

- Ask students to explain how they found the mean of the data.
- Ask students to explain which value is the closest to the mean and which is the farthest.
- Ask students to interpret the data values as close or far away from the mean.

Differentiating Instruction:

Struggling Students: Mean absolute deviation is a very difficult concept for sixth graders. Help struggling learners find mean absolute deviation (MAD) with the four main steps they will need to follow. (1) Find the mean of a collection of data. (2) Find the distance between each data value and the mean. (3) Take the absolute value of the distances. (4) Find the mean of the absolute values of the distances. Sometimes creating a table where students can enter the first three steps of the algorithm for MAD is helpful. After discussing each step, have students create a visual list of the four steps with examples to display as a bulletin board. Struggling learners will need many repetitions of practice to internalize the concept and procedure used for mean absolute deviation.

Extension: Students who understand the concept of mean absolute deviation can be challenged to collect their own data and use the interquartile range from a box and whisker plot to describe the variability of a data set.

Notes

Statistics and Probability

Cluster A: Develop understanding of statistical variability.

Standard:

Standards for Mathematical Practice:

Goal:

Planning:

Materials:

Sample Activity:

Questions/Prompts:

Differentiating Instruction:

Struggling Students:

Extension:

Statistics and Probability

Cluster B: Summarize and describe distributions.

Standard:

Standards for Mathematical Practice:

Goal:

Planning:

Materials:

Sample Activity:

Questions/Prompts:

Differentiating Instruction:

Struggling Students:

Extension:

Statistics and Probability
7.SP.A*

Use random sampling to draw inferences about a population.

STANDARD 1   **7.SP.A.1:** Understand that statistics can be used to gain information about a population by examining a sample of the population; generalizations about a population from a sample are valid only if the sample is representative of that population. Understand that random sampling tends to produce representative samples and support valid inferences.

STANDARD 2   **7.SP.A.2:** Use data from a random sample to draw inferences about a population with an unknown characteristic of interest. Generate multiple samples (or simulated samples) of the same size to gauge the variation in estimates or predictions. *For example, estimate the mean word length in a book by randomly sampling words from the book; predict the winner of a school election based on randomly sampled survey data. Gauge how far off the estimate or prediction might be.*

*Supporting cluster

Statistics and Probability   7.SP.A

Cluster A: Use random sampling to draw inferences about a population.
Grade 7 Overview

In this cluster students learn about sampling populations. Specifically, they learn that a sampling must be representative of a population in order to make valid inferences and generalizations. Students conduct multiple samples of the same size from populations with an unknown characteristic to measure variation in estimates or predictions about the characteristic.

Standards for Mathematical Practice
SFMP 2. Reason abstractly and quantitatively.

Students make generalizations and predictions based on random samples.

SFMP 3. Construct viable arguments and critique the reasoning of others.

Students use statistical methods as justification for predictions and inferences.

SFMP 4. Model with mathematics.

Students develop probability models and use them to find probabilities of events.

SFMP 5. Use appropriate tools strategically.

Students use organized lists, tables, tree diagrams, and simulation tools.

Related Content Standards

6.SP.A.1   8.SP.A.4   HSS.IC.A.1   HSS.IC.B.3

STANDARD 1 (7.SP.A.1)

Understand that statistics can be used to gain information about a population by examining a sample of the population; generalizations about a population from a sample are valid only if the sample is representative of that population. Understand that random sampling tends to produce representative samples and support valid inferences.

Sampling is taught in this standard as a statistical tool used to gain information about a population without examining the entire population. Sampling is the process of taking a subset of subjects that is representative of the entire population and collecting data on that subset. The sample must have sufficient size to warrant statistical analysis. Samples need to be representative of the population in order to make valid generalizations and, therefore, should be randomly selected. A random sampling guarantees that each element of the population has an equal opportunity to be selected in the sample. An example of a random sample is taking a list of names at a school and selecting every fourth person to be in the sample to represent the population of the school.

What the TEACHER does:

- Facilitate a discussion about statistics as an introduction. Ask students questions such as, *"What is statistics? Why do we study it? How is it useful?"*

- Propose a generalization about students at your school such as, *"Students at our school do at least 5 hours of homework per night."* Sample discussion questions include, *"How do I know that is true? Is it true? Is this a valid generalization?"* Facilitate a whole class discussion about sampling. Model vocabulary: *sampling, population,* and *valid generalization.*

- Ask students to work with a partner to brainstorm three ways to collect a sampling of data. Share the methods and facilitate a class discussion with questions that lead to the importance of random samples. Sample questions may include the following: *"Is it possible to ask everyone at the school? Are all grade levels included in the sample? Are all the elements of the entire population represented in the sample? Are the elements represented proportionally? Should there be the same number of boys and girls in the sample? Define random sample and how it is representative of a population."* Allow students to offer random sampling ideas.

- Provide a list of sampling examples for students to critique. Ask students, *"Are they random?"* Look for students to use appropriate vocabulary in their critiques.

What the STUDENTS do:

- Critique examples of random sampling as statistical tools using precise mathematical vocabulary: *random sampling, population,* and *valid generalizations.*

- Design random samplings to collect the data given statistical questions. Defend the samplings as random.

Addressing Student Misconceptions and Common Errors

This domain has many vocabulary words for students to learn and use. Use word walls and the Frayer model (see Reproducible 2). For words that are easily confused, have students create foldables.

The concept of random is difficult for some students. It may be necessary to physically demonstrate a random versus non-random sampling to eliminate misconceptions for these students. For example, a non-random sampling in the classroom would be to ask all the girls to stand up to answer a question about video game preferences. A random sample would be to ask every third student to stand up and answer the same question. Ask students how the answers were different in the girls sampling than the mixed sampling and how the generalizations would be different from each group.

Use data from a random sample to draw inferences about a population with an unknown characteristic of interest. Generate multiple samples (or simulated samples) of the same size to gauge the variation in estimates or predictions. For example, estimate the mean word length in a book by randomly sampling words from the book; predict the winner of a school election based on randomly sampled survey data. Gauge how far off the estimate or prediction might be.

This standard connects to 7.SP.A.1 by using the sample data collected to draw inferences. Generate multiple samples of the same size from a given population to examine the variation in estimates or predictions. This standard provides an introduction to variability. An example of data to collect is two random samples of 100 students about school lunch preferences.

School Lunches Preferred				
Sample	Burgers	Salad	Pizza	Total
#1	13	13	74	100
#2	12	11	77	100

What the TEACHER does:

- Use random samples from examples done in class to draw inferences. Ask students to draw inferences and valid generalizations and make predictions whenever random data are collected in class. Expect students to use appropriate vocabulary when explaining the sampling process and their generalizations.

- Collect multiple samples. Using examples, discuss why someone would want to use this technique and why the samples need to be the same size.

- Give students practice collecting multiple samples after making estimates or predictions for given situations such as estimating the mean word length in a book. Gauge how far off estimates are.

What the STUDENTS do:

- Draw valid inferences and generalizations from random samplings of populations and justify their inferences and generalizations as valid using appropriate vocabulary.

- Explain the variability in multiple random samples and gauge how far off an estimate may be.

Addressing Student Misconceptions and Common Errors

Students may have difficulty understanding why it is necessary to conduct multiple samples of the same size. A misconception is that only one of the samples is correct. Conduct multiple data collections in class so that students realize that none of the samples are exactly the population, but together they provide a good picture of the population.

Notes

Statistics and Probability
7.SP.B

Draw informal comparative inferences about two populations.

STANDARD 3 **7.SP.B.3:** Informally assess the degree of visual overlap of two numerical data distributions with similar variabilities, measuring the difference between the centers by expressing it as a multiple of a measure of variability. *For example, the mean height of players on the basketball team is 10 cm greater than the mean height of players on the soccer team, about twice the variability (mean absolute deviation) on either team; on a dot plot, the separation between the two distributions of heights is noticeable.*

STANDARD 4 **7.SP.B.4:** Use measures of center and measures of variability for numerical data from random samples to draw informal comparative inferences about two populations. *For example, decide whether the words in a chapter of a seventh-grade science book are generally longer than the words in a chapter of a fourth-grade science book.*

Statistics and Probability   7.SP.B

Cluster B: Draw informal comparative inferences about two populations.
Grade 7 Overview

In the previous cluster students worked with one population. In this cluster students draw valid comparable inferences about two populations using measures of center (mean, median) and measures of variability.

Standards for Mathematical Practice
SFMP 2. Reason abstractly and quantitatively.

Students compare statistical measures on two populations.

SFMP 3. Construct viable arguments and critique the reasoning of others.

Students use statistical methods as justification for inferences.

SFMP 5. Use appropriate tools strategically.

Students use statistical functions on graphing calculators for large data sets.

SFMP 6. Attend to precision.

Students calculate measures of center and variability with accuracy.

Related Content Standards

6.SP.A.3   6.SP.B.5   7.SP.A.2

Informally assess the degree of visual overlap of two numerical data distributions with similar variabilities, measuring the difference between the centers by expressing it as a multiple of a measure of variability. For example, the mean height of players on the basketball team is 10 cm greater than the mean height of players on the soccer team, about twice the variability (mean absolute deviation) on either team; on a dot plot, the separation between the two distributions of heights is noticeable.

Students compare statistics on two data sets for the first time. Build on their understanding of graphs, mean, median, mean absolute deviation (MAD), and interquartile range from sixth grade. Students understand that variability is responsible for the overlap of two data sets, which can be visible when the data are presented in graphic form—two dot plots or box-and-whisker plots, for example. With two data distributions with similar variability, students will express the difference between centers (mean, median, mode) as a multiple of a measure of variability. For an example see Reproducible 4.

What the TEACHER does:

- Build on students' understanding of graphs, mean, median, mean absolute deviation, and interquartile range from Grade 6 by beginning with one data set and adding a second for comparisons.

- Display two data sets presented on dot plots and ask students what they notice. Ask about the variability of the sets. Guide the discussion to point out that the greater the variability, the more overlap visible in a graph. Facilitate a discussion about why that makes sense to them.

- Provide numerical data sets that are of interest to students. Data can be found in fact books and online about sports, the environment, and government statistics—local, state, and federal. Use of contextual examples allows students to understand how to not only calculate the measures of center and variability but also understand their meaning in the given context.

- Use the example from the standard to model measuring the difference between the centers by expressing it as a multiple of a measure of variability. For a detailed example, see Reproducible 4.

- Provide opportunities for students to calculate with and without graphing calculators. Large data sets can be compared using graphing calculators.

What the STUDENTS do:

- Compare two data sets for variability by comparing graphs.

- Explain orally and/or in writing why it makes sense that the greater the variability, the more visible the overlap on graphs presenting two numerical data sets.

- Use statistical functions on graphing calculators for large data sets.

- Model and compare two real-world data sets by measuring the difference between centers and expressing it as a multiple of a measure of variability.

Addressing Student Misconceptions and Common Errors

Comparing two data sets and expressing the difference between centers as a multiple of a measure of variability has several steps. Some students become overwhelmed and need the teacher to break down the steps so they make sense. These students may need access to the graphing calculator for smaller data sets.

Measures of center and measures of variability are easily confused. Spend time concentrating on the difference between these two concepts. A foldable may help students separate the two concepts.

Notes

STANDARD 4 (7.SP.B.4)

Use measures of center and measures of variability for numerical data from random samples to draw informal comparative inferences about two populations. For example, decide whether the words in a chapter of a seventh-grade science book are generally longer than the words in a chapter of a fourth-grade science book.

Draw valid comparative inferences about two populations. The inferences are drawn from using measures of center (mean, median, mode) and variability (range, mean absolute deviation, and interquartile range) from random samples. This standard differs from the previous in that students are now drawing inferences. Using the examples from the previous standard where the data were collected will unify this work.

What the TEACHER does:

- Introduce the example by comparing it to the example from standard 7.SP.A.2 about word length in books. Ask the students how the two questions differ. (In 7.SP.A.2, there is only one data set and you are looking for only one statistic.)

- Walk through the example with the class, asking questions along the way such as, *"What should we do first? Next?"*

- Encourage students to practice using precise vocabulary as they answer the questions: *measures of center, measures of variability, mean, median, mode, range, interquartile range,* and *mean absolute deviation.*

- Present other data sets to students in different formats (dot plots, box and whisker plots, etc.) and have them determine which measures to use to compare the sets. Comparative inferences are phrases such as, *"Set A has more variability than Set B"* or *"Group 1 has the larger mean."*

- Share data sets and inferences with students and have them determine if the inferences are valid. Ask students to justify their determinations.

What the STUDENTS do:

- Identify what the question asks. This is a key step in problem solving.

- Use appropriate vocabulary when explaining key concepts and computations.

- Select the correct measure(s) of center or variability in comparing two data sets.

- Draw valid comparative inferences for two data sets.

- Identify valid inferences and justify why they are valid (or why other inferences are not valid).

Addressing Student Misconceptions and Common Errors

This standard requires the use of many new vocabulary words. This may be overwhelming to some students. Use word walls, foldables, and graphic organizers to help students become fluent in the use of these words.

Notes

Statistics and Probability
7.SP.C*

Investigate chance processes and develop, use, and evaluate probability models.

STANDARD 5

7.SP.C.5: Understand that the probability of a chance event is a number between 0 and 1 that expresses the likelihood of the event occurring. Larger numbers indicate greater likelihood. A probability near 0 indicates an unlikely event, a probability around $\frac{1}{2}$ indicates an event that is neither unlikely nor likely, and a probability near 1 indicates a likely event.

STANDARD 6

7.SP.C.6: Approximate the probability of a chance event by collecting data on the chance process that produces it and observing its long-run relative frequency, and predict the approximate relative frequency given the probability. *For example, when rolling a number cube 600 times, predict that a 3 or 6 would be rolled roughly 200 times, but probably not exactly 200 times.*

STANDARD 7

7.SP.C.7: Develop a probability model and use it to find probabilities of events. Compare probabilities from a model to observed frequencies; if the agreement is not good, explain possible sources of the discrepancy.

a. Develop a uniform probability model by assigning equal probability to all outcomes, and use the model to determine probabilities of events. *For example, if a student is selected at random from a class, find the probability that Jane will be selected and the probability that a girl will be selected.*

b. Develop a probability model (which may not be uniform) by observing frequencies in data generated from a chance process. *For example, find the approximate probability that a spinning penny will land heads up or that a tossed paper cup will land open-end down. Do the outcomes for the spinning penny appear to be equally likely based on the observed frequencies?*

STANDARD 8

7.SP.C.8: Find probabilities of compound events using organized lists, tables, tree diagrams, and simulation.

a. Understand that, just as with simple events, the probability of a compound event is the fraction of outcomes in the sample space for which the compound event occurs.

b. Represent sample spaces for compound events using methods such as organized lists, tables and tree diagrams. For an event described in everyday language (e.g., "rolling double sixes"), identify the outcomes in the sample space which compose the event.

c. Design and use a simulation to generate frequencies for compound events. *For example, use random digits as a simulation tool to approximate the answer to the question: If 40% of donors have type A blood, what is the probability that it will take at least 4 donors to find one with type A blood?*

*Supporting cluster

Statistics and Probability   7.SP.C

Cluster C: Investigate chance processes and develop, use, and evaluate probability models.
Grade 7 Overview

This cluster focuses on probability and is the first time students encounter this topic formally. Students learn the likelihood of chance events and approximate probabilities. They investigate chance using probability models they develop. The cluster begins with single events and builds up to finding the probability of compound events using tree diagrams, lists, tables, and simulations.

Standards for Mathematical Practice
SFMP 2. Reason abstractly and quantitatively.

Students use reasoning to determine the likelihood of an event.

SFMP 4. Model with mathematics.

Students construct and use probability models for chance events.

SFMP 5. Use appropriate tools strategically.

Students select from tree diagrams, organized lists, tables, and simulations to determine probabilities.

SFMP 6. Attend to precision.

Students calculate probabilities.

Related Content Standards

6.RP.A.1

Notes

STANDARD 5 (7.SP.C.5)

Understand that the probability of a chance event is a number between 0 and 1 that expresses the likelihood of the event occurring. Larger numbers indicate greater likelihood. A probability near 0 indicates an unlikely event, a probability around $\frac{1}{2}$ indicates an event that is neither unlikely nor likely, and a probability near 1 indicates a likely event.

This standard introduces students to the concept of chance with events that are likely, unlikely, or neither likely nor unlikely. Students learn to use a scale from 0–1 representing probabilities that range from impossible to certain as in the scale from 0–1 below:

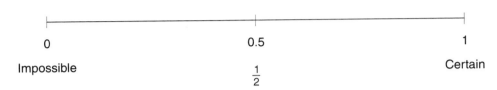

Numerical probabilities are numbers from 0–1, and the larger the number (the closer to 1), the more likely the event is to occur. A number near 0 (i.e., $\frac{1}{50}$) indicates an unlikely event and a number in the middle (≈ 0.5) is neither likely nor unlikely. A 0 probability is an impossible event, and a 1 is a certainty. Probabilities are expressed as ratios of the number of times an event occurs to the total number of trials performed. Probabilities can be represented as fractions, decimals, and percents.

What the TEACHER does:

- Promote discussion about events in the students' lives and how likely they are to occur. For example, *"How likely is it that lunch will be served today at 3:00?"*

- Display a scale from 0–1 and have students add the events they discussed previously to the scale based on their chance of occurring.

- Present students with blank scales and have them add daily events.

- Give students specific events to categorize as unlikely, likely, or neither likely nor unlikely. Present students with a list of events and their probabilities and ask students to justify them. Include some probabilities over 1 to be certain students understand the 0–1 scale and that anything over 1 is not a probability.

- Conduct simple probability experiments. Examples include tossing dice, flipping coins, marbles in a bag, and so on. Use these calculations (expressed in fraction, decimal, and percent forms) to determine if the events are likely, unlikely, or neither likely nor unlikely.

What the STUDENTS do:

- Understand that probabilities are numbers from 0–1 that express the likelihood of the event occurring. That probabilities closer to 1 are likely, and those closer to 0 are unlikely.

- Use reasoning to determine where a probability lies on the scale when the probability is expressed as a fraction such as $\frac{5}{8}$.

- Understand that the probability of 1 is certain and 0 is impossible.

- Justify the categorization of events as likely, unlikely, or neither likely nor unlikely and use appropriate vocabulary and the concept of probability being from 0–1.

- Conduct simple experiments and calculate probabilities.

Addressing Student Misconceptions and Common Errors

Students who do not have a solid concept of fractions will have difficulty deciding if a probability is closer to 1 or 0. Encourage these students to convert fractions to decimals or percents.

Some students may decide that selecting a blue marble from a bag with 2 blue marbles and 3 red has a probability of 2 instead of $\frac{2}{5}$. Refer these students back to the scale that only goes from 0–1.

STANDARD 6 (7.SP.C.6)

Approximate the probability of a chance event by collecting data on the chance process that produces it and observing its long-run relative frequency, and predict the approximate relative frequency given the probability. For example, when rolling a number cube 600 times, predict that a 3 or 6 would be rolled roughly 200 times, but probably not exactly 200 times.

Students collect data on chance events so that they can estimate the probability of the event. Students learn the difference between theoretical probability (probability that is calculated mathematically) and experimental probability (actual outcomes of an experiment). Seldom are the theoretical and experimental probabilities equal, although the more a simulation is repeated, the closer the theoretical and experimental probabilities become.

Relative frequency is the observed number of successful outcomes in a set number of trials. It is the observed proportion of successful events. Students learn to make predictions about the relative frequency of an event by using simulations.

GRADE 7

What the TEACHER does:

- Conduct a simple experiment with a large number of trials (i.e., spinning a spinner, marbles in a bag, coin toss). Let the students determine the theoretical probability first, and then collect data individually and compile class data. Use these data to introduce the terms *theoretical* and *experimental probability.*

- Simulate chance events in class with students collecting the data using physical objects (marbles in a bag, spinners, etc.). Students can perform experiments multiple times and pool data with other groups to look at the long-run relative frequencies.

- Have students observe the long-run relative frequency of the outcomes and predict the approximate relative frequency given the theoretical probability. For example, when rolling a number cube 600 times, predict that a 3 or 6 should be rolled 200 times (experimental probability) but probably not exactly 200 times.

- Introduce students to the use of simulations with technology to collect data on chance events. Students can collect data using graphing calculators or computer simulations found on the web (random number generators are an example).

What the STUDENTS do:

- Explain the difference between experimental and theoretical probability using appropriate vocabulary and examples.

- Collect data on chance events (hands-on events such as spinning a spinner and simulations) and approximate the relative frequency of an event given the probability.

Addressing Student Misconceptions and Common Errors

Students may want to express the relative frequency as a probability. Point out that the probability helps to determine the approximate relative frequency.

Notes

Part 6 Statistics and Probability **225**

Develop a probability model and use it to find probabilities of events. Compare probabilities from a model to observed frequencies; if the agreement is not good, explain possible sources of the discrepancy.

    a. *Develop a uniform probability model by assigning equal probability to all outcomes, and use the model to determine probabilities of events. For example, if a student is selected at random from a class, find the probability that Jane will be selected and the probability that a girl will be selected.*

    b. *Develop a probability model (which may not be uniform) by observing frequencies in data generated from a chance process. For example, find the approximate probability that a spinning penny will land heads up or that a tossed paper cup will land open-end down. Do the outcomes for the spinning penny appear to be equally likely based on the observed frequencies?*

Standard 7.SP.C.7 is broken into two parts (7.SP.C.7.a–b). We will consider them together since they are so closely related.

Overall, students develop and use probability models to find the probability of events. Uniform probability models are those where the likelihood of each outcome is equal. For example, there are 17 children in the class. What is the probability that Sam will be chosen?

Using theoretical probability, students can predict frequencies of outcomes. In part b of this standard, students look at the experimental probability to develop a model.

What the TEACHER does:

- Present numerous opportunities for students to find the theoretical probability of an event. Have students compare their theoretical probabilities to the experimental probabilities (observed frequencies). Students should be guided to conclude that the number of trials affects the closeness of the experimental probability to the theoretical. Experiments can be hands-on or use a variety of random generation devices, including spinners, number cubes, coin tosses, and colored chips. Students can collect simulation data using graphing calculators or computers for web-based simulations. Students can also develop models for geometric probability such as the following: The square has a side length of 16. If you choose a point in the square, what is the probability that it is not in the circle?

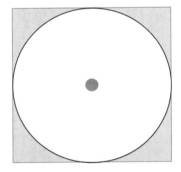

- Set up probability experiments for students to find the approximate probabilities from observed frequencies. Ask questions such as, "*Do the outcomes appear to be equally likely? Why do you think the experimental probability was not close to the theoretical in this case? What could cause the discrepancy? What could we do to get different results?*"

- Provide students many opportunities to explain their thinking aloud and/or in writing.

What the STUDENTS do:

- Determine the probability of events by developing uniform (and non-uniform) probability models (theoretical probability).

- Compare the models to the observed frequency and explain their reasoning, orally and in writing, for the discrepancy between the model and the observed frequency using appropriate vocabulary.

- Develop probability models by observing frequencies and approximating the probability using hands-on experiments and simulations.

Addressing Student Misconceptions and Common Errors

The new vocabulary in this cluster can be overwhelming for some students. Review the words frequently and use them repeatedly in class discussions. Word walls are helpful. Students may not be familiar with simulations and may need time working with them. Sometimes, in simulations, not all of the outcomes are shown. This can confuse students since all outcomes need to be taken into consideration when developing the probability. When an outcome does not appear in a simulation, make this a point for a class discussion.

Notes

Find probabilities of compound events using organized lists, tables, tree diagrams, and simulation.

a. *Understand that, just as with simple events, the probability of a compound event is the fraction of outcomes in the sample space for which the compound event occurs.*

b. *Represent sample spaces for compound events using methods such as organized lists, tables and tree diagrams. For an event described in everyday language (e.g., "rolling double sixes"), identify the outcomes in the sample space which compose the event.*

c. *Design and use a simulation to generate frequencies for compound events.* For example, use random digits as a simulation tool to approximate the answer to the question: If 40% of donors have type A blood, what is the probability that it will take at least 4 donors to find one with type A blood?

Standard 7.SP.C.8 is broken into three parts (7.SP.C.7.a–c). We will consider them together since the parts are very closely related.

Students move to compound events by building on their knowledge of single events. Compound events are those where two or more events are happening at once. For example, what is the probability that you forgot to study last night *and* there will be a surprise quiz in class today? Students select tools such as organized lists, tables, and tree diagrams to represent sample spaces for compound events. Ultimately, students design their own simulation for a compound event.

What the TEACHER does:

- Compare compound events to simple events, drawing on students' background knowledge. Provide students the opportunity to find the similarities and differences between the two types of events, stressing that the probability of a compound event is the fraction of outcomes in the sample space for which the compound event occurs, just as it is for single events.

- Provide students opportunities to express their understanding of compound events orally and in writing using appropriate vocabulary: *compound event, single event, sample space, outcomes, journals,* and *entrance and exit slips* are some examples of opportunities.

- Give students many opportunities to read/answer questions from sample spaces, and create sample spaces for compound events using organized lists, tables, and tree diagrams. Students identify the outcomes. The following example shows a tree diagram: What is the probability of rolling an even number and heads on a coin toss? (See diagram.) The answer is $\frac{3}{12}$ or $\frac{1}{4}$. Highlights in the diagram indicate the outcomes in the sample space that make up the event.

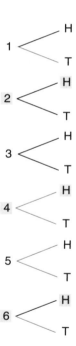

- Provide many opportunities for students to use simulations to collect data on compound events. Once students are comfortable with simulations, have them design their own to model a compound event and generate frequencies (data) so that students can approximate probabilities for their event. Examples of student-designed simulations are using a graphing calculator to generate random numbers to represent certain random characteristics of a population such as the question posed in the standard about blood types.

What the STUDENTS do:

- Explain orally and in writing the similarities and differences between single and compound events.

- Read and create sample spaces as organized lists, tables, or tree diagrams to determine the probability of a compound event.

- Select the appropriate tools for a simulation for a compound event and use the data it generates to approximate the probability of an event. Explain orally and/or in writing how the simulation was selected, why it models a compound event and not a single event, the data it generated, and how the probability was approximated.

Addressing Student Misconceptions and Common Errors

When using tree diagrams students may have difficulty keeping the lines straight and cannot read their final product. Encourage students to use graph paper so they can keep the outcomes apart from each other and/or use a ruler to read across the diagram. When using lists, some students will need additional help keeping them organized rather than random. When students create lists randomly, there is a greater chance that they will miss listing one or more outcomes.

Notes

Statistics and Probability

Cluster C: Investigate chance processes and develop, use, and evaluate probability models.

Standard: 7.SP.C.5. *Understand that the probability of a chance event is a number between 0 and 1 that expresses the likelihood of the event occurring. Larger numbers indicate greater likelihood. A probability near 0 indicates an unlikely event, a probability around $\frac{1}{2}$ indicates an event that is neither unlikely nor likely, and a probability near 1 indicates a likely event.*

Standards for Mathematical Practice:

SFMP 2. Reason abstractly and quantitatively.

Students reason about the error made by a fictional student.

SFMP 3. Construct viable arguments and critique the reasoning of others.

Students justify why a conclusion made by a fictional students is incorrect.

SFMP 6. Attend to precision.

Students communicate their justification precisely using appropriate vocabulary.

SFMP 7. Look for and make use of structure.

Students apply general mathematical rules about probabilities being expressed as a number between 0 and 1.

Goal:

Students use what they have learned about expressing probability and apply that knowledge to a new situation. Students express their thoughts in writing using appropriate vocabulary terms.

Planning:

Materials: situation cards, paper and pencil

Sample Activity:

- Provide pairs of students with one situation card each. The cards should look like the following sample:

Mike was given the following question:

  There is a bag with 6 marbles. Three marbles are blue, 2 are red, and 1 is green. What is the probability that you will randomly select a red marble? A green marble? What is the likelihood of those probabilities?

Mike answered: The probability of selecting a red marble is 2 and that is likely. The probability of selecting green is 1 and that is certain.

Mike is incorrect. Explain in writing what mistakes Mike made and justify your reasoning. Give the correct answers.

- Students work in pairs to complete the task.

Questions/Prompts:

- How are probabilities expressed?
- Make a list of the probability words we have been using in class to help you express your thoughts.
- Do Mike's answers make sense? How?

Differentiating Instruction:

Struggling Students: Students may need to have hands-on materials to help them understand the bag pull experiment. Students with writing difficulties may be able to explain their answers orally.

Extension: Give students a specific probability such as $\frac{2}{3}$ and ask them to design an experiment that would yield that probability. Have them justify their experiment.

Notes

Statistics and Probability

Cluster A: Use random sampling to draw inferences about a population.

Standard:

Standards for Mathematical Practice:

Goal:

Planning:

Materials:

Sample Activity:

Questions/Prompts:

Differentiating Instruction:

Struggling Students:

Extension:

Statistics and Probability

Cluster B: Draw informal comparative inferences about two populations.

Standard:

Standards for Mathematical Practice:

Goal:

Planning:

Materials:

Sample Activity:

Questions/Prompts:

Differentiating Instruction:

Struggling Students:

Extension:

Statistics and Probability

Cluster C: Investigate chance processes and develop, use, and evaluate probability models.

Standard:

Standards for Mathematical Practice:

Goal:

Planning:

Materials:

Sample Activity:

Questions/Prompts:

Differentiating Instruction:

Struggling Students:

Extension:

Notes

Statistics and Probability
8.SP.A*

Investigate patterns of association in bivariate data.

STANDARD 1 **8.SP.A.1:** Construct and interpret scatter plots for bivariate measurement data to investigate patterns of association between two quantities. Describe patterns such as clustering, outliers, positive or negative association, linear association, and nonlinear association.

STANDARD 2 **8.SP.A.2:** Know that straight lines are widely used to model relationships between two quantitative variables. For scatter plots that suggest a linear association, informally fit a straight line, and informally assess the model fit by judging the closeness of the data points to the line.

STANDARD 3 **8.SP.A.3:** Use the equation of a linear model to solve problems in the context of bivariate measurement data, interpreting the slope and intercept. *For example, in a linear model for a biology experiment, interpret a slope of 1.5 cm/hr as meaning that an additional hour of sunlight each day is associated with an additional 1.5 cm in mature plant height.*

STANDARD 4 **8.SP.A.4:** Understand that patterns of association can also be seen in bivariate categorical data by displaying frequencies and relative frequencies in a two-way table. Construct and interpret a two-way table summarizing data on two categorical variables collected from the same subjects. Use relative frequencies calculated for rows or columns to describe possible association between the two variables. *For example, collect data from students in your class on whether or not they have a curfew on school nights and whether or not they have assigned chores at home. Is there evidence that those who have a curfew also tend to have chores?*

*Supporting cluster

Statistics and Probability   8.SP.A

Cluster A: Investigate patterns of association in bivariate data.

Grade 8 Overview

Grade 8 focuses on bivariate data and the patterns of association such as clustering, outliers, positive or negative association, and linear or nonlinear association. Students informally assess a model fit for a line and solve problems involving bivariate data, slope, and intercepts. Students also work with bivariate categorical data using relative frequency.

Standards for Mathematical Practice

SFMP 1. Make sense of problems and persevere in solving them.

Students solve problems using a linear model in the context of bivariate data.

SFMP 2. Reason abstractly and quantitatively.

Students informally assess a line of best fit to data.

SFMP 4. Model with mathematics.

Students use a linear model to solve problems.

SFMP 6. Attend to precision.

Students solve problems efficiently, accurately, and with the degree of precision appropriate for the context of the problem.

SFMP 7. Look for and make use of structure.

Students look for structure in word problems to find linear patterns.

SFMP 8. Look for and express regularity in repeated reasoning.

Students understand the broader application of patterns in bivariate data and see the structure in similar situations.

Related Content Standards

8.F.A.3   8.F.B.4   8.F.B.5   7.EE.B.4.a

Notes

STANDARD 1 (8.SP.A.1)

Construct and interpret scatter plots for bivariate measurement data to investigate patterns of association between two quantities. Describe patterns such as clustering, outliers, positive or negative association, linear association, and nonlinear association.

Students study scatter plots of bivariate data by constructing and interpreting them in terms of patterns they can see. They look for the patterns of clustering, outliers, positive or negative association, and linear or nonlinear association. Examples of scatter plots below show positive and negative associations, clustering, and an outlier.

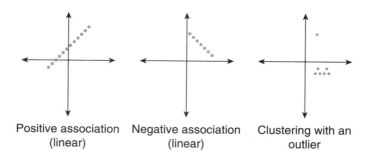

Positive association   Negative association   Clustering with an
(linear)   (linear)   outlier

What the TEACHER does:

- Provide students with many examples of scatter plots showing bivariate data to help them understand what bivariate data are versus univariate data. Encourage students to collect their own bivariate data on a topic of interest to them. These activities can range from suggestions by individual students to group projects involving the collection and organization of the data into a scatter plot. This helps students clarify their understanding of what constitutes bivariate data.

- Use several different scatter plots that show clustering; outliers; positive, negative or no association; and linear or nonlinear associations. One approach is to let students sort the different scatter plots by what they see (i.e., positive or negative association patterns, linear or nonlinear associations, graphs with outliers). The scatter plots should be a mix of those that have no labels and those that do. This adds to the meaning of the different associations. For example, a scatter plot that has no association may have points scattered around, but that association brings meaning when the data are identified as the number of hours eighth graders sleep versus the number of hours they spend playing sports.

- Plan for students to explain the patterns in writing and orally using the correct terminology.

What the STUDENTS do:

- Model bivariate data in a scatter plot showing the different types of associations.

- Describe orally and/or in writing different patterns of association when presented with scatter plots of bivariate data. Explain what the different patterns mean in specific contexts.

Addressing Student Misconceptions and Common Errors

Sometimes when a scatter plot shows no association, students are confused. Give them examples of data that may have no association to provide a context for reasoning why there would be no association. An example is the length of a person's hair and his or her final grade in mathematics.

Know that straight lines are widely used to model relationships between two quantitative variables. For scatter plots that suggest a linear association, informally fit a straight line, and informally assess the model fit by judging the closeness of the data points to the line.

Students focus on linear patterns of association in scatter plots and understand that linear models (straight lines) are commonly used to model linear relationships. Then they begin to informally fit a straight line to the data and learn to assess its fit by judging the closeness of the line to the data points. The most appropriate line is the one that comes closest to most data points. The use of linear regression is not expected at this grade.

What the TEACHER does:

- Facilitate a discussion about straight lines being widely used to model relationships between two quantitative variables in the real world. Ask students questions to involve them in the discussion such as, *"Do you know of any situations where linear models are used? What do you remember about the lines we have been graphing in class? Name some examples from class. Why do you think linear models are used so often?"*

- Pose problems for students to solve using linear models. Encourage students to make predictions based on their lines.

- Display a few scatter plots that show a linear association. Ask students to informally fit a straight line. Students should informally draw a line of fit for a scatter plot and informally measure the strength of fit. Discussion should include questions such as, *"What does it mean if a point is above the line? Below the line?"* Students should interpret the slope and intercept of the line of fit in the context of the data.

What the STUDENTS do:

- Understand that straight lines are widely used to model relationships between two quantitative variables in the real world and can name some examples.

- Model real-world linear relationships on a graph.

- Construct straight lines to fit data presented in scatter plots, informally.

- Justify a fit line as a good fit (or not).

- Explain orally and/or in writing the meaning of the fit line and its properties in terms of the context of the graph.

Addressing Student Misconceptions and Common Errors

A common misconception students have is that a line of fit must go through at least some of the data points on the scatter plot. Expose students to examples where a line of fit goes through all of the data points and those where it does not go through any but both lines are good fits.

Notes

Use the equation of a linear model to solve problems in the context of bivariate measurement data, interpreting the slope and intercept. For example, in a linear model for a biology experiment, interpret a slope of 1.5 cm/hr as meaning that an additional hour of sunlight each day is associated with an additional 1.5 cm in mature plant height.

Students practice solving contextual linear problems. The problems involve situations using bivariate measurement data such as those collected in a biology experiment. This standard connects with what students have learned about models of linear equations, slope, and intercept.

What the TEACHER does:

- Present students with measurement data on two variables and ask them to use a linear model to answer questions that involve interpreting slope and intercept. Ask the students to create a scatter plot, informally fit a line, and use the line to create a linear equation. Students will need the slope and intercept of the line to create the equation. Then students can answer questions or make predictions about the data. For the example, questions could be, *"What could we expect with 3 more hours of sunlight each day? How much sunlight could we continue to add before the graph is no longer useful for the situation?"*

- Pose problems like this example:

"In a mathematics class, the teacher kept a record of absences and grades.

Absences	Grades
2	87
4	75
0	99
1	95
1	92
3	65
2	89
5	50
2	85
2	90
3	80

Show these data on a scatter plot and fit a line to the data. Determine an approximate linear equation for this line. What does the slope of this line say about the relationship?"

What the STUDENTS do:

- Solve problems using a linear equation to model bivariate measurement data in context.

- Fit a line to the data, interpret the slope and intercept for the context, write the linear equation, and make predictions from the line.

Addressing Student Misconceptions and Common Errors

There can be many steps before a student is ready to answer the specific questions asked in these problems. For struggling learners, scaffold the questions until they can make sense of the steps themselves.

Understand that patterns of association can also be seen in bivariate categorical data by displaying frequencies and relative frequencies in a two-way table. Construct and interpret a two-way table summarizing data on two categorical variables collected from the same subjects. Use relative frequencies calculated for rows or columns to describe possible association between the two variables. For example, collect data from students in your class on whether or not they have a curfew on school nights and whether or not they have assigned chores at home. Is there evidence that those who have a curfew also tend to have chores?

Standard 4 asks students to switch from using numerical data to categorical data and use frequencies to answer questions about possible associations (linear/nonlinear, positive/negative/no association). Students construct and interpret tables that display categorical data on two different variables from the same subjects. A two-way table is a table that shows categorical data classified in two different ways. An example of a two-way table that records possible data from the example in the standard about chores and curfews may be the following:

CURFEW

		YES	NO
CHORES	**YES**	44	20
	NO	20	44

One interpretation of the chart is that of the students who answered yes, they had a curfew, 44 had chores and 20 did not. Of the students who answered no, they did not have a curfew, 20 had chores and 44 did not. From this sample, there appears to be a positive correlation between having a curfew and having chores.

What the TEACHER does:

- Present information on two categorical variables in a two-way table such as the example in the standard. Facilitate a discussion that leads students to conclude that categorical data can also be described numerically through the use of a two-way table.

- Pose the question, *"Do you see a pattern in the responses to indicate an association in the data? What type of association?"*

- Provide many opportunities for students to interpret categorical data presented in two-way tables.

- Give students time to collect categorical data, create their own two-way table, and justify any patterns of association they find.

What the STUDENTS do:

- Understand the use of a two-way table to display bivariate categorical data.

- Collect categorical data on two variables from the same group of people, display them in a two-way table, and interpret the data for associations. Justify orally or in writing the association using precise mathematical language.

Addressing Student Misconceptions and Common Errors

As students collect their own data, be aware of them asking the same two questions of the same people. Some students may ask each person only one question. Students may have to use tally marks for frequency while collecting the data. Many students will be content with asking a few friends. Students should understand they need a significant sample size to find an association and the sample should be random.

GRADE 8

Statistics and Probability

Cluster A: Investigate patterns of association in bivariate data.

Standard: 8.SP.A.2. *Know that straight lines are widely used to model relationships between two quantitative variables. For scatter plots that suggest a linear association, informally fit a straight line, and informally assess the model fit by judging the closeness of the data points to the line.*

Standards for Mathematical Practice:

SFMP 3. Construct viable arguments and critique the reasoning of others.

Students explain how well their fit line matches the data and then critique the presentations of the other students.

SFMP 4 Model with mathematics.

Students model a linear relationship by informally fitting a straight line to a scatter plot.

SFMP 6. Attend to precision.

Students use correct vocabulary as they explain their line of fit.

Goal:

Students informally fit a line to a set of bivariate data and explain in words how well the line fits the data.

Planning:

Materials: a prepared data set, large graph chart paper (one sheet per pair), markers

Sample Activity:

- Present a set of data to pairs of students. Ask them to create a scatter plot of the data, and informally create a fit line on the large graph paper. An example of data that may be of interest to eighth graders is the following:

# Absences	3	5	1	1	3	6	5	3	0	7	1	9	5	0	2	8	5	1	3
Final Grades in Science	66	51	90	97	80	35	75	55	99	20	85	45	60	95	88	50	62	95	70

- Students post their work and explain how well their line fits the data.
- Use the posters for a whole class discussion about how the fit lines were the same/different among all the posters.

Questions/Prompts:

- If students seem stuck, ask them to talk through the steps they have already completed.

- For students who seem overwhelmed by the data, ask, *"How would you explain the data in your words?"* or *"Describe the relationship between the variables."*

- Are students having trouble fitting a line? Ask, *"Do you remember how we did this in class for the data on _____?"*

Differentiating Instruction:

Struggling Students: Some students may need more time to complete the task than others. Give them a few less data points to graph. For students struggling to find a fit line, give them a piece of spaghetti or something similar to use as a line they can manipulate.

Extension: Using their line, have these students offer predictions or make some general statements about the relationship of absences to final science grades.

Notes

Statistics and Probability

Cluster A: Investigate patterns of association in bivariate data.

Standard:

Standards for Mathematical Practice:

Goal:

Planning:

Materials:

Sample Activity:

Questions/Prompts:

Differentiating Instruction:

Struggling Students:

Extension:

Reflection Questions: Statistics and Probability

1. Discuss how the study of data will apply directly to students' lives now and in the future.

2. Brainstorm topics that would be of interest to middle school students where they can ask questions and investigate the answers through statistical analysis.

3. The formal study of probability does not appear in the content standards until Grade 7. Discuss how this is advantageous. Consider the students and the curriculum.

Resources

Table 1 Standards for Mathematical Practice

Standard for Mathematical Practice	What the Teacher Does	What the Students Do

1. Make sense of problems and persevere in solving them.	• Provide students with rich tasks and real-world problems that focus on and promote student understanding of an important mathematical concept.
	• Provide time for and facilitate the discussion of problem solutions.
	
	   ○ What are you asked to find?
	   ○ Have you solved a similar problem before?
	   ○ What is your plan for solving the problem?
	   ○ Can you explain how you solved the problem?
	   ○ Does your answer make sense?
	   ○ Did you use a different method to check your answer?
		• Actively engage in solving problems by working to understand the information that is in the problem and the question that is asked.
		• Use a variety of strategies that make sense to solve the problem.
		• Try a different strategy if the first strategy does not work.
		• Ask themselves if they used the most efficient way to solve the problem.
		• Ask themselves if their solution makes sense.
		• Solve real-world problems through the application of algebraic and geometric concepts.

2. Reason abstractly and quantitatively.	• Provide real-world scenarios to use real numbers and variables in mathematical expressions, equations, and inequalities. • Help students decontextualize to manipulate symbolic representations by applying properties of operations. • Help students understand the meaning of the number or variable as related to a problem.	• Use varied strategies, models, and drawings to think about the mathematics of a task and example. • Represent a wide variety of real-world situations through the use of real numbers and variables in mathematical expressions, equations, and inequalities. • Contextualize to understand the meaning of the number or variable as related to the problem and decontextualize to manipulate symbolic representations by applying properties. • Examine patterns in data and assess the degree of linearity of functions.

3. Construct viable arguments and critique the reasoning of others.	• Provide tasks that encourage students to construct mathematical arguments.
	• Expect students to explain their strategies and mathematical thinking to others.
	• Expect students to listen to the reasoning of others and respond to their thinking.
	• Help students to compare strategies and methods by asking questions such as:
	
	   ○ How can you prove that your answer is correct?
	   ○ What do you think about _____'s strategy?
	   ○ How is your method different from _____'s? How is it similar?
	   ○ Why is this true? Does it always work?
		• Explain orally or in writing their strategies and thinking using models, drawings, or symbolic representations.
		• Critique and evaluate their own thinking and the thinking of other students.
		• Ask questions to one another and to the teacher to clarify their understanding.
		• Look for similarities among different ways to solve problems.
		• Construct arguments using verbal or written explanations for expressions, equations, inequalities, models, and graphs, tables, and other data displays.

Standard for Mathematical Practice	What the Teacher Does	What the Students Do

4. Model with mathematics.	• Provide a variety of materials for students to use as they work to make sense of mathematical ideas and solve problems.
	• Pose real-world tasks to apply proportional reasoning to plan a school event or analyze a problem.
	• Provide experiences to explore covariance and represent two quantities simultaneously.
	• Provide experiences to connect and explain connections between different representations.
	• Encourage students to use models as they create mathematical arguments and explain their thinking to others.
	• Ask questions such as:
	  ○ Can you show me how you solve this using a _____?
	  ○ Can you draw a model to explain what is happening in the problem?
	  ○ Is this working or do you need to change the model?
		• Put the problem or situation in their own words.
		• Check to see if an answer makes sense and change a model when necessary.
		• Model the problem situations symbolically, graphically, tabularly, and contextually.
		• Use the mathematics they know to solve problems for everyday situations.
		• Use measures of center and variability and data displays to draw inferences about and make comparisons between data sets.
		• Solve systems of linear equations and compare properties of functions provided in different forms.

5. Use appropriate tools strategically.	• Encourage students to use physical objects or models in constructing mathematical arguments. • Provide a variety of materials for students to use as they develop mathematical ideas.	• Select models that help develop understanding. • Determine if mental computation, concrete models, or paper and pencil are the most efficient way to solve a problem or task. • Use physical objects or applets to construct nets and calculate the surface area of three-dimensional figures. • Use physical objects or applets to generate probability data and use graphing calculators or spreadsheets to manage and represent data in different forms.

6. Attend to precision.	• Support students in developing an understanding of mathematical vocabulary by explicitly introducing terms and expecting students to use them.
	• Repeat a student's explanation using accurate vocabulary when necessary.
	• Support students' precision by asking the following questions:
	  ○ What does _____ mean?
	  ○ What labels could you use with your answer?
		• Communicate precisely using appropriate mathematical vocabulary when referring to rates, ratios, geometric figures, data displays, components of expressions, equations or inequalities, number system, and functions.
		• Work to carefully formulate clear explanations.
		• State the meaning of symbols; calculate accurately and efficiently.

(Continued)

Table 1 (Continued)

Standard for Mathematical Practice	What the Teacher Does	What the Students Do
7. Look for and make use of structure.	• Provide experiences for students to discern a pattern or structure. • Allow students to examine patterns in tables and graphs to generate equations and describe relationships.	• Look for patterns or structures to model and solve problems. • Discover patterns in ratio tables, recognizing both the additive and multiplicative properties. • Compose and decompose two- and three-dimensional figures to solve real-world problems for area and volume. • Examine tree diagrams or systematic lists to determine the sample space for compound events and verify that they have listed all possibilities. • Apply properties to generate equivalent expressions and solve equations.
8. Look for and express regularity in repeated reasoning.	• Provide a variety of examples that explicitly focus on patterns and repeated reasoning. • Help students make connections between covariance, rates, and representations showing the relationships between quantities.	• Notice repeated calculations to understand algorithms and make generalizations about patterns. • Continually evaluate the reasonableness of their answers and their thinking. • Create, explain, evaluate, and modify probability models to describe simple and compound events. • Use iterative processes to determine more precise rational approximations for irrational numbers.

Source: Adapted from Principles to Actions, National Council of Teachers of Mathematics (2014).

Table 2 Effective Teaching Practices

Teaching Practice	Purpose	What the Teacher Does	What the Students Do

1. Establish mathematics goals to focus learning.	• Set the stage to guide instructional decisions.
	• Expect students to understand the purpose of a lesson beyond simply repeating the words in the Standard.
		• Consider broad goals as well as the goals of the unit and the lesson, including:
		  ○ What is to be learned?
		  ○ Why is the goal important?
		  ○ Where do students need to go?
		  ○ How can learning be extended?
			• Make sense of the new concepts and skills, making connections to previously learned Grades 6–8 concepts.
			• Experience connections among the Standards and across domains.
			• Deepen their understanding and expect what they are learning makes sense.

2. Implement tasks that promote reasoning and problem solving.	• Provide opportunities for students to engage in exploration and make sense of important mathematics.
	• Encourage students to use procedures in ways that are connected to understanding.
		• Choose tasks that:
		  ○ are built on current student understandings,
		  ○ have various entry points with multiple ways for the problems to be solved,
		  ○ are interesting to students.
			• Work to make sense of the task and persevere in solving problems.
			• Use a variety of models and materials to make sense of the mathematics in the task.
			• Convince themselves and others the answer is reasonable.

3. Use and connect mathematical representations.	• Lead students to connect conceptual understanding of procedural skills using models and representations.	• Use tasks that allow students to use a variety of representations. • Encourage the use of different representations, including concrete manipulatives, models, and symbolic representations that support students in explaining their thinking and reasoning.	• Use materials to make sense of problem situations. • Connect representations to mathematical concepts and the structure of big ideas for ratios and proportional relationships, expressions, and equations, the number system, statistics, and probability, geometry, and functions.
4. Facilitate meaningful mathematical discourse.	• Provide students with opportunities to share ideas, clarify their understanding, and develop convincing arguments. • Allow discussion to advance mathematical thinking for the whole class.	• Engage students in explaining their mathematical reasoning in small group and classroom discussions. • Facilitate dialog among students that supports sense making of a variety of strategies and approaches. • Scaffold classroom discussions so that connections between representations and mathematical ideas occurs.	• Explain their ideas and reasoning in small groups and with the entire class. • Listen to the reasoning of others. • Ask questions of others to make sense of their ideas.

(Continued)

Table 2 (Continued)

Teaching Practice	Purpose	What the Teacher Does	What the Students Do
5. Pose purposeful questions.	• Reveal students' current understanding of a concept. • Encourage students to explain, elaborate, and clarify thinking. • Make the learning of mathematics more visible and accessible for students.	• Ask questions that build on and extend student thinking. • Be intentional about the kinds of questions asked to make the mathematics more visible to students. • Use wait time to provide students with time to think and examine their ideas.	• Think more deeply about the process than only focusing on the answer. • Listen to and comment on the explanations of others in the class.
6. Build procedural fluency from conceptual understanding.	• Provide experiences with models to allow students to make sense of important mathematics and flexibly choose from a variety of methods to solve problems.	• Provide opportunities for students to reason about mathematical ideas. • Expect students to explain why their strategies work. • Connect student methods to efficient procedures as appropriate.	• Understand and explain the procedures they are using and why they work. • Use a variety of strategies to solve problems and make sense of mathematical ideas. • Do not rely on shortcuts or tricks to do mathematics.
7. Support productive struggle in learning mathematics.	• Allow productive struggle for students to grapple with ideas and relationships. • Productive struggle is significant and essential to learning mathematics with understanding.	• Support student struggle without showing and telling a procedure but rather focus on the important mathematical ideas. • Ask questions that scaffold student thinking. • Build questions and lessons on important student mistakes rather than focusing on the correct answer. • Recognize the importance of effort as students work to make sense of new ideas.	• Stick to a task and recognize that struggle is part of sense making. • Ask questions that help students to better understand the task. • Support each other with ideas rather than telling others the answer or how to solve a problem.
8. Elicit and use evidence of student thinking.	• Elicit and use evidence of student thinking to help assess learning progress and make instructional decisions during lessons and for future lessons. • Use formative assessment through students' written and oral ideas to assess thinking and understanding.	• Determine what to look for in gathering evidence of student learning. • Pose questions and answer student questions that provide information about student understanding, strategies, and reasoning. • Use evidence to determine next steps of instruction.	• Accept that reasoning and understanding are as important as the answer to a problem. • Use mistakes and misconceptions to rethink their understanding. • Ask questions of the teacher and peers to clarify confusion or misunderstanding. • Self-assess and progress toward developing mathematical understanding.

Source: Adapted from *Principles to Actions*, National Council of Teachers of Mathematics (2014).

CCSS Where to Focus Grade 6 Mathematics

CCSS
WHERE TO FOCUS
GRADE 6
MATHEMATICS

MATH · 6 · F

MATHEMATICS · GRADE 6 · FOCUS

This document shows where students and teachers should spend the large majority of their time in order to meet the expectations of the Standards.

Not all content in a given grade is emphasized equally in the Standards. Some clusters require greater emphasis than others based on the depth of the ideas, the time that they take to master, and/or their importance to future mathematics or the demands of college and career readiness. More time in these areas is also necessary for students to meet the Standards for Mathematical Practice.

To say that some things have greater emphasis is not to say that anything in the Standards can safely be neglected in instruction. Neglecting material will leave gaps in student skill and understanding and may leave students unprepared for the challenges of a later grade.

Students should spend the large majority[1] of their time on the major work of the grade (■). Supporting work (☐) and, where appropriate, additional work (◉) can engage students in the major work of the grade.[2,3]

MAJOR, SUPPORTING, AND ADDITIONAL CLUSTERS FOR GRADE 6

Emphases are given at the cluster level. Refer to the Common Core State Standards for Mathematics for the specific standards that fall within each cluster.

Key: ■ Major Clusters   ☐ Supporting Clusters   ◉ Additional Clusters

6.RP.A	■ Understand ratio concepts and use ratio reasoning to solve problems.
6.NS.A	■ Apply and extend previous understandings of multiplication and division to divide fractions by fraction.
6.NS.B	◉ Compute fluently with multi-digit numbers and find common factors and multiples.
6.NS.C	■ Apply and extend previous understandings of numbers to the systems of rational numbers.
6.EE.A	■ Apply and extend previous understandings of arithmetic to algebraic expressions.
6.EE.B	■ Reason about and solve one-variable equations and inequalities.
6.EE.C	■ Represent and analyze quantitative relationships between dependent and independent variables.
6.G.A	☐ Solve real-world and mathematical problems involving area, surface area, and volume.
6.SP.A	◉ Develop understanding of statistical variability.
6.SP.B	◉ Summarize and describe distributions.

HIGHLIGHTS OF MAJOR WORK IN GRADES K–8

K–2	Addition and subtraction – concepts, skills, and problem solving; place value
3–5	Multiplication and division of whole numbers and fractions – concepts, skills, and problem solving
6	Ratios and proportional relationships; early expressions and equations
7	Ratios and proportional relationships; arithmetic of rational numbers
8	Linear algebra and linear functions

REQUIRED FLUENCIES FOR GRADE 6

6.NS.B.2	Multi-digit division
6.NS.B.3	Multi-digit decimal operations

STUDENT ACHIEVEMENT PARTNERS

Find additional resources at achievethecore.org

1 At least 65% and up to approximately 85% of class time, with Grades K–2 nearer the upper end of that range, should be devoted to the major work of the grade. For more information, see Criterion #1 of the K–8 Publishers' Criteria for the Common Core State Standards for Mathematics www.achievethecore.org/publisherscriteria.

2 Refer also to criterion #3 in the K–8 Publishers' Criteria for the Common Core State Standards for Mathematics www.achievethecore.org/publisherscriteria.

3 Note, the critical areas are a survey of what will be taught at each grade level; the major work is the subset of topics that deserve the large majority of instructional time during a given year to best prepare students for college and careers.

Source: Created by Student Achievement Partners (SAP). http://achievethecore.org/content/upload/SAP_Focus_Math_6.pdf

CCSS Where to Focus Grade 7 Mathematics

CCSS
WHERE TO FOCUS
GRADE 7
MATHEMATICS

MATHEMATICS · GRADE 7 · FOCUS

This document shows where students and teachers should spend the large majority of their time in order to meet the expectations of the Standards.

Not all content in a given grade is emphasized equally in the Standards. Some clusters require greater emphasis than others based on the depth of the ideas, the time that they take to master, and/or their importance to future mathematics or the demands of college and career readiness. More time in these areas is also necessary for students to meet the Standards for Mathematical Practice.

To say that some things have greater emphasis is not to say that anything in the Standards can safely be neglected in instruction. Neglecting material will leave gaps in student skill and understanding and may leave students unprepared for the challenges of a later grade.

Students should spend the large majority[1] of their time on the major work of the grade (■). Supporting work (☐) and, where appropriate, additional work (●) can engage students in the major work of the grade.[2, 3]

MAJOR, SUPPORTING, AND ADDITIONAL CLUSTERS FOR GRADE 7

Emphases are given at the cluster level. Refer to the Common Core State Standards for Mathematics for the specific standards that fall within each cluster.

Key: ■ Major Clusters ☐ Supporting Clusters ● Additional Clusters

7.RP.A	■ Analyze proportional relationships and use them to solve real-world and mathematical problems
7.NS.A	■ Apply and extend previous understandings of operations with fractions to add, subtract, multiply, and divide rational numbers.
7.EE.A	■ Use properties of operations to generate equivalent expressions.
7.EE.B	■ Solve real-life and mathematical problems using numerical and algebraic expressions and questions.
7.G.A	● Draw, construct and describe geometrical figures and describe the relationships between them.
7.G.B	● Solve real-life and mathematical problems involving angle measure, area, surface area, and volume.
7.SP.A	☐ Use random sampling to draw inferences about a population.
7.SP.B	● Draw informal comparative inferences about two populations.
7.SP.C	☐ Investigate chance processes and develop, use, and evaluate probability models.

HIGHLIGHTS OF MAJOR WORK IN GRADES K–8

K–2	Addition and subtraction – concepts, skills, and problem solving; place value
3–5	Multiplication and division of whole numbers and fractions – concepts, skills, and problem solving
6	Ratios and proportional relationships; early expressions and equations
7	Ratios and proportional relationships; arithmetic of rational numbers
8	Linear algebra and linear functions

STUDENT ACHIEVEMENT PARTNERS

Find additional resources at achievethecore.org

---

1 At least 65% and up to approximately 85% of class time, with Grades K–2 nearer the upper end of that range, should be devoted to the major work of the grade. For more information, see Criterion #1 of the K–8 Publishers' Criteria for the Common Core State Standards for Mathematics www.achievethecore.org/publisherscriteria.

2 Refer also to criterion #3 in the K–8 Publishers' Criteria for the Common Core State Standards for Mathematics www.achievethecore.org/publisherscriteria.

3 Note, the critical areas are a survey of what will be taught at each grade level; the major work is the subset of topics that deserve the large majority of instructional time during a given year to best prepare students for college and careers.

Source: Created by Student Achievement Partners (SAP). http://achievethecore.org/content/upload/SAP_Focus_Math_7.pdf

CCSS Where to Focus Grade 8 Mathematics

CCSS
WHERE TO FOCUS
GRADE 8
MATHEMATICS

MATH · **8** · **F**

MATHEMATICS · GRADE 8 · FOCUS

This document shows where students and teachers should spend the large majority of their time in order to meet the expectations of the Standards.

Not all content in a given grade is emphasized equally in the Standards. Some clusters require greater emphasis than others based on the depth of the ideas, the time that they take to master, and/or their importance to future mathematics or the demands of college and career readiness. More time in these areas is also necessary for students to meet the Standards for Mathematical Practice.

To say that some things have greater emphasis is not to say that anything in the Standards can safely be neglected in instruction. Neglecting material will leave gaps in student skill and understanding and may leave students unprepared for the challenges of a later grade.

Students should spend the large majority[1] of their time on the major work of the grade (■). Supporting work (□) and, where appropriate, additional work (⬤) can engage students in the major work of the grade.[2,3]

MAJOR, SUPPORTING, AND ADDITIONAL CLUSTERS FOR GRADE 8

Emphases are given at the cluster level. Refer to the Common Core State Standards for Mathematics for the specific standards that fall within each cluster.

Key: ■ Major Clusters   □ Supporting Clusters   ⬤ Additional Clusters

8.NS.A	□ Know that there are numbers that are not rational, and approximate them by rational numbers.
8.EE.A	■ Work with radicals and integer exponents.
8.EE.B	■ Understand the connections between proportional relationships, lines, and linear equations.
8.EE.C	■ Analyze and solve linear equations and pairs of simultaneous linear equations.
8.F.A	■ Define, evaluate, and compare functions.
8.F.B	■ Use functions to model relationships between quantities.
8.G.A	■ Understand congruence and similarity using physical models, transparencies, or geometry software.
8.G.B	■ Understand and apply the Pythagorean Theorem.
8.G.C	⬤ Solve real-world and mathematical problems involving volume of cylinders, cones, and spheres.
8.SP.A	□ Investigate patterns of association in bivariate data.

HIGHLIGHTS OF MAJOR WORK IN GRADES K–8

K–2	Addition and subtraction – concepts, skills, and problem solving; place value
3–5	Multiplication and division of whole numbers and fractions – concepts, skills, and problem solving
6	Ratios and proportional relationships; early expressions and equations
7	Ratios and proportional relationships; arithmetic of rational numbers
8	Linear algebra and linear functions

STUDENT ACHIEVEMENT PARTNERS

Find additional resources at achievethecore.org

1 At least 65% and up to approximately 85% of class time, with Grades K–2 nearer the upper end of that range, should be devoted to the major work of the grade. For more information, see Criterion #1 of the K–8 Publishers' Criteria for the Common Core State Standards for Mathematics www.achievethecore.org/publisherscriteria.

2 Refer also to criterion #3 in the K–8 Publishers' Criteria for the Common Core State Standards for Mathematics www.achievethecore.org/publisherscriteria.

3 Note, the critical areas are a survey of what will be taught at each grade level; the major work is the subset of topics that deserve the large majority of instructional time during a given year to best prepare students for college and careers.

Source: Created by Student Achievement Partners (SAP). http://achievethecore.org/content/upload/SAP_Focus_Math_8.pdf

Reproducibles

Directions: Cut out two wheels on cardstock. Cut along the dotted line to the center of each wheel. Insert the wheels into each other through the cuts. Position the wheels so the lines face out. You should be able to see the lines on each side when the wheels are together.

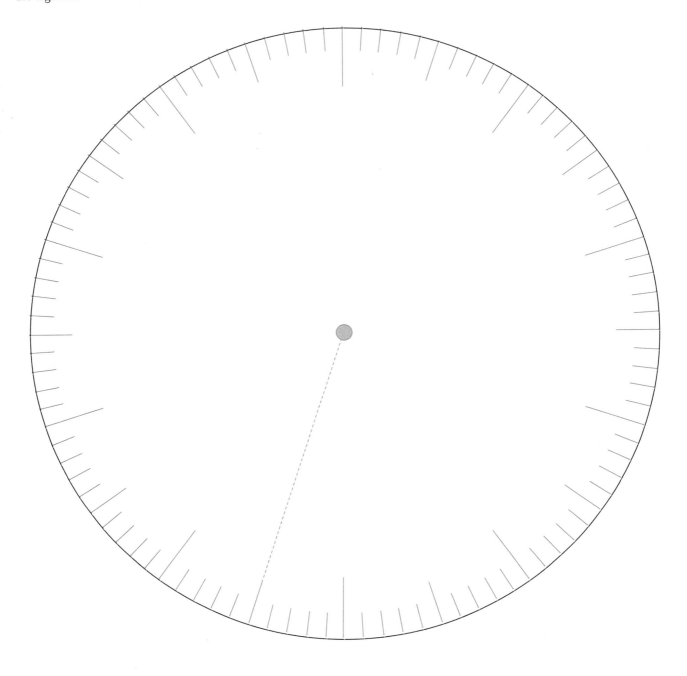

Available for download at **resources.corwin.com/mathematicscompanion6-8**

Copyright © 2016 by Corwin. All rights reserved. Reprinted from *The Common Core Mathematics Companion: The Standards Decoded, Grades 6–8: What They Say, What They Mean, How to Teach Them* by Ruth Harbin Miles and Lois A. Williams. Thousand Oaks, CA: Corwin, www.corwin.com. Reproduction authorized only for the local school site or nonprofit organization that has purchased this book.

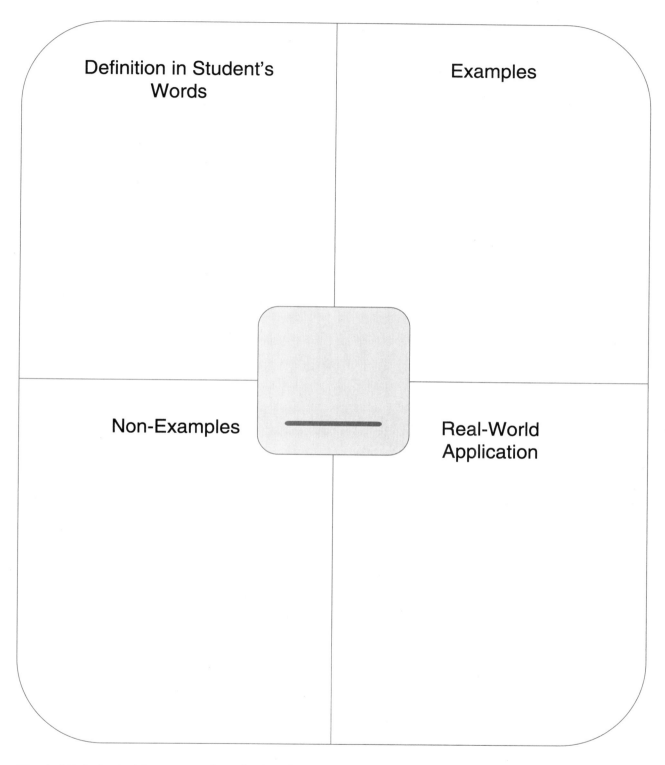

Definition in Student's Words

Examples

Non-Examples

Real-World Application

Available for download at **resources.corwin.com/mathematicscompanion6-8**

Source: Adapted from "The Frayer Model." Frayer, D., Frederick, W., & Klausmeier, H. (1969). *A schema for testing the level of cognitive mastery.* Madison, WI: Wisconsin Center for Education Research.

Reprinted from *The Common Core Mathematics Companion: The Standards Decoded, Grades 6–8: What They Say, What They Mean, How to Teach Them* by Ruth Harbin Miles and Lois A. Williams. Thousand Oaks, CA: Corwin, www.corwin.com. Reproduction authorized only for the local school site or nonprofit organization that has purchased this book.

Directions: Cut out the shape along the outside edges. Fold along the inside dotted lines.

Available for download at **resources.corwin.com/mathematicscompanion6-8**

Copyright © 2016 by Corwin. All rights reserved. Reprinted from *The Common Core Mathematics Companion: The Standards Decoded, Grades 6–8: What They Say, What They Mean, How to Teach Them* by Ruth Harbin Miles and Lois A. Williams. Thousand Oaks, CA: Corwin, www.corwin.com. Reproduction authorized only for the local school site or nonprofit organization that has purchased this book.

Reproducible 4. Example for MAD (Mean Absolute Deviation)

Compare the mean height of male basketball players on the men's team to the mean height of female players on the women's team. Display the data on a dot plot. Discuss the variability in height within each team and between teams.

Men's Basketball Team

Height of male players in inches:

75, 73, 76, 78, 79, 78, 79, 81, 80, 82, 81, 84, 82, 84, 80, 84

Women's Basketball Team

Height of female players in inches:

73, 73, 73, 72, 69, 76, 72, 73, 74, 70, 65, 71, 74, 76, 70, 72, 71, 68, 71, 78

To compare the mean heights, simply find the mean of each data set.

Men's Mean Height = 79.75 inches   Women's Mean Height = 72.05 inches

There is a difference of 7.7 inches between the men's and women's basketball teams' mean heights.

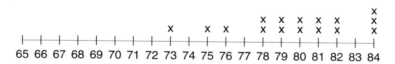

Heights of Players on Men's Basketball Team

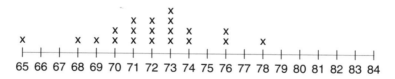

Heights of Players on Women's Basketball Team

From looking at the two distributions, we can see some overlap. Both teams have players with heights between 73 and 78 inches. We will use the mean and mean absolute deviation to compare the sets of data. Arrange the data in tables.

(Continued)

(Continued)

Heights of male players	Deviation from the mean (in.)	Absolute deviation from the mean (in.)
75	−5	5
73	−7	7
76	−6	6
78	−8	8
79	−1	1
78	−2	2
79	−1	1
81	1	1
80	0	0
82	2	2
81	1	1
84	4	4
82	2	2
84	4	4
80	0	0
84	4	4

Heights of female players	Deviation from the mean (in.)	Absolute deviation from the mean (in.)
73	1	1
73	1	1
73	1	1
72	0	0
69	−3	3
76	4	4
72	0	0
73	1	1
74	2	2
70	−2	2
65	−7	7
71	−1	1
74	2	2
76	4	4
70	−2	2
72	0	0
71	−1	1
68	−4	4
71	−1	1
78	6	6

The mean absolute deviation (MAD) is calculated by taking the mean of the absolute deviations for each data point. The difference between each data point and the mean is recorded in the second column of each table. This is the deviation from the mean. (The means were rounded to 80 for the men's team and 72 for the women's team to find the differences.) The absolute deviation, which is the absolute value of the deviation from the mean, is recorded in the third column. The absolute deviations are summed and divided by the number of data points in the set to get the MAD for each set.

The men's team's mean absolute deviation is 3. The women's team's mean absolute deviation is 2.15. This shows a moderate variability in both sets, with more variability in the men's team.

The difference between the heights of the teams is approximately two and a half times the variability of the data sets ($7.7 \div 3 = 2.57$).

Available for download at **resources.corwin.com/mathematicscompanion6-8**

Copyright © 2016 by Corwin. All rights reserved. Reprinted from *The Common Core Mathematics Companion: The Standards Decoded, Grades 6–8: What They Say, What They Mean, How to Teach Them* by Ruth Harbin Miles and Lois A. Williams. Thousand Oaks, CA: Corwin, www.corwin.com. Reproduction authorized only for the local school site or nonprofit organization that has purchased this book.

Additional Resources

Online

http://www.corestandards.org

A complete copy of the Common Core Standards by grade level is available on this site. Other supporting resources include background on the development of the standards, videos, documents, FAQ, and much more.

http://community.ksde.org/Default.aspx?tabid=5646

This site includes instructional strategies and examples for each standard for Grades 6–8 as well as links to other valuable resources.

http://ime.math.arizona.edu/progressions

The series of progressions documents written by leading researchers in the field summarizes the standards progressions for specific CCSS domains.

http://illustrativemathematics.org

This site is a variety of videos, tasks, and suggestions for professional development accessible to all teachers.

http://www.pta.org/parents/content.cfm?Item Number=2583

The Parents' Guides to Student Success were developed by teachers, parents, and education experts in response to the Common Core Standards. Created for Grades K–8, high school English language arts/literacy, and mathematics, the guides provide clear, consistent expectations for what students should be learning at each grade to be prepared for college and career.

http://www.achievethecore.org

Practical tools designed to help students and teachers see their hard work deliver results. http://www.achievethecore.org was created in the spirit of collaboration and includes planning materials, professional development resources, assessment information, and implementation support.

Books

Principles to Actions, NCTM (ISBN **978-0-87353-774-2**)

The Common Core Mathematics Standards: Transforming Practice Through Team Leadership, Hull, Harbin Miles, and Balka (ISBN 978-0-87353-715-5)

Realizing Rigor in the Mathematics Classroom, Hull, Harbin Miles, and Balka (ISBN 978-1-4522-9960-0)

The Common Core Mathematics Companion: The Standards Decoded, Grades 3–5, Gojak and Harbin Miles (ISBN 978-1-4833-8160-2)

Uncomplicating Fractions to Meet Common Core Standards in Math, K–7, Marion Small (ISBN 978-0-80775-485-6)

Elementary Mathematics: Teaching Developmentally, John van De Walle (ISBN 0-205-48392-56)

About the Authors

Ruth Harbin Miles coaches rural, suburban, and inner-city school mathematics teachers. Her professional experiences include coordinating the K–12 Mathematics Teaching and Learning Program for the Olathe, Kansas, public schools for more than 25 years; teaching mathematics methods courses at Virginia's Mary Baldwin College; and serving on the Board of Directors for the National Council of Teachers of Mathematics, the National Council of Supervisors of Mathematics, and the Kansas Association of Teachers of Mathematics. Ruth is a coauthor of seven Corwin books, including *A Guide to Mathematics Coaching*, *A Guide to Mathematics Leadership*, *Visible Thinking in the K–8 Mathematics Classroom*, *The Common Core Mathematics Standards: Transforming Practice Through Team Leadership*, *Realizing Rigor in the Mathematics Classroom*, and *The Common Core Mathematics Companion: The Standards Decoded, Grades K–2* and *The Common Core Mathematics Companion: The Standards Decoded, Grades 3–5*. Ruth is an International Fellow with the Charles A. Dana Center working with classroom teachers in Department of Defense Schools, helping them implement College and Career Ready Standards. As co-owner of Happy Mountain Learning, Ruth specializes in developing teachers' content knowledge and strategies for engaging students to achieve high standards in mathematics.

After teaching mathematics in Grades K–8 for 20 years, **Lois A. Williams** served as the middle school mathematics specialist for the Virginia Department of Education. Here she worked on curriculum and teacher professional learning. She served the Virginia Council of Teachers of Mathematics and was a board member for the local Jefferson Council of Teachers of Mathematics. After receiving her doctorate in curriculum and instruction at The University of Virginia, she began serving as adjunct faculty to Mary Baldwin College and is in her 15th year working with preservice teachers. Currently, Lois is an International Fellow with the Charles A. Dana Center working with classroom teachers in the Department of Defense Schools helping them implement their College and Career Readiness Standards. Among her recognitions are a Fulbright Teacher Exchange and Virginia Middle School Mathematics Teacher of the Year.

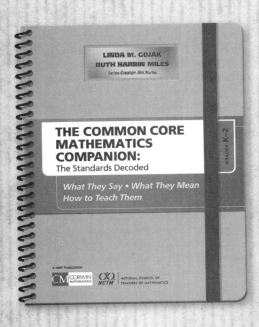

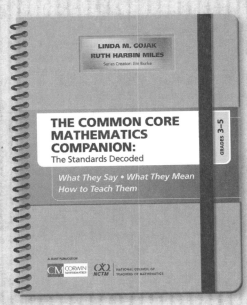

CORWIN MATHEMATICS

BESTSELLERS!

The Common Core Mathematics Companion:
The Standards Decoded, Grades K–2 and 3–5

What They Say, What They Mean, How to Teach Them

Linda M. Gojak and Ruth Harbin Miles

CONSULTING

Don't spend another minute poring over the mathematics standards. Gojak and Miles have already done the heavy lifting for you. Focus instead on how to teach them, page by page, *The Common Core Mathematics Companions* clearly lay out:

- The mathematics embedded in each standard for a deeper understanding of the content
- Examples of what effective teaching and learning look like in the classroom
- Connected standards within each domain so teachers can better appreciate how they relate to each standard
- Priorities within clusters so teachers know where to focus their time
- The three components of rigor: conceptual understanding, procedural skills, and applications
- Vocabulary and suggested materials for each grade-level band with explicit connections to the standards
- Common student misconceptions around key mathematical ideas with ways to address them

Grades K–2: 256 pages, 978-1-4833-8156-5
Grades 3–5: 320 pages, 978-1-4833-8160-2
Grades 9–12: (Coming in September 2016) 978-1-5063-3226-0

"The Common Core State Standards in mathematics needed to be deciphered! After reading this book, teachers will have acquired an abundance of realistic steps to achieve fantastic outcomes! Well done!"

—Susan E. Schipper, Elementary Teacher
Charles Street School

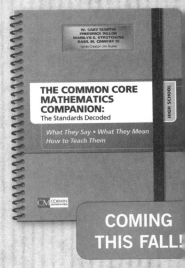

COMING THIS FALL!

To order your copies, visit **www.corwin.com**

Standards-Aligned Solutions, District-Wide Implementation

The key to raising district-wide achievement is purposeful, potent, standards-based instruction—all year long in every classroom. That's where the Common Core Companion series can help. Series creator Jim Burke and an all-star team of authors walk you step-by-step through what the standards say, what they mean, and how to teach them. Ensure that every student in your district has the critical skills they need to succeed on test day, in school, and in life.

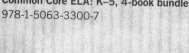

Common Core ELA: K–5, 4-book bundle
978-1-5063-3300-7

Need a K–12, district-wide implementation plan? Call your account manager for a district discount.
800-831-6640

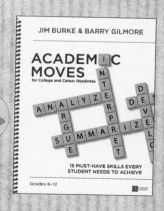

Common Core ELA: 6–12, 3-book bundle
978-1-5063-3301-4

Corwin educator discount
20% off
every day

N162C6

A SAGE Publishing Company

Helping educators make the greatest impact

CORWIN HAS ONE MISSION: to enhance education through intentional professional learning.

We build long-term relationships with our authors, educators, clients, and associations who partner with us to develop and continuously improve the best evidence-based practices that establish and support lifelong learning.

NATIONAL COUNCIL OF
TEACHERS OF MATHEMATICS

The National Council of Teachers of Mathematics is the public voice of mathematics education, supporting teachers to ensure equitable mathematics learning of the highest quality for each and every student through vision, leadership, professional development, and research.